Overcoming Shattered Dreams

Ouch! That Hurt!

Carrie Mathis

Order this book online at www.trafford.com/08-1456
or email orders@trafford.com

Most Trafford titles are also available at major online book retailers.

Note for Librarians: A cataloguing record for this book is available from Library and Archives Canada at www.collectionscanada.ca/amicus/index-e.html

Printed in Victoria, BC, Canada.

ISBN: 978-1-4251-9072-9 (soft)

ISBN: 978-1-4251-9073-6 (dj)

ISBN: 978-1-4251-9074-3 (e-book)

We at Trafford believe that it is the responsibility of us all, as both individuals and corporations, to make choices that are environmentally and socially sound. You, in turn, are supporting this responsible conduct each time you purchase a Trafford book, or make use of our publishing services. To find out how you are helping, please visit www.trafford.com/responsiblepublishing.html

Our mission is to efficiently provide the world's finest, most comprehensive book publishing service, enabling every author to experience success. To find out how to publish your book, your way, and have it available worldwide, visit us online at www.trafford.com

www.trafford.com

North America & international
toll-free: 1 888 232 4444 (USA & Canada)
phone: 250 383 6864 • fax: 250 383 6804 • email: info@trafford.com

The United Kingdom & Europe
phone: +44 (0)1865 487 395 • local rate: 0845 230 9601
facsimile: +44 (0)1865 481 507 • email: info.uk@trafford.com

10 9 8 7 6 5 4 3 2 1

"If life throws you lemons, gather them and make a big, big pitcher of lemonade well sweetened to be shared and enjoyed with others."

Acknowledgements:

To: Cleo Brookins-Pearson, my mother.

Her favorite song that she sang to her children (me and my siblings), "If I could hear my mother pray again."

To: Tommie Lee Pearson, Sr., my Daddy

To: Armonia Spears-Mathis, my mother-in-law.

She sang off-key but it was music to my ears. "Oh Mary, don't you weep, don't you moan, oh Mary why don't you sing your song.

Special Dedication:

To: Joe Henry Mathis, Jr., "JoJo" my son;

To: Vanessa Mathis, "Van", my daughter.

Both of which saw me through my tangled web.

To all of my siblings in chronological order:

Lottie Jean Pearson-Poe;

Tommie Lee Pearson, Jr.;

Joyce Elizabeth Pearson-Anderson;

Bennie Cleo Pearson-Watson;

James Edwin Pearson;

Willie Gray Pearson;

Janie Ruth Pearson-Anthony;

and in memory of our sister, Janet Pearson.

To my grandparents:

Carrie Bell Brookins;

Rev. James S. Brookins;

Lillian "Pinky" Pearson-Cherry;

Papa Walter.

Honorable mention:

Ana Garza-Mathis, the mother of my two grandchildren at the time that these events took place;

"Connie" Constance V. Brookins-Gathright;

Tommie Gathright;

To the family of Mrs. Iva Murray;

To my honorary "Uncle Ben", Benny Robert Brookins, my cousin who resembles my favorite Uncle Robert;

To Phillip Mathis, my favorite brother-in-law;

To Matthew Mora, my pest controller.

To Joe Henry Mathis, Sr., the father of my two children without whom there would not be a stronger me.

Contents

Prologue

It was one of the coldest nights that I could ever remember in the fifteen years that I had been on this earth. At one point I felt that "I must be in hell." I must have been the enemy on that God-forsaken land where time had obviously been forgotten. There was no getting around it, I was being punished by that satanic being (my father-in-law, Bigman). He must have known that I did dare to marry his beloved spoiled son. I must have been out of my cotton pickin' mind to try to come between the sick love that those two had for each other. Their relationship was one that I would never really understand.

"This must be what a hunted rabbit feels like," I thought. I began to understand what my great grandmother account of her forefather's attempts to run away for the freedom from their slave masters. Although they were scared, they had attempted many times to escape. They were hunted then brought back after being shot down like a wild jack rabbit. The masters wouldn't kill them, just maim them a little where they couldn't run "no mo'." She added, "Day wuz they property and a dead nigger wuz no good to da masah." She would explain further that the field hand was the most valuable because farming was how the white folks made their living down in these parts. She would get that far-away look in her hazel colored eyes that would well up with tears. I could always tell that she didn't like to talk about that aspect of her family (it was my family too).

My thoughts were jarred back when I heard the gun blast in the distance. POW! POW! POW! I thought, "well that crazy old man must be out his fucking mind!" He had gotten so drunk and I had irritated him purposely because I wasn't his property nor was I his daughter. I had lost my respect for him as being a so called human being. My respect for his son (my new husband, Joe Henry) was dwindling.

Again, I took off running. There was as much chance as a snowball in hell for me to survive that damnable hell hole. My white flannel night gown had been torn in several places. The long sleeve of the right arm was practically pulled off the entire arm hole. I was shivering uncontrollably. It seemed to have gotten colder. My shoes had filled with something wet and gooey. I looked down and saw that I was stuck in a ditch that had recently been dug for a fire lane. I fell forward as I tried to get out of the knee-deep mud. My gown was totally soaked with the red mud all the way up past my breast. The last down pour of rain had made it into what seemed like a small pond. I remained stuck for a moment trying to pull my shoes back on to protect my painful feet. I didn't know the depth of the water and I couldn't swim. There seemed to have been only two choices for me: either I could drown or get a bullet in my back. God gave me another choice: I chose life. Something inside of me said, "get up girl, run little girl, they can't catch you." During my falling and wallowing in the red clay, I had blended well into my surroundings of the dreadful unfamiliar woods. The mist of the fog was upon my face. Suddenly I felt that I had wings beneath my feet – "God have mercy on me!" as I heard several gunshots seemingly much closer. POW! POW! POW! POW! I had to gather my wits about me. Breathing deeply and quieter. My chest and throat were so painful with each inhalation. I stopped and looked all around me. The only things that I could discern were the shadows of the tall trees. It was better for me that the moon wasn't shining that night. I forced myself to stop breathing and listened. I didn't hear any footsteps behind me so I changed my course away for the small fish pond (that I knew was somewhere in the vicinity; Boot had brought me down this way to look for fat pine that they used to help start the fire in their wood burning heater; Joe Henry and I had ventured down this way and had made love on a bed of pine straw only two week ago) and away from the blast of gun fire. Gun that would eventually rule, tame and rear me a fifteen year old girl who had made a bad choice.

I walked for what seemed like an eternity. Wishing that I had not married and left the safety of my home. Neither of my parents had never used profanity except for an occasional "oh shit!" from my mother who many times had burned toast. She would try again and more than likely it would burn again – you got it – "oh shit!" as she flung it playfully into our dining room. My daddy on the other hand owned a hunting knife and a hunting rifle that he used for hunting critters like squirrels, rabbits, and opossum for his children. He would never use a curse word, even if there were matches between his toes and was set afire.

That wasn't the case for my new found in-laws. I heard a male voice call out loudly and close by, "Carrie! Carrie! Where is she?! I wi' ki' dat God-dammed bitch if'n I git my hands on huh." Another round of shotgun blast rang out and broke the silence. I had through that I was home free. I didn't want to die, not like that. So I took off running again. Finally I saw lights in the distance. As I neared the light I noticed that it was coming from an old shack. I ran through a corn field that looked familiar then climbed under a fence. There weren't any cars on the roadway so I ran toward the house as I looked back over my shoulders.

There was dim light on in the front room that could be seen from outside. Smoke was coming from the chimney. I banged on the door. Someone peered through the window. The door opened. Soooo….

Chapter I

Introduction of My Family

Sooo…we all have a story to tell. I may put you to sleep or maybe I can awaken something deep inside of you that perhaps you thought was dead and buried inside your soul. I've often pondered about multiple things that occurred in my life. One phenomenon that happened has caused me many sleepless nights. There was no rational reason for me to have lived so long with a man who was a womanizer. Oh there were the fringe benefits (perks) to living with a man such as he was. I became a strong (er) more positive and above all much wiser because of or in spite of him. I believed that at every corner our lives were going to get better. I had made so many excuses for staying with him. In retrospect, I felt that he was just too young. Or he'd grow out of it. My personal favorite was, "a man is going to be a man" and last but not least, "he's just feeling trapped." I obviously believed that there was some truth to all of the above reasons. I had to take a stand in life or the two children that I had always dreamed about would never be born and he wouldn't be the father that I felt that he could be. All of my dreams were based on a man who had shown me many times that I was not the woman for him.

My story doesn't really begin with Joe Henry Mathis. I was a person before I met him – so let's step backwards a few years in time to approximately the year of 1949.

My first recollection of who I was I believe that I was about four years old. I can't be precise because during the era of The Great Depression and living in Mississippi during those times, birthdays were the least celebrated special occasions, unless you just happen to be white or if your family was well off. Perhaps being an only child, then there were more chances to make a big deal out of a being born. Most families that I knew were rather large. They usually had grandparents thrown into the mix. Staying alive was our ultimate goal.

During those lean times we coloreds (as we had been so eloquently labeled by whites AKA Negros short for niggers) was mostly interested in getting our basic psychological needs met, that included food, air, water, temperature, elimination, rest and pain avoidance. We (my family) were having difficulties getting those necessities met on a daily basis. Apparently it was assumed that if we stayed in our places and remain inferior to the whites, we were allowed to live in a hand to mouth state of being. We were taught that anything or anyone above ground was a good thing. Birthday parties weren't part of the equation. It was much further up on the hierarchy of needs. We were happy just to be able to eat buttermilk and corn bread that we had for our supper on many nights. It was really delicious and felt even better when our stomachs were full. Mother would bake a large pan of bread that she made from scratch. She crumbled the hot bread in individual bowls, then poured fresh churned buttermilk over the bread that had a nice brown crust. The inside was moist and steamy with a buttery taste and fragrance. I liked to put sugar in mine. Some of us put a pinch of salt to taste. My parents liked theirs plain.

My daddy would take us for long drives in his old Ford truck. He had a makeshift camper that he had made. It was a canvas that he had tied on to four posts that kept the wind and weather from his children. We were in awe of the white neighborhoods. Their houses were so much different than ours. They sometimes had large gatherings out on their front lawn with elaborate banners that could be seen from the street. It read "Happy Birthday." All of their children were running wildly squealing for happiness. I could only hope that one day I would have a surprise birthday party. It was getting cold on the back of our truck. I got under the blanket and went to sleep and dreamed of better days.

Our neighbors went all out for the Fourth of July (Independence Day). They would light the sky with fireworks. I found out later that some of the sounds we heard were actually gunfire. Firecrackers didn't' make that kind of noise. I've yet to fully embrace that holiday because I don't feel free.

We grew up with both of our parents. They had so much love to give all of us. My mom gave birth to eight live babies and one who died at birth. A girl, whom my mom named Janet. She was born at home in the attendance of a mid wife. Her birth weight was fifteen pounds. During the difficult birth, she strangled on the umbilical cord – it had been said that had she been born in the hospital, she would have lived – my mother almost died during her delivery.

Mother – and I use the term so dearly – always spoke of Janet as if though she had lived. I know that she missed her because she had bonded with her during the full term of pregnancy. She talked about how pretty that she was. She and daddy had a quiet burial for her. I wasn't allowed to attend it.

Mother was proud of her three boys, Tommy Jr., James and Willie the youngest. She was equally proud of her five girls, who included the oldest Lottie, then Joyce, then came Bennie, yours truly, Carrie, last but not least was Janie.

Please allow me to take this time to give a proper introduction for all of my family because I've always felt that there's something in a name. we were all basically named for someone special or in memory of a family member who had past on.

My fathers full name was Tommy Lee Pearson, Sr. He and my mother, Cleo Oralee Brookins-Pearson, married at the age of nineteen years old. She took his last name and dropped her maiden name.

#1. Their first born child was Lottie Jean Pearson. Please note that my daddy was away during her birth. He came in after she had been named. He was the man and wanted to do his part so he had them to add Mary to it. She became Mary Lottie Jean and that was enough said. Warning: please don't ever ask Lottie about her name. she might turn on you.

#2. Their second child was Tommie Lee Pearson, Jr. Now! Where am I going with this you might ask? Well, in the deep south especially in Mississippi, Alabama and lets not forget Louisiana, it was a known fact that we had a vast array of family folks that mother and daddy could choose from no matter what the gender of their newborn. However, there was only one of my siblings whom I feel escaped from their madness for naming us (God please forgive me). Their third child was named Joyce Elizabeth Pearson. There wasn't anybody else in my family circle whom she may have been named after. I'm sure that my oldest brother (aka Boy Baby or Boy ay – my oldest sister did this to him when she was two years old – she was being taught to call him Baby Boy, it came out Boy Baby it stuck to him for so many years). Lottie still insists on calling him Boy ay. I'm still leaning toward their love and respect for family traditions.

#3. It must have been clockwork because in two years my mother gave birth to their third child, Joyce Elizabeth who I explained earlier had not been named after any of our family. She had always been bright and outspoken and sometimes felt that she was special because of her name, and that daddy loved her more because of her personality. I beg to differ – an assertive person can get another person to say anything. We all were taught that mother and daddy loved all of us dearly (in different ways) and that none of us were any better than the others.

#4. My sister Bennie (Bennie Cleo) who was named after our beloved Uncle (Bennie Robert). He was happy that one of his sisters' babies had been named a portion of his name. I don't think that Bennie liked it. Our cousins were taught to say the full name so Bennie Cleo it was to most people outside of our family. Mother and Daddy, what were you thinking?

#5. Now, James Edwin was their masterpiece as far as looks goes of all their children. He needed something to pad the blow of being hard rock or hard headed that daddy called him constantly. James didn't seem to mind the scolding and the belt didn't help either. I don't think his looks mattered to Deddy who carried that belt like Matt Dillon on Gunsmoke. I just went on a tangent and now I'm back. Oh yes! James was named after my mothers father (James Sir Clarence Brookins). I never did ask nor did I want to know where he got his weird middle name…one thing I do know we had to respect him because he was our grand-dad – we called him Gran.

#6. I'm on pins and needles to get to the good sweet child. The one who's staying up to the wee hours of the night to tell her story. Tah dah! I'm the sixth child (not 666). I was born on July 13, 1945 during The Great Depression obviously my parents weren't depressed and I digress. The midwife who delivered me was m mother's cousin, Ailie. Right after birth she counseled my mother that she would have to be careful with raising me. She warned her that I would probably have bad luck throughout my life because of my birth day being on Friday the 13th. My mother somehow reinforced that superstition onto me because she believed it to be my fate. I'm still trying to dispel the myth. I was named Carrie Ann Pearson after my grandmother Carrie Bell Brookins and my Aunt – Carrie Mae Bolden (who was married at the tender age of 15).

Both of those women have made positive impacts on my life. Especially my Aunt who taught me that although she was considered different (she had darker skin and brown eyes) her siblings were just the opposite. She always knew that she was a special person with so much pride except for her two failed marriages.

I never did get a real clear picture of who married whom and who divorced whom. I do know that on several occasions Aunt Carrie Mae tried to tell me about spousal abuse that she had endured while she was married and that she could not or would not take it from either of her husbands anymore. She must have known that her words of wisdom would one day save my life.

My photos won't portray who I really am. Some see me as beautiful while others as cute. Right now the only thing that I can say about me is brave, strong, wise and a tad bit naughty – the attributes that I'm working on are intelligence, vibrant, funny, God-fearing, adorable, respectable, accountable, exciting, elegant, artistic, honest and above all else, blessed. The question is what do you need to drink to wash all of this down – it's all true, I promise. It hasn't always been so. I will explain later after I complete my introduction of my siblings.

#7. Mother gave birth to her third son named Willie Gray. I'm sure that it was inevitable that he would be named after – you guessed it – after two of my daddy's sisters (they had the same father and different moms). Their names were Lillie Gray and Willie Mae – no, silly they weren't twins. It's just that people didn't really put too much thought and originality into a child's name that would hang onto their tiny little chicken necks like an albatross for the rest of their lives.

I've heard that one of our distant cousins was in the process of changing his name because he couldn't take it anymore – it was Mozell – he never did resurface again. It's best to leave certain things alone. If ones grandma gave you a name it's yours to keep whether you like it or not. Oh yes, Mozell's name fitted him like a glove. He wasn't a handsome man. He moved and talked slower than molasses. He was also dim-witted. One thing about Mozell, he did love him some women. When even he attempted to approach me, I would just mosey over to the other side of the street. I knew that it would take him a while to catch up with me. It must have been something weighing him down. He always walked wide legged. I'd heard that he was the father of many and daddy of none. I'm sure that some women loved them some Mozell too no matter what I thought. There is a man for many women – I've side tracked again.

Janet as I explained earlier was born with the cord wrapped around her neck (she was actually the eighth of my siblings). She was delivered by a mid-wife. I used to hear my mother rationalize her death. "If I would have..." or "I should have..." She later found out that she was a diabetic and that problem would always be with her.

#8. Last but not least of my siblings was Janie Ruth. I'm sure that your anticipation of who named her is too much. She was named after my daddy's sister (Aunt Janie) and my mother's cousin (Ruth Jones). I've always given myself a pat on the back for being intelligent; however, it was so obvious that I was so naïve to not have suspected that my mom was pregnant with Janie.

My baby sister had been brought home from the hospital by my mom and dad on a cold and rainy day on March the tenth. She had been born on the third of that month in 1952. The month of March should have been so full of promises of spring but old man winter didn't want to let go of the cold gruesome weather since the ground hog had just seen its shadow.

We, my family, had been living in an old shack that was indescribable as far as the color goes. Okay! I'm going to try. Please, picture a dull grey with a tinge of brown that after many years of sun baked, rain, wind and snow. There was no crayon to match it. It was still standing with the nine of us crammed into all of its nook and crannies. There were two bedrooms, a kitchen and an entry way that was later made into a sitting room/bedroom. Yes! There were seven of us and our two parents, one of which was pregnant, and I was none the wiser.

There was an urgency for my dad to build a house for us. My mother must have nagged him since she "didn't want another baby born in that old house," (I wasn't listening) "we need to move before it's born, Tommy, do it now!" (la la la, totally clueless). I guess that she didn't want to get my hopes up again after the death of Janet.

My dad was a self made brick mason by trade. He had had a second grade education only. However, he was an amazing mathematician. He didn't know how to read nor write yet, he was able to learn his trade and figure out house plans using his form of arithmetic – he provided for his family. He drew up the blue prints for our new house that he built (the man was brilliant). He and the boys dug the foundation, put up the frame. He had his friends to do the plumbing and electrical work. My daddy laid the block and assisted with plastering the walls. There were three small bedrooms, one bathroom (the cesspool had to be redone several times until the city ran a sewer system that was accessible to my family). Our kitchen was built with no sink, however there was a faucet (I'm finding it so difficult to go on with the description of my life because it saddens me to think that there are so many, many families today who don't have what we didn't have then). Deddy got a good deal on an old gas stove. The Frigidaire had been found by the road side discarded. It was still in good running condition. It needed to be defrosted practically every other day because we (including myself) were constantly opening the door and just looking inside. There was never enough ice in the metal ice trays only crystal because we drank the cold water from the ice trays constantly.

One of the fringe benefits that our house had was a hot water heater that had to work overtime for all of our baths. We had a faucet in the front and back yard. Quite frankly looking back, I felt that we had landed in a palace. Our address was Route 3, Box 33, Meridian, Mississippi. The phone number was 4318.

The house was built on two acres of flat land that had been practically given to my parents by my grandparents who lived next door to us. My great grandmother Lottie Roberts (Muhmuh's Mother) lived next door to Muhmuh and Gran. Yes! There were a lot of folks and a lot of love – but not enough when everybody in the family knew that I was going to have a baby brother or baby sister – I sometimes get a mild pang of anger when I think about so many secrets that had been kept from me – let's move on…

When I first saw Janie she looked just like a strawberry. She was crying and had turned completely red. I was so proud of her. I knew that one day she would be my playmate, until then I attempted to help take care of her. She was so pretty with very fair clear (high yellow) skin, bluish grayish greenish color eyes – depending on what she was wearing.

Yesiree! We made it to our new house just in time for her birth by c-section (by the doctor's insistence and mother had her tubes tied against my daddy's wishes).

Can you say and spell Mississippi? I lived there many years. I didn't have the sense of pride whenever I spoke of my birth place. I couldn't hold my head up high and smile. I was ashamed but made up so many excuses for the citizens of Meridian.

There were many times that I saw that things that happened in our small town that just didn't seem right, even to a naïve little girl that I was. A girl who had always tried to be sweet and be a good girl, to do unto others, to do good to those who mistreat you! Blah, blah, blah. I had received a very good upbringing by my parents. Of course I can't prove it by the way that I just defiled the Golden Rules.

We were definitely Christians and was brought up in the church where Gran (grandfather) was pastor for so many years. We all went to church on Sunday (not sent) and attended Sunday school and afternoon preaching services. The children attended the two weeks of vacation bible school that was held during the hottest, most humid, and sometimes rainy downpours. No matter what, all eight of us had to go for the exception of Janie if she didn't feel like it because she was the baby. We had no access to a car so, you guessed it, we walked the five to ten miles (depending on the short cuts, that Boy Baby would lead us). Some of the short cuts would be in pastures along the way, all of which had cattle and usually a bull who wanted to charge us. And there were warning signs of "No Trespassing." Another route was along the railroad tracks. I was terrified of trains. It was a ritual that Boy Baby would reenact each time we were on an area that had the trestle only it was over a body of water. It appeared that the train would appear right out of the blue – while we were crossing over the body of water that had an approximate drop of fifty feet. The conductor would blow that God-awful horn to warn us – Boy Baby would pretend that he was going to get ran over by the train. He would jump off of the tracks just in the nick of time. There was about three feet that we had between us and the fast moving train. It was so loud that it drowned out my screaming. I laugh about it now but it wasn't funny then.

It was extremely difficult walking in shoes that were either too tight or too loose, either way I'm sure that a person could imagine who has the blister scars on her heels. But I complain not, nosirree Bob. Bunions and blisters aren't' funny either.

Speaking of church, we also attended our yearly revival meetings to bring more members into the fold. I was young but realized there were other purposes for those meetings. It was required that the church members feed the guest speaker. It was my parents turn to do the honors. My mother and Lottie prepared a feast befitting a king with extra large portions. The minister and his family (wife and five children) arrived "hongry." The man was a huge butterball and so was his wife and five piggies. They all sat down and blessed the table with all of the grown ups eating first. By the time that bugger had asked for seconds and then "maybe I'll have smo' " there were some scraps left for the children. I could tell that Deddy wasn't pleased by the scowl on his face. We didn't attend revival meetings that night because Deddy was so wound up about what had happened. He and mother discussed it and decided there wouldn't be any more revival ministers eating at or house again. Deddy went to town and bought back some food that he got from a café that he frequented.

The last and equally important church function was the every Wednesday night prayer meetings. I must add, our community needed it badly. I saw a lot of things that went on outside just a few yards from where we knelt to pray. Some of the members' husbands would wait outside, passing the white lightening bottle around. I don't want to name names out of respect for the dead or for those alive who may be worthy of respect. Oh! I can't hold it, it was Mr. S. Chood and his older brother. I even saw Mr. Milson all of whom lived in the same vicinity of the church.

Community was so important to most of the people that I felt connected to. It brought so many things to my mind. Such as a group of people working together for a common goal. I saw it different for that particular group who were striving for much more than eternal life. They were dealing in dirt and claimed it in the name of the Lord. For example our prayer meetings as mentioned before, should have been for restoring the soul and begging for forgiveness from the Master who sees all. I'm sure he saw in the darkness of night where the bottle of liquor was passed among those who thought that we little children going to the outhouse didn't see what was happening. My body would cringe whenever I saw them looking me up and down just like hungry wolves on the prowl. They would be whispering as they drooled and eye-balled me. I made sure that I would pass by quickly and had someone to accompany me to the dark, snake-ridden outhouse. We were overrun with (human) snakes of all kind staking out, in wait of their next victim. I got some relief when I finally told my mother about the eerie feeling. She said she felt the same and that I needed to be careful.

So prayer meetings aren't what they are cracked up to be. Please don't get me wrong, there were some who went for asking atonement for their sins and who knows…maybe they have gotten lucky with some of those hot spicy church sisters…hmmm. I'm not a judge.

I've always had the utmost regards and adoration for my dad. Being that he was a great provider and had the most fantastic sense of humor. There were no strangers to him, if they were, they wouldn't be for long. He made sure that his family was well rounded in all aspects, that include our spiritual need. He made sure that we all got baptized and saved. It was later on in life while I was growing up at home, it was revealed that just going to church wasn't all that Deddy wanted. I'm sure that he made peace with his maker – it's not easy, but the truth will sooner or later be told. So here goes – my daddy was having an affair with my mother's cousin named Wilona Milson who was four years older than me. Deddy admitted it to mother who was so ashamed of him for his infidelity. He was dismissed from Pleasant Hill Baptist Church. I felt bad about it because he had been a long standing member and that he had been the main brick mason who was on the building committee. The building was previously an old dilapidated structure made of the same wood that our old house had been built with (ghastly grey). After it was erected his name was engraved on the outside cornerstone. We all were so proud of his accomplishment. I was so glad that I was no longer a member when they dispelled him.

No matter what the hardships were, my family seemed to always land on our feet. It must have been because of our need to have laughter in our home. Both my parents had such a keen sense of humor. Sometimes the jokes were a bit harsh coming from my dad. He tended to tease those who were sensitive to the brunt of his jokes. I was sometimes on the hot seat but I knew that I had to respect him even if he would go too far. On the flip side of the coin he and mother were generous. It was hard for either of them to say no to anyone. Looking back over the years I remember my daddy must have had more to give to women (mostly younger) who flirted with him shamefully and he returned the gesture even when I was present. He seemed to like introducing us to his friends and bragged about his beautiful daughters. We knew the old cliché "children should be seen but not heard" so we would play and no questions were asked as he entertained his lady friend(s).

Through all of the accusations of infidelity and one-outside-bastard child, my parents stayed together for the family's sake, not because it's cheapa to keepa. Over the years my mom would find many excuses to drop everything to visit family members for the birth of a baby, Fourth of July, National Ground Hogs Day. She was dubbed Grandma Globe Trotter.

With all that was going on down south I found it hard growing up into an intelligent well informed young lady. My parents were holding back on providing me with information that I would eventually require. There weren't any sex education classes at school yet and I was about to burst because I could feel that something was stirring in my little body that I couldn't explain. I felt so excited most of the time. I remember rocking in the rocking chair, back and forth listening to music on the radio (my favorite pastime). Thoughts about the time that I had heard my older sisters and my cousin Connie (she lived with Muhmuh who had raised her since she was about six months). They began whispering whenever I was within hearing range. They refused to tell me anything because, "you're not grown enough, you're still wet behind the ears, or too green." They didn't trust me because I would probably tell mother. Well, somebody had better tell me something, and soon. So I continued to listen through the open door but none of the information made any sense. My decision was to experiment for myself. I began touching my budding nipples, oh so gentle. The pleasure that I felt was indescribable. I had goose bumps. I became so warm and almost an out of body experience when I got up enough nerve to touch the few hairs that were sprouting on my vagina (I later renamed it to Too-Too because that's what my little sister had named hers and my mother said that's what it's called – anything to camouflage the truth).

I can't imagine how my mom and dad had ever gotten together, to get it on. God forbid to have intercourse. They were such prudes, prim and proper. For Pete's sake they had nine children together. The subject was still off limits (taboo). Whatever the case may have been there was so much laughter after they were in bed for a while. He must have told one of his funny jokes? He could be heard snoring so loudly throughout the night then awaken the next morning so happy.

It was generally quiet in our rural (country) neighborhood, especially in the summer nights. There was always a chorus of crickets, with an occasional blood curdling call from a hoot owl, the frog would join in with their sounds of a screeching door hinge that needed oiling and an occasional wild cat. I stand corrected. It was a noisy swampy place to grow up in. I forgot about the mosquitoes that would make a fine buzzing noise just as they had targeted my tender flesh to suck the blood for their snack. The gnats took a back seat and got the leftovers. They tended to like certain kids, and I was it.

Me and my four sisters shared a bedroom. There was just enough room for two full size beds and a night stand separated them. We five girls shared a modest size dresser. Sometimes Janie would sneak into our parents' room. That may have worked out better for them because she became a barrier between them. Although I must say that they kept up a good charade of being happy since the cat was out of the bag about daddy's unfaithfulness. Mother suffered in silence.

My three brothers were more fortunate than us girls. Tommy had his own single bed, James and Willie had to share a full size bed. Poor Willie caught it from James who would tease and tantalize him unmercifully from the time they awakened until Willie couldn't stand it anymore. James was relentless. He would say or do something so bizarre that my youngest brother wouldn't be able to eat or sleep for days. James personal best was telling Willie details about our cow who had been infested by a worm like critters that burrowed itself under the skin of our cow, we called it a woffie. They grew quite plump the longer that they stayed in the cows flesh. James explained the process of removing the varmint and even demonstrated it in Willie's presence. The boy was traumatized and the rest was history. Willie's weak stomach prevented him from eating okra (its consistency was slippery slimy and green). He lost so much weight during those times. It mostly happened during our supper time – we were kids and we laughed ourselves silly.

Life in the country could not have been any better as a child. I always thought that I would stay there forever but as I began to grow up, the grass seemed to be greener elsewhere.

We lived a quarter of a mile from my Aunt Gladys (she was the sister of Gran). She stayed married sixty years to the same old geezer – Uncle Brother – formally Frank Robert, Sr. They had ten children one of whom was found drowned in a nearby pond one Sunday morning. He knew how to swim very well. It was said that the white folks who owned the property were responsible for his death. There was never an investigation because he was found trespassing and he "was a nigger on white people's property." Our folks knew not to question any decision made by whites because it was the law of the land. That was in the late forties. Our lives throughout the fifties were just as unpredictable and unbearable. But like a child (adults included) who was either spanked or whipped for misbehaving – you had to take it.

Aunt Gladys and Uncle Brother were deeply hurt and extremely angry because of the loss of their thirteen year old son and the sense of powerlessness that coloreds endured in Mississippi. They would talk in hushed voices when we were visiting. I don't believe that they ever found closure – justice wasn't served. They found solace in each other and the rest of their children.

Aunt Gladys had a grandchild about my age. Her name – you guessed it! Gladys! We were the best buds both of us were growing and budding into big girls. We played all day in the woods. We had to be creative since there were no toys to play with. Picture this: we made dolls out of a coke bottle with ice string for hair. Can you say desperate? We were happy – really! We were. However things started to change as we began maturing and budding (breasts). Gladys asked me to sleep over. I noticed that my boy cousins seemed to have been spying on as we were preparing to go to bed. They suggested that we strip. She and I began to bear all until Aunt Gladys came and broke up the strip tease party. She made us all some cool aid and fresh baked tea cake – FLASH – the very idea of any of my cousins acting fresh with me makes my flesh crawl…eeew!

Every summer I continued to visit my Aunt when Gladys was visiting from Memphis for the holidays. Their house was a humungous two story about seven bedrooms that were constantly being remodeled by Aunt Gladys' older sons. Their house was much nicer than ours or any other colored family that I knew. One thing about it, there wasn't a bathroom or running water initially. It had a well that was a part of the house in the front (I did mention earlier that I'm afraid of my shadow).

Well, for someone who was an admitted scaredy-cat, I was drawn to go back for more from my cousin Arthur Hugh who was well known by all of us to be the story teller of the family. He had promised us little ones that he was going to hire the headless horseman to catch us and throw us all in their deep well the next time we walked through the woods. He had us so frightened to look over our left shoulder. If we dared to do so we would see a ghostly spirit and it would overtake our little bodies. The ultimate weird story that he told us was, "If you ever smell burned oatmeal while walking through the woods, it was for sure that there were ghosts near by that were cooking a big pot of oatmeal." They are waiting for you little ones especially because you are so slow." We all screamed so loud. The more we screamed, the more pleasure that he got from his gruesome stories. Arthur was a twin boy to Minnie Lou. His nickname was Chew Baby because Minnie Lou couldn't say Hugh Baby when she was a toddler. It must have sounded so cute to my Aunt Gladys because he was saddled with it until he married and moved out of the state. Some of us refused to let it go. We were gluttons for punishment and you have just met the president. I can honestly say with conviction that, me, my siblings and our cousins were entertained superbly for many hours up at Gladys' house and in the ghost infested woods of Mississippi that would raise the hairs on our heads.

Please, don't get me wrong. Although I professed to be a tad bit skittish, puny and yes scared of my shadow, there was a daring side to me. I needed to prove that I could overcome my fears.

There was another occasion when I was feeling womanish (boys were manish). My cousin Georgia Mae was sleeping over at my house for a few days. We had played as many childhood games that we could think of including hopscotch, tag, a rock game, hide and go seek, another game that rhymed – see, see, see, I am a funny little Dutch girl. As funny as funny can be, and all the boys around my house sing pretty little songs to me – it didn't have to make sense, it was fun as we said the words, together and clapped our hands in a rhythmic routine that was done with skill and precision. We had tired ourselves out and became bored. She was used to city life and didn't really like all of the wonders that the woods had to offer that I enjoyed so much. We decided after a lot of coaxing from me to learn how to smoke. My oldest brother, Boy Baby (Tommy Jr.) had just returned back home from the army. He had been stationed in Germany. We (Georgia and I) noticed that he had a carton of Marlborough's in his knapsack. "He's not going to miss a pack" I said with enthusiasm. He had no idea that his innocent sweet little sister would dare to take his smokes – that was not hidden, that was beckoning to be smoked – so that's what we did. I had watched my grandmother and great grandmother (my mother was their look out woman) as they smoked some weird smelling smokes. They claimed that it was rabbit tobacco…hmmm! They had made some home brew and homemade wine. I perfected the latter of the two because the process was simpler. About a month prior to Georgia's visit I decided to make some wine from my favorite fruit. I washed and peeled then sliced the luscious peaches that were in season. I had obtained a large mason jar that I washed carefully. I put the fruit with some water and sugar carefully not to close the lid too tight so that the fermenting process could breathe and not explode. I had watched it for weeks as if though it was a baby. It was kept in my secret hiding place. It began foaming, bubbling and was making a gurgling sound as it emitted an odoriferous putrid smell. It must have been ready when the fruit floated to the top and the liquid was at the bottom of the jar. It was time for the next step to strain the contents. I took it outside in the backyard to strain it into another prettier jar. The fruit flies and gnats must have gotten wind of my efforts so they waged war on me and my long awaited wine. I was the victor as I closed the jar tightly. There it was finally – the fruit/liquor of my labor – a jar of pure peach wine ready to be sampled while me and Georgia Mae would be partaking of those enticing cigarettes. We were alone in the house. We knew that we would surely get our hides tanned severely if we were found smoking or even have the odor of cigarettes on our breath or clothes. I shiver to think about it, but we had come that far with our plans of becoming worldly women. The wine was chilled, clear and ready to be sampled. And that was what we did. I found two small glasses from my mothers company glass ware. I poured the strong odor liquid and filled both our glass. We toasted each other. I gulped mine. It was so strong and was unlike anything that I had ever tasted. Georgia Mae had taken a few sips then gave me the nod of "okay." We polished off about a half of the wine. We became so giddy and giggling a lot at basically nothing and everything. I was bound and determined to complete everything that we had set out to do before my parents returned back home from wherever they said that they were going. Ha ha ha ha! Everything was getting so fuzzy. The floor seemed to have gotten closer each step that I made. We were cracking up at how we were reacting to the wine but were still in control. We searched high and low and finally found a small box of matches.

We literally floated up the path into the woods. It was amazing that we had found a clearing in the woods far enough where no one could hear us and God forbid to smell the cigarette smoke. There were no leaves nor straw to catch fire so we sat down on the ground. We had so much to talk about for one, no two, oh hell it had to have been at least three hours. We had lit and smoked up the whole pack of cigs one right after the other. Yes! Count them, twenty of the most strongest cancer sticks consumed in one sitting – sick – that's exactly what both of us were feeling. We made it back down the hill on a wing and a prayer. Can you say or spell floating which we couldn't stop. I don't know which one of us vomited the most. We were found by my parents, oh so sick. I had developed diarrhea and Georgia Mae continued to upchuck (she hadn't consumed as much wine as I had). We both looked so pitiful to my parents. Two little girls in the country trying to grow up too fast. Deep down, I knew that mother and daddy must have known what had happened to us and that we had already punished ourselves enough. They never said anything to my face or even out loud, however, I had heard them snickering to themselves on several occasions whenever they saw me or when I mentioned that maybe having Georgia Mae to visit again. Aunt Janie knew that something was wrong with her baby girl. Georgia Mae was never allowed to sleep over again.

Now Boy Baby was never informed of that episode. He was seen searching high and low for that one missing pack in which he should have known that one of his rug rat siblings had taken.

You would think that after such a horrific experience that there should have been some lesson learned by me. Well, for you or maybe you all but, not for me. You see, there was so many hours in a day which seemed much longer while living in the country (where are the violins?) Again, we had no bikes, no skates, no teen centers, parks or swimming pools. We did, however, have neighbors – white folks – who lived up the road (not the street). We weren't' allowed to play with their children. some of them wanted to join us as we played those who were younger and hadn't been poisoned with the hate and bigotry that their parents had instilled into their minds. The older kids that I saw across the creek that divided our property would holler out loudly. It made an echo that made it sound far worse, "hey niggers, you can't play with us. We are better than you!" I made up in my mind that I would one day be as good as and hopefully better than…

Tolerance was taught by my parents at an early age. I didn't really understand it as I nodded my head, "yes." It didn't make any sense to me. The bottom line was that they were white and superior to us. "Carrie you have to make sure that you say yes sir and no sir, don't forget to say mister if you are talking to a white man, and with the white woman you have to say Mrs. They don't like for us to look at them straight in their eye or question anything that they say." I saw early on in my childhood that there was a disparity with coloreds and whites. They had things better than me. I saw their little girls my age had beautiful clothes that looked store bought. It was instilled in us that since my daddy was struggling "to pu' food on tha table and to sen' ya'll ta schoo' sos ya'll kin do bet'n than we done."

There were plenty of times that I had the pleasure of getting nice stylish garb as hand-me-downs or used clothes. Bennie absolutely refused to wear something that somebody else had worn. Since Janie was the baby, she was more privileged to also have new attire. I got used to getting rather nice skirts and blouses that mother would buy for a small fee from white people that she or Muhmuh worked for. Although they were second handed they were a cut above the clothes that my parents could ever afford. I became tolerant and somewhat indifferent not really feeling good about who I was. I "made do" as my father had often said, "you have to make do or do wid ou'" His philosophy would always be etched into my brain as I tried so hard to fit into a mold of a child that was inferior. I DIDN'T want to accept seconds and to settle for less.

The last encounter of playing with my cousin Gladys was when I was about twelve years old. It was the year of 1957. we really didn't play games as we did when were much younger children. you see we were about to become TEENAGERS which was a milestone for most girls our age back in the day. There was so much excitement when we got together to catch up on our growth, such as, "did you get your period yet?" and no, I had not! I was emphatic about it. I knew that there must be something wrong with me. Maybe I'm cursed because of something I had done wrong in my lifetime – the curse came later that summer – I was so happy! You can't believe it? I truly was on my way to becoming a grown woman, I could hardly wait Yaaaaah Hooooo.

During her visit we sat on the swing on the back porch of Aunt Gladys' house. The days would be filled with stories or fantasies of the future. Neither of us had ever had any experiences with a boy but OH BOY we could hardly wait. My other cousin Connie who was older than us had told me what boys and girls did when they had intercourse. I listened to her with my eyes bucked and my mouth wide open in disbelief about all the stuff that she told me. I thought, "you must be out of your cotton-pickin' mind!" I was so gullible when she told me that "each month, when you get your period, you'll have bleeding from your navel." She said it as she laughed knowing that I was ripe and ready to believe anything that anybody would tell me or anything that I could get my hands on about having sex and "where do baby's come from?" It was assumed that since I was still a child and didn't need any formal information on the matter. My mother would flush when the subject was brought up. So I passed all of my unreliable information on to Gladys who was also in the dark and wasn't able to fill in the blanks.

We had just finished eating supper that Aunt Gladys had prepared. She always had some delicious dessert. On that day she had baked a blackberry (fresh-picked) pie. I have to pause for a while to reflect back. The crust was perfect, so crispy/flaky, it melted in my mouth. There was no need for it to be topped with ice cream nor whipped cream. The pie said it all.

We both loved singing, swinging and talking. It was so much fun and relaxing. We were both giggling about a joke that I past on to her when we were interrupted by my cousin (Gladys' Aunt). She sat on the swing right in the middle of us. I thought that it was very strange because she was about six years older than us. Her age group usually wouldn't give us the time of day or associate with us younger kids. All of a sudden, there she was. She moved in closer to me. Well! I thought maybe she was going to tell us a story as she had often done in the past when we had both family children together. She had a different menacing expression on her face. She said to me, "it looks like you have something sprouting there" as she gently touched my tiny right breast bud (they were about the size of a door knob and were so tender). She must known because she even mentioned, "they probably hurt a little, huh?" I sat there speechless and so was Gladys who remained seated at the far right of the swing. That was certainly new territory that she and I had never discussed in all of the visits that she had made to her grandma's house. They had all been fun filled encounters that little girls played. Suddenly I had a great urge to go to the toilet. There was so much pressure in my bowels. I felt sick at the stomach. I had to literally run down the path to their outhouse or it wasn't going to be a pretty sight. The small outhouse was about 200 yards away from the main house. It was almost in the woods. It was a two seater. They even had a roll of toilet paper and regular toilet seats with lids. It still had a yucky odor. I slammed the door behind me. There wasn't a latch to lock it. I was soaking in perspiration as I fumbled to pull down my Bermuda shorts then my panties. Sweat was pouring down my face. I noticed that my tiny dark nipple could be seen through my drenched white tee shirt (my mom hadn't bought me a training bra yet). I sat there for a while. It must have been a false alarm with the #2. as I was drying my too-too the door flung open (no locks) and there she stood before I could completely pull up my panties. She was in front of me kneeling and whispering insistently, "I want to see it." I knew that up until then that I was an innocent naïve girl but I knew with all of the fiber as a good girl that that was wrong. She said it again. I tried to be ignorant as I was trying to get my sweat soaked panties all the way up. I said, "do you mean you want to see me pee?" She became irritated by the look on her face and the sound of her voice. "No!" she snapped, "I want to touch that" as she pointed to my vagina. Loudly I said, "NO!" I jumped up still pulling up my shorts as I went past her.

I don't know how I was able to redress or what wing that was again under my feet. I ran home alone through the woods with no thoughts of all the ghosts and goblins that had never, ever attacked me. I felt that I would be safer with them than with…

Everybody had eaten supper when I got to my house. I was out of breath but safe. It was so quiet. Most of my family were in the living room listening to the radio (we found entertainment in the story hour, The Shadow Knows). I found my mother in their bedroom reading the bible as was her practice. She looked up as I said her name, "Mother." Her face reflected concern as she closed the book. She must have known something dreadful had happened. I closed the door because I was so embarrassed and didn't want any of my siblings to hear what I had to tell her. Tears were streaming down my face. I was breathing so irregular and heavy I thought I was about to faint. "What's wrong Carrie?" she asked. I was still out of breath, gasping for air. When able, I told her the whole story. She remained calm. I thought that she would lose it or scream, "how dare her!" but she didn't. instead she said quietly, "I'm going to talk with Aunt Gladys and that will never happen to you ever again." I felt that she must have known that my cousin had those tendencies. Thinking back and looking deeper, she didn't want to involve my daddy for he was like still waters that ran deep. It was no telling what he would have done if he knew that someone had touched me in such a manner. It was a taboo subject. So I'm not sure if any of my sisters had ever had encounters such as what I experienced.

I felt so embarrassed for the next few weeks. It would take some time before I could go back up to my favorite Aunts house. It was so hard to look Delia in the face (Aunt Gladys obviously didn't break it (her face) as I had wanted. It must have been something that I did because a crime had been committed and I didn't see anybody being punished but me.

I was becoming more and more critical of myself, mainly because of being compared to my two cousins that I was close to and growing up with. Georgia Mae who was simply beautiful and so was Gladys. Georgia would get compliments when we were together, "She's filling out so well." I waited for a glimmer of "and so is Carrie" but it never came. I began to feel insecure and inadequate. I do know for a fact that my Aunt Janie fed Georgia Mae spoonful of real butter to "make her fat and fine" as folks used to say. It was stylish to be over weight. Old people used to worry if a person was average or thin. I was compared so much until my mom made an appointment with Dr. Polk who was one of the few colored doctors in Meridian. He told my parents that "Carrie is a petite average size for her age" and he only guessed that my cousin may have been above average. I never did divulge that information to her because we were so close and I needed a friend.

Church continued to be the focal point to my family. I loved to sing. It brought me so much joy that I could carry a tune and harmonize with who ever could sing soprano or a lead singer. I tried out for our church choir. I needed them and they needed me. After joining I found that it was quite boring. Our song selections were so plain. Lottie and Muhmuh did their best as they alternated playing the piano. They were able to play but it didn't have that oomph that most Baptist church choirs had. One of our members had heard a young man play piano at a concert. He was excellent and was available to be hired. He was creative, he knew that no one else could top him.

Singing in the choir had become so special to me. Our church members were so filled with the Holy Ghost with every song that we performed on Preaching Sunday (1st and 3rd Sundays). There were a lot of amen's and shouting as some southern Baptist ladies were known to do. I could almost always tell which member would start shouting (they screamed, kicked, waved their arms about out of control sometimes hitting other members). The ushers were the ones who were harmed the most. The shouter would have to be carried outside the church – rarely in the winter time. The point was: those shouters would have arrived at church questionably angry with – you guessed it – their husbands. So it must have been good therapy for them (a punching bag). I never did see my mother express herself in that manner.

We had choir rehearsal every Tuesday night. All of Aunt Gladys' children – those who were living at home (except for Lee) could sing and was a member of our church choir. My family would all be ready and waiting to catch a ride with cousin Melvin (Aunt Gladys' oldest son) who was the choir director Willie and Janie were my siblings who weren't member. We would all crowd into the small car like sardines. Sometimes we would hitch a ride in Marvin Crue's car – Mr. Piano Man – he was so professional and overly polite. He was able to tickle the ivory without reading music and it was always a performance of pure finesse and flare. He seemed to like me to a certain degree. I on the other hand didn't feel any attraction for anybody (for that matter) who was termed high yellow (colored term for fair skin). He stood about five feet, nine inches and had a medium build. He always wore either a nice suit or clean cut casual wear that was well coordinated. His voice, mannerisms and the way that he walked just didn't seem to capture my idea of manliness, but who was I to judge him because I hadn't had any experience of being a sophisticated woman of the world. I still wanted to be in the know. I didn't want to make any snap decisions about anybody. My problem was, I was too impatient with the process of life. Things needed to happen faster for me.

Marvin began talking to me gradually after our choir rehearsal. He was so shy as he was attempting to make conversation with me. It was making me so uneasy because he really wasn't saying anything that would have interested me. I finally gathered that he was trying to ask me out. My parents had made it perfectly clear to me that I could start dating when I reached sixteen years old and at that time I was only fourteen. Daddy wasn't going to allow it.

Muhmuh called me over to her house one morning. It was close to the Thanksgiving holiday. She told me that Marvin's mother had called her and asked her if she would be instrumental to get permission from Mother and Deddy for me to accompany Marvin to a dinner engagement that he had been invited to and he could bring a guest. Mrs. Crue had even called me and had practically begged me to accompany her son to the gala. It would appear that everybody and their grandma knew what path that Marvin was taking in his life, and I must have been the chosen one to veer him from his course. I must have been their last ditch effort. As for me, just getting out of the house with a person who truly needed a friend was my motive. I felt so sad for him that I had been thrown in the middle to try to force him to be attracted to the opposite sex. It was as clear as the nose on my face, it wasn't his idea. He was so called going along with the program for his mothers' sake and with my grandmother's interference.

I too was having mixed feelings. It felt like a lose-lose situation. You see, I had recently met another handsome boy at Muhmuh's house a week ago. There weren't too many opportunities for a country girl such as myself to meet and – God forbid – for me to be asked out on a date at my age. Finally I said "yes, I'll go since my parents gave their permission."

I was definitely not attracted to Marvin but desperate times made desperate measures. My patience for life hadn't been developed yet, however, on the other hand I was becoming a very popular girl and wasn't that what life was all about, to be liked and desired by many especially by the opposite sex? Now, that I could attest to. Oh, how

I wished that I coulda woulda shoulda. My street smarts hadn't been developed yet, so most of my decision making processes were made while my hormones were raging a war from within. I was having cravings of a sexual nature that were animalistic. It had practically taken over my every thought. My body was betraying me. I had been taught early on to love the Lord and above all else to follow His commandments (found in Exodus, chapter 34). The one that was causing me so much problems was "Thou shall not commit adultery." Up until then I hadn't performed the actual act only in my mind but it would be only a matter of time that I knew that if there was an opportunity, I would do it gladly then suffer the consequences later.

The mirror had become my best friend. I styled my hair constantly. I studied my facial features finding flaws. With make up I found that I could camouflage some of my imperfections. I loved putting on lipstick especially the red and shiny ones (Royal Crown hair grease was a good lip gloss). There were times that I tried on so many outfits. Most of them belonged to my older sisters, "they wouldn't mind" I thought (yes they would). I found a one piece bathing suit that had been given to us by white folks. I wouldn't be able to wear it to the pool because we didn't have access to a pool in our neighborhood for coloreds. None of us had learned to swim (it was later on in Meridian that the city opened a park for coloreds and it had a pool. Our parents didn't trust it so we were forbidden to get in it. We could watch the kids swimming from afar).

Picture me prancing around throughout our home posing uninhibited. My body was shaped nicely my booty was not too big as most girls my age wanted, but – nicely packed for sexiness and that made me proud of myself. My legs were my greatest attribute. I had had so many compliments from so many people. I had been told on several occasions by my paternal grandmother, Lillian "Pinky" Pearson. She was so nice to me – yet extremely hateful to mother. She had often said in her slower than molasses, southern drawl "Carrie Ann, you sho' do have niz legs, jus' lak yo' daddy." She seldom complimented anybody. She would look at me and smile with so much pride (I hoped also with joy). She didn't have to say a word. I just knew that she approved of me. Little did she know that her sweet little Carrie Ann was about to embark upon the road to destruction.

It had become so difficult for me to get ready for the upcoming date. There was so much pressure from his family and from mine as well for me not to break the date. That dreadful evening finally came. I put on a rather dressy outfit, an A-lined black and white plaid skirt with a white blouse. I put on a black wool jacket, my shoes were a plain low heeled pumps. My stockings were a must that were held up by adjustable rubberized garters worn above my knees. I put on just a little make up as I wasn't really trying to impress or turn him on. By the time that he arrived, I was a nervous wreck. I looked out of our window as he parked his car in our driveway. He got out with so much style and grace. I thought, "how could I measure up to him?" He knew who he was and wasn't ashamed of it. He had something in his hands. I opened the front door and gave him a smile. My face must have lit up when he pinned a beautiful white corsage onto my jacket. He fumbled with what had started out as a hand shake that progressed to a hug. He didn't seem to know where to place his arm around me. He gave me a light peck on my cheek. I thought, "now that wasn't so bad."

It took us almost an eternity to drive across the city to the ghastly building that the gala had been held. It was totally dark outside and was dimly lit inside at which time I was able to get a better glimpse of Marvin. He was sporting a black suit that was trimmed with silky satin lapel and a white silk scarf that was in his jacket pocket. His shirt and tie was awesome. He did look good. However he was the most nervous person that I had ever seen. It was probably due to my demeanor. The look on my face was most likely a dead giveaway that I didn't want to be there and he must not have wanted the same. I wondered, "was this a life sentence? God please let this night be over."

Marvin did the honors to introduce me to the few people who remained in the barren ballroom. You see somebody had gotten the wires crossed and forgot to tell him that the time of the gala had been changed to begin one hour earlier. He was so apologetic to me. I pasted a smile on my face that I wasn't used to wearing. It must have looked fake. "I want to get out of here!" I wanted to scream but refused to be so rude to a person who was really trying hard to make the best of it – and I wasn't. The room and buffet looked as if there had been a herd of hogs that was on a scavenger hunt, eating everything within their path. I felt so bad for Marvin because he really did try to impress me. I was too hungry to even concentrate. I looked around and saw that there was a big bowl of potato salad that had a mini lake of potato juice in the middle. It had most likely been sitting there for hours just waiting to give me food poisoning. There was some remnants of wilted lettuce. I couldn't pretend any longer. I refused to eat there and so did he. We were both famished and was getting cold.

Marvin reluctantly suggested that we go over to his house. He assured me that it was safe since I had made up so many excuses that I didn't want to go. He wanted me to meet his mom who I had spoken to on the phone. Upon entering their living room she came out in her gown (she was preparing to retire for the night). The room was so dim. There were three other couples about his age. They had music on that was soft and slow. Marvin asked me to dance. He was light on his feet and commanded the art very well. We danced for a few minutes until I excused myself to go to the bathroom. When I returned I noticed that there was a pint of scotch that was being passed around. I wondered what in the world had happened to his mom with the grub that she had promised us as she left the room earlier. It was getting late. I found a few salted peanuts and a coke. I saw Marvin take a long swig from the bottle. He then handed it to me. I took a gulp and within minutes I was feeling warmer and uninhibited.

His body was closer to mine as we danced. I didn't like the way that he was kissing me. It was as if it was his first time. I was fresh out of ideas on how to teach an eighteen year old man/boy how to kiss. He kept whispering in my ear, "I want to! I want to! Give me some crim!" I became so sober with that last request. The other couples were kissing and necking – please don't get me wrong, I wanted to have sex but not with a person who I had no sparks of desire as I thought that there should be. He was brought back to reality with my abrupt request that was firm and polite, "will you take me home now?" He looked so shocked and hurt. He heard the determination in my voice and saw the way that I was gathering my jacket and pocket book. I felt so sorry for him and yes, somewhat irritated at my grandmother and his mom for interfering in our lives by trying to set us up with each other.

Our drive back to my house was as bad or worse than a funeral procession. We uttered just a few words. We both knew that we had given it our level best for the sake of our loved ones. I didn't blame him for who he was (I'm not a judge). We pulled up into my parent's driveway. It appeared that everybody had gone to bed already. They had forgotten to leave the front stoop light on for me.

Marvin jumped out of the car to rush around to open the car door for me (what a gentleman). He was perspiring profusely although it was freezing cold. I just wanted to get into my house and end the horrific evening (if only he was if he would?) he was who he was. People change when they have a need and desire to change. He asked me for a hug which I allowed. He began to moan again. I tried to pretend "I don't know what you're talking about, crim?" He tried to kiss me again and I broke free and rushed into my house locking the door behind me. I felt so many emotions as I relived the evening. Deep in my heart and soul I knew that I was powerless to change the course of Marvin's life. We all had choices and he chose who he wanted and what he wanted. I could only be accountable for myself (or am I my brother's keeper?). I remained saddened because he wasn't into girls at least not in the way that I wanted and needed.

I was absolutely famished. I warmed up the leftovers of chicken, greens and macaroni & cheese – all of my favorites – and a glass of cold kool aid.

It took me a long time to finally calm myself down. I went to sleep that night with a clear conscious about all of my actions which were all for the best – so I thought. Muhmuh called me early the next day. She had just gotten off the phone with Mrs. Crue who was beside herself because Marvin was upset. As she was talking I thought, "how dare both of you parents to place such a burden on my shoulders in hope that I could change something that Marvin may have been born with." I received several calls from him. I refused most of them. The last call I got was answered with an attempt at diplomacy. That didn't work so I had to use "don't you ever call here again" and that worked. It became a strain for both of us since he was still employed by my church to play for our wonderful choir. He remained as our pianist for another six months. Thereafter he moved up north where he was in multiple concerts. He had a fabulous career.

Marvin is no longer with us due to reported complications from respiratory problems. All of the "should have" will not bring him back. He brought so much joy with his talent of playing the piano. I hope that he found happiness during his lifetime on earth. May God be with you, Marvin. ■

Chapter II

On Becoming a Woman

It was the year of 1959 and in the frigid cold month of November. The bedroom where I slept was still freezing although Lottie or Joyce had lit the gas heater that was connected to a gas outlet just outside of our closet full of clothes (fire hazard). It had a sputtering sound when it was lit and there was a mild odor of natural gas that was escaping and filtered into the air…It generally took about two hours to heat the room up because the opening to the (crawl space) loft opened to our closet. We had hung a curtain to the doorway opening. Daddy never did get (a round tuit) motivated to put in a door which would have been feasibly impossible to install anyway.

I had stayed up past my ten o'clock curfew the night before and was so sleepy and practically frozen. We were all out of school for the Thanksgiving vacation. I had amused myself by reading several short stories from magazines that had been forbidden by my mom for me to read. I waited until everybody was asleep before I started reading and transforming myself into the main characters of the story(ies). True Confessions and Modern Romance were two popular magazines among girls my age. We all were curious about subjects that was on most of teen agers minds. I obtained a lot of important information that I would eventually need when the time was right. I had insomnia after reading then going into a day dreaming state. I finally drifted off and I dreamed of meeting a wonderful boy who I fell in love with. We were about to kiss…

My youngest sister was already up and playing. I had hoped that she would grow up quickly so that I could have a built in playmate when I was a little girl. That didn't happen so she became my personal little pest and the family's greatest tattle-tell. I believed that somebody was bribing her to spy on me because there she was just like clock work from early morning till late at night. She was quicker than grease lightening whenever I veered from the straight and narrow path that my parents had me on. She would say, "oooh! I'm gonna tell!" One thing about it I couldn't stay mad at her because she was so cute with those big green inquisitive eyes. She was no doubt quite spoiled. I don't remember ever getting away with bloody murder when I was the baby girl of our family.

It had become apparent that I wasn't going to get any more much needed sleep with all of the racket that Janie was making. I got up quickly and ran to the bathroom because I was about to flood my pad. I slammed the door and latched it. Daddy had finally put a simple latch on the door since there had been so many embarrassing moments when one of the family members would knock and before there was a response, they would burst into the functionally, no frills (grand central station), bathroom. There weren't any frosted glass encasements or a shower no need for a shower curtain. Again, it somehow served its purpose for the eight of us and our parents.

Janie had followed me and remained outside the door until I came out. She was always such a happy child and could keep me entertained for hours if I allowed it. Well, that day was not one of them. I knew that she must have been hungry. We walked to the kitchen – at least I did, she skipped – there was some cooked grits with butter on the stove. I found a clean skillet to fry some bacon and eggs. I made some toast in the broiler area of the stove. She wanted some jelly on it, so be it. I got her settled at the counter in the kitchen. We said our blessings as was our family's practice for each meal. To make sure that she was settled I poured her a big glass of cold milk. She certainly was hungry.

While she wasn't looking, I slapped two pieces of bacon on the toast. I hurried past her, "Oh, Janie, I'll be right back, I need to tell Connie something." She began eating faster. I said, "slow down, you're going to choke." She looked at me so pitifully and so betrayed but – I made my great escape. I literally flew over to Muhmuh's house. Connie was busy as usual cleaning up the house. I could hardly catch my breath after that sprint. I knew that I had to talk fast. I heard our grandparents talking in their bedroom. They must have heard my voice. Muhmuh yelled out softly, "Yoo hoo, Carrie Ann, is that you?" I answered musically "yes ma'am." I walked quickly through the house to where they were, leaving Connie to continue to do her chores. She had always been rewarded by Muhmuh for doing such a good job either with new clothes, presents or by word of mouth. Connie had on several occasions bragged to us that our grandmother loved her more than us. I felt the love that she had for me, and that was all that mattered.

The house was spotless. Usually I could detect the smell of food that had been cooked from their breakfast. I smelled only the strong scent of pine oil. Their dishes had been washed and put away. I thought to myself, "no goodies over here." I had to go home and wash the mountain of dishes at home.

Before entering their bedroom, knock, knock, knock! Then I opened the door to say hello. Muhmuh was on the telephone talking to her half sister, aka Auntee/Eddie Mae Wilson – who was about five feet tall and looked to be about five feet wide. She and Muhmuh were as different as night and day. I saw Auntee one day after she had just taken a bath. There was not a shame bone in her body. She came out of the bathroom…she had only a towel that was held up by her tits that were humongous. They hung down to her navel (that picture of her was etched in my little girl memory bank). She was darker skinned with brown eyes that always seemed to look so tired because she worked "in the white folks kitchen." She had told some stories that made me ill. She hated her job yet she was always in demand from many white folks who wanted her rolly polly ass to work for them. The woman could cook and she certainly could eat.

Auntee had mentioned on several occasions when some of her folks she worked for would insist that she do other chores other than cooking, she would do "things" to pay them back "I'm a cook, not a dam babysitter." She said that as she made their toast she put plenty of butter then she would smear it with love (that was spit – eew!). How gross! I thought as I hid inconspicuously from Auntee and Muhmuh pretending that I wasn't listening to their conversation.

Muhmuh was crying as she generally did when she talked with Auntee. The subject of their mother (Mama) would always be a part of their conversation. She never really seemed to have gotten over Mama's death (Lottie Roberts). It had happened so tragically. You see Mama was hit by one of those damnable speeding cars soon after we moved into the home that Deddy had built. Me, James and Willie were up the hill feeding and watching the hogs and their piglets as they ate and smacked on the slop. We all heard an ear piercing scream, "Mama!" We threw the slop basket down on the ground. There was a loud screeching sound from a car out of control during an attempt to put on the brakes. It lasted for a few seconds. We basically flew home. I thought that something had happened to my mother. I ran inside with my brothers looking for mother who was nowhere to be found. I was about to run out of the front door when Lottie stopped me, "No! Carrie you can't go out there!" I was frantic and began crying, "where is Mother?!" Lottie was pacing the floor and was still trying to calm us down. She answered, "Mother is okay. It's Mama, we'll wait in here until Mother comes back." We all knew that we had to mind Lottie. She took charge when Mother was away.

There was so much commotion on the roadway in front of our house. Most of the cars were stopping (looky-loos who only wanted to see what was happening with the niggers).

A white man had gotten out of his car and was sobbing and moaning uncontrollably, "oh auney, auney (a term used by whites as a term for so called respect for older colored women). I'm sorry, I'm so sorry, please forgive me. I didn't see you!" As Mama lay on the side of the road, her body was still, she must have been dead? we all thought. The whining sound of the ambulance could be heard from a distance. It became louder and louder as it approached my great grandmother.

The police were there and had stopped traffic both ways. Muhmuh could be heard crying continually unable to be consoled. Mother was by her side doing the best that she could to no avail. The ambulance attendant got out quickly to stabilize Mama. She still wasn't moving. They finally got her positioned on the stretcher as we all looked on from Mother's bedroom window. The ambulance took off slowly then gradually picked up speed with a police car in front and in the rear. The sirens could be heard even after they were out of sight. I thought she would never ever return back home to where she had lived for so many years. She would never see her family whom she loved so dearly. She and Muhmuh were so close. Mama had always thought so much about my mom and there was nothing that she wouldn't do for us.

We didn't go to school that day. I cried each time that I thought about Mama and when my siblings would mention her. Our parents wouldn't allow us to visit her in the ICU at the hospital. Later on that night, our parents came home, both looking so sullen. They gathered all of us in the living room where they broke the news to us that "Mama never did regain consciousness." They told us how she had been talking out of her head. We were told that Mama went home with the Lord and that she wouldn't have to suffer anymore. I wondered would she come back, "no, she's not coming back; Mama's dead." My mother said as she cried in the arms of Deddy. I understood that very well because we (me and my siblings) had seen animals/pets who had died out in the roadway, after being struck by a car. We would have their funeral then bury them. It hurt so badly that it was final for a person who had been such an inspiration of love. She had given herself and never asked for anything in return. Her two bedroom house had been opened up to us when I was a newborn. She later welcomed us back again after my dad had moved us to a poverty stricken lean – to for about six months.

So, that was it. She was gone. One more thing I overheard my parents discussing "Mama was tired of living." She had become increasingly depressed and had often said to Muhmuh and Mother "I wants to go home with Papa (her husband)" my parents said in hushed voices. That Mama was crossing the road as she had always done in the early morning to go and milk her cow. Thereafter she would lead the cow out to pasture for the day (the pasture belonged to a white man who allowed Mama to allow the cow to graze with his cattle. His arterial motive was to purchase land that she and papa had further down in the country. It was about twenty acres. She sold it for about $200.00 – Later a large lake was put on the property). Mama must have known that the cars always picked up speed just above her house and continued beyond about five miles past my parent's house. Most of the drivers would be so irritated by the slow moving auto during their drive through the hairpin curves. It was bound to happen we had seen so much road rage and speeding cars not really going anywhere. We had so many of our pets (dogs, cats) and chickens who had been mowed down by the speeders.

The point was Mama had been witnessed acting angry and overheard her say, "I'm tired I wanna go home." On that fateful morning, she had been seen by my mom with her milk bucket in her hand. She had on her usual garb. The only thing different was an old jacket that had belonged to Papa.

There weren't many cars passing on the road yet. My mother said that she saw Mama who waited until there was a car that wasn't going too fast. She had just milked White Face, her cow. She then jumped out in front of it from behind a thick growth of shrubbery that had concealed her "Mama had committed suicide."

Muhmuh hung up the rotary dial phone and was trying to refocus. She stood up and gave me one of her loving hugs. Her beautiful face lit up. She stood about five feet eleven inches (she was about three to four inches taller than Gran). She had fair skin however through the years it was taking on a darker hue. She had the most beautiful eyes that were grayish green. Her lips were the thinnest lips that I had ever seen for a colored woman. Her nose was the only facial feature that was a dead give away that kept her and the whites in reality that she was negro – it had always been said that a drop of negro blood labeled that person a negro. There was only one thing that she and Auntee had that resembled each other and that was their cooking style. They were like twins.

My grandmother (Muhmuh) was a retired school teacher. She had been one of the first women (colored and white) in Meridian to learn how to drive and to purchase her own car – Gran never did learn to drive a car. He did, however, know how to ride his mule, Ol' Bill. She was indeed a woman of great substance who was on a mission, a woman of means we all knew that she mean what she said and said what she meant.

There was a lecture that was brooding and she was the one who was about to deliver it. I could feel it in my bones like looming gloom and quite frankly I didn't feel receptive to listen to it.

Their bedroom was extremely warm. It had a pungent odor of tobacco juice like the juice that had been placed so close to their gas heater. Obviously Gran had placed it there last night before he went to bed. He had absolutely refused to give up his awful chewing tobacco habit. Ever since the church had retired him he had become a semi-invalid. He sat for hours during the day in his rocking chair just staring into space, rubbing his knees. If by chance he would stop rocking, he would go to sleep and the brown slime from the tobacco juice would drizzly down the corner of his mouth. When he awakened he would aim to spit in the Prince Albert's can that he kept with him at all times. Sometimes he made it, most of the time, not. His quest in life seemed to have gone from being the pastor of a growing church that he had built to vegetating at home and running my grandmother ragged. She had taken her vow when she married him for better or worse for richer or poorer, in sickness…

Get one thing straight, Gran wasn't sick, he was seemingly angry and had given up because he had been replaced by popular vote with a younger minister whose style and message was completely different from Gran. He would have all of the household wait on him (pity party). He even had Muhmuh to help dress him. Afterwards he would take off to go visit the Wilson's next door. He seemed to like the company of Mrs. Wilson the most. She would return the visit. He liked to have her rub him on his bald head. It must have been innocent or Muhmuh would have put a stop to it. She explained that her being run ragged was what women had to do to stay with their husbands.

It sounded like a big plate of bullshit. It seemed that people made up their rules and regulations to fulfill their own purpose. Out of respect for Muhmuh I listened to her like a sweet/good girl supposed to, no questions asked.

"How you doin' Gran?" I asked with enthusiasm when I saw him blinking. Suddenly I was sorry that I had asked him a question because he was always sooo slow to respond. His speech was even slow and deliberate than when he was walking "oh God! I'm going to be stuck here all day waiting to get a simple answer (well I did ask)" I thought, maybe if I stay perfectly still, he would hopefully forget the question. He motioned for me to get his spit can that was warming nicely next to the heater. I got up quickly from his rocking chair to get the can. He was lying (perched) on the side of their full size bed that he shared with Muhmuh. It would appear that he would fall off but he never did. I've never seen anyone sleep so close to the edge of a bed. It was as if he was trying to stay as far from Muhmuh as possible. Maybe she had pushed him over the edge – but not quite. Gran finally spit the wad that he had packed in the side of his mouth. I knew the routine i.e. glass of water for rinsing and a glass of ice water for his thirst. He thanked me slowly. I was still waiting for his response for the question that I had posed earlier – then it came. It would have been so rude of me to leave. "Oh! I'm doing tolerably well" a few moment lapsed then at last, "how you do'n this mon'n Carrie Ann?" I answered quickly "I'm good thanks" careful not to ask anymore questions. The room was becoming unbearably hotter by the minute. Muhmuh had turned up the heater, "(Jemes) I'll get your bath water." She began helping him shave. She took off his p.j. top and his socks after she had assisted him to sit up on the side of the bed. She was singing an old hymnal – Down at the Cross – she could sing so good (that's how we all learned to sing). She came back into their room with a wash basin, towels, soap and a clean change of p.j.s.

We walked out of their steam room to the kitchen that was next door. She stopped and faced me, "Carrie Ann, I'm sorry that things didn't go well with you and Marvin." (I was sure that I had closed the book on that chapter of my life). She explained that she had only wanted what was best for me. She had hopes that I would one day have a good husband (I'm so glad she didn't say like me). I said, "Muhmuh, I'm still in school and have a long ways to go." Perhaps she knew something that I didn't know. I was soft hearted, mannerable girl who had always tried to live by the Golden Rule. Was Muhmuh trying to reveal something to me that would be beneficial to me later on in my life? If she was, it would certainly have to wait.

My name was being called by my little sister – saved by the bell – Muhmuh was about to get into second gear to lecture me on, "the family's expectation for all of you girls". Janie was getting impatient as she always did. She wedged in between me and Muhmuh and interrupted abruptly. "What cho do'n? I was so glad to see her at the moment. She was persistent, that's what made her special. Muhmuh became distracted from me because Gran was in the room wailing loudly, "Carrey! Carrey!" I could see the irritation on Muhmuh's face but then it softened as she turned around to attend to Gran's needs. She was honestly a caring and doting wife. I thought, "I could never be that kind of wife if I ever married." Janie began tugging at my jacket which I had kept on. I stopped short with her directly on my heels, "what do you want?" I asked. I knew that I had better change my tone of voice and my bad attitude or she would feel hurt. I looked at her and her eyes were still clear so she obviously hadn't been offended by me. She was skipping behind me and was looking so disheveled. Her hair was in such disarray her clothes were mismatched and wrinkled. "Mother said for you to comb my hair." She said after she saw me looking her over. It sounded too much like an order but I wasn't buying it. "Okay Janie," I said "let's go back home and I'll give you a nice hairstyle." She smiled up at me. I thought, "now that was easy enough, now the next thing I had to do was get a message to Connie who was still busy sprucing up their house. We often used a special code language that Janie hadn't learned yet. Pig Latin came in handy when there were little tattle-tells around. I asked her if her boyfriend (Tommie Gathright) was coming over to see her that night and above all, was his cute friend Joe Henry Mathis going to show up as he had done the last week. She stopped what she was doing and smiled at me.

Connie was always taunting and teasing me because she knew that I couldn't stand it. She asked – out of the blue – "sooo, what happened to Marvin? I thought that you two looked so good together." I was becoming furious. "Connie, stop it." I snapped playfully under my breath so that Janie wouldn't hear the conversation. Instantly I asked, "well is he coming here tonight or not?" She continued to tantalize me as she smiled then said, "Yes, Tommie said that he wanted to meet you ever since he saw you at a distance." My heart stopped beating briefly then started beating too fast. She said, "I'll call you when he gets here." I squealed ever so quietly as I didn't want to alarm my grandparents who were still behind their closed bedroom door.

Suddenly we were having summer weather in the middle of November. At least that was how my body felt. I was so hot when I left Muhmuh's house I literally floated back home with Janie right behind me. I was in such a daze for the rest of the day. I figured that I must have done all of my chores right. I combed and plaited Janie's hair. She had on neatly pressed clothes that I had found for her.

Time was passing so slowly. I walked around as if though I was a zombie. "Supper's ready" my family gathered for our evening meal as we generally did except for Saturday. I wasn't hungry at all because I was full of butterflies. I picked at my food that tasted like cotton. I asked to be excused. The anticipation was killing me. I had to get a grip on myself.

I knew what I would wear tonight. It was my best looking outfit which was a red and black plaid form fitted skirt, a black sweater and black leotards. I had just gotten my hair washed, pressed with the back curled under slightly. I wore bangs that were cut straight across my forehead with a bit of body to shape my thin oval face. My mother came into the room. I pretended that I was reading. I assured her that everything was okay. It's probably my period. She suggested that I take some aspirins for the cramps. She was walking out the door. I blurted out, "mother, I'm going over to Muhmuh's later to talk with Connie," who was also a good girl and I would be in the safety of Muhmuh's house.

We had only the telephone in our living room and in mother's room. I went and sat next to the one in the living room then went to the boys room to peer out of their window to see what was going on over at Muhmuh's house. After doing that several times, I realized "I'm not dressed yet!" It was only six o'clock in the evening. I had literally become a basket case. The next problem that I was faced with was waiting my turn to get into the Grand Central Station (bathroom). Deddy had the first dibs on it. He was going to his mason's meeting that was held on Friday nights. He used most of the hot water and left the bathroom in such disarray. He never did let the water out of the tub which had the most gross greasy ring around it. He knew that one of his children would clean up after him. We all knew not to question anything that he did. If we dared to venture onto his territory, there would certainly be a dear price to pay. My personal favorite was the old lecture, "I'm da boss in dis heah houz. I pays da coss ta be da boss!" The other price (remember the belt, no switch).

I could remember only two times that my father had used his belt to punish me and that was two times too many for me and for my mom. She wouldn't allow him to punish the girls, however, the boys weren't off limits. They all turned out to be good law abiding men.

Well, all of the grime was finally cleaned out of the tub that Deddy had left. There was no such thing as soaking or getting a leisure bath in our tub. I did get lost a tad in my thoughts then knock! Knock! Knock! "Carrie, I need to use the bathroom" I wonder who could it be – it was Janie of course. I got out of the tub that was so deep and it had four legs. It was a challenge for me and my petite (short) legs. I put a towel around me and opened the door. She was dancing around like she was going to wet herself. She seemed to have some kind of radar implanted in her head. She knew each time that someone was using the bathroom. Maybe it was a good thing because she had basically trained the whole family to hurry up and get out of there. She sat quickly on the commode as she watched me still wet and cold. She had a half a smile on her face. That time I didn't return it. I could hear only a trickle of pee. She was turning red as she was straining to squeeze cheese which never happened. I stood impatiently watching her performance. She dried off the tooky, "I'm finished," she said meekly. I couldn't help but smile to myself. She slowly walked out. I locked the door behind her then finished toweling off.

There was an old mirror that had been mounted on the bathroom wall. It was obviously hung for someone much taller than me. I wanted to see how much progress that I'd made. I was about 5 feet 2 inches and weighed about 90 pounds. My skin color was caramel. I had been told that I had a beautiful color skin. My legs were my greatest attribute as far as Grandmoh (paternal grandmother) was concerned. She mentioned them each time she visited us.

She said in her slow southern drawl, "you got legs jus' lak' yo' daddy." My breasts were still developing but not yet big enough to suit me. They did, however, stand at attention. I noticed that I had gotten more pubic hairs and also under my arm pits. I used the Tussy deodorant that we all used, it was about empty. There was no more sanitary napkin that I used from the Kotex box that all of the girls used except for Janie. We needed more.

Bam! Bam! Bam! "Carrie are you coming out of there? There are other people who need to use the bathroom." I put on my makeshift house coat. James was standing outside the door. "Well, it's about time" he said playfully. He and I had always played so well together as we were growing up. I thought back to the time when we were living in the old house. He must have been about seven years old and I about five years old (again) since there weren't any toys (no bicycles, skates, we had to be resourceful with what we had. There was one thing that we both found amusing (no, not star gazing). It was striking and watching matches as they burned up. Oh, it wasn't for lighting cigarettes or lighting a bon fire. It was simply just lighting matches just to see how long that we (he) could hold it without burning our (his) fingers. Now, James was the instigator – the brains for the operation. He would strike it as we muffled our laughter, our play area that we (he) had chosen was under our wood framed house. The one that was dried out till it had no color yes, a fire hazard that should have been condemned. We (I) found plenty of matches in the kitchen in those large match boxes. I was the worker bee – the follower, the look-out person. My assignment was, "Carrie, you go inside when nobody's watching and get a handful of matches." I was getting so weary because I had made several trips inside and down the stairs from the house then under the house where James awaited my return. Playing was wearing me out. He would scratch and watch the flame then – my mother found out what we were doing because Joyce was curious and had hid out of my sight. She was the culprit who told on us. Surprisingly the old house was spared but James and I weren't. we got a good spanking and sent to bed early without eating supper (our family over the years especially Joyce would never let us live down that near disaster).

James asked "what are you up to sis?" I thought for a moment because at that time, I didn't want him to be a part of lighting a fuse that would burn – I answered, "I'm just going over to Muhmuh's to talk to Connie, you know girl talk."

My hands were shaking so badly as I was putting on the forbidden make up. Mother would tan my hide if she knew about the red lip stick so I rammed it into the pocket of my jacket. My clothes were in the extremely small closet that was crammed pack with all of the girls' clothes. Don't ask! We did what we had to do and it worked.

My family – for the exception of Deddy who was at his "meeting" – were enjoying a TV program. It was wonderful to have the table model black and white TV. There was usually a pang of jealousy on my part whenever we passed the neighborhood whites who had color televisions. The burst of laughter from my family brought me back to reality. They must have been watching the Jack Bennie show. We had so much laughter in our family all derived from clean fun and wholesome family values. Laughter was the least thing on my mind at that moment. I began to pace the floor from the girl's room to the living room and then ring! ring! ring! It was for Deddy. Somebody wanted to speak to him about lining up a potential job. Lottie took the message I heard her say, "yes sir, no sir (a pause as she was writing down the message for Deddy. I became about unglued. I hated to hear her sound so subservient. I felt so above it all and had been disciplined by both my parents about my being insubordinate. "Carrie, your daddy has to work with white people. When you answer the phone you can't just say yes or no. You have to show respect to white folks or we won't be able to live here." There was a way around it but I didn't have any answers yet. I was coming unglued and nobody knew it. The phone rang again. Ring! Ring! Ring! "Carrie, it's for you. It's Connie." I ran and answered quickly, "Hello? Is he there?" She said, "Yes, Carrie and calm down." I slowly floated back to the bedroom, put on that ugly red carcoat over my shoulder, on a quick check in the mirror. I lost all of my confidence. "I don't think he will like me" but I was compelled to meet Tommy Gathright's friend.

Growing up in our community up until then was very simple. We all went to school during the week days and worshipped on Sunday. There were a very few people at Pleasant Hill who weren't cousins. There had been occasions when even my cousins would try to flirt with me. I thought, "eew! That's nasty!" Joyce had met and was dating Robert Gathright (not a cousin) and Connie at about the same time had begun seeing Tommy Gathright (Robert's younger brother). Their family was well known and respected by the community and by our church. Their family was in the logging business. Both of those young men were known by many to be the pillar of the earth and would probably make a good husband to some lucky woman. I saw the relationship of Joyce and Robert as it was blossoming. He had asked her to marry him and she had conceded. They talked about their wedding plans each time he came to visit her. I was always in hearing distance – to make sure that they stayed on track and that they did until one fateful day – there was phone call to Joyce, it seemed that there had been an accident. The logging truck that Robert Gathright was driving had veered off the slippery, winding hairpin curve that was about one and a half miles from our house. The message continued that the driver had lost control of the truck. He was thrown from his truck. It didn't have a door on the driver side and of course no seat belts. He died instantly.

That incident shook up so many families. It hurt me so much to see my sister suffer. I cried for her and her loss. I questioned why would God allow something like that to happen to such a wonderful man (the Lord giveth and the Lord taketh – blessed be the name of the Lord) whose life was just beginning. So, now it's all over except for those left behind. Connie was also suffering because she was in love with Robert's brother. A young man who had come from the same righteous family. Connie and Tommy had tried to get me interested in his younger brother (my mo-jo didn't work on him) I must say I did my best but without any luck. So, what's a girl to do?

I saw Tommy's car parked over in Muhmuh's driveway. It was dark but I was still able to see another vehicle parked behind his. The dim street light in front of our house (the last one on 22nd Avenue) didn't illuminate too much further than objects right under it. Fifty feet beyond it was pitch black. I was able to avoid the small stream (I jump across it) that flowed between the two properties right next to their driveway.

Connie had left the front porch light on. I stopped short before knocking and put on the lipstick that was hidden in my pockets. I had had so much practice in the mirror I didn't worry that it may be smeared. I knew that it was on perfect. I pulled off the car coat, "now I'm ready." I thought as I slithered up the front steps. I didn't want to appear too eager. I had remembered, "stay calm, be cool" Connie had whispered earlier. Knock, knock, knock. Connie asked teasingly, "who is it?" I wanted to strangle her – I answered, "It's me, Carrie." I walked inside the house that seemed to be hotter than usual (or was it me?). I said, "Hi" to Connie and Tommy. I then focused my attention to the person/the young man/the boy that stole my heart at that moment. Tommy said, "Carrie this is Joe Henry Mathis" Joe Henry asked quickly looking at me, "What's yo' name?" Timidly I answered, "I'm Carrie." I walked over to where he was standing next to the upright piano. I held out my hand for a polite handshake – he took both my hands in his then kissed them ever so lightly (that had never happened). His hands were so warm and massive. He looking down at me with a broad smile that was melting my poh' little heart. He stood about one foot taller than me. I would say, six feet. His body was slender with broad shoulders that was somewhat slumped. His eyes were like no other that I had ever seen. They were small, brown, and slightly slanted. Those eyebrows were perfectly shaped as if they were plucked. He had eye lashes that most women would die for they were so thick. The color of his skin and texture was smooth chocolate brown with a ruddy hue to it. He was sporting a goatee and mustache that was trimmed (like a well manicured lawn) so perfectly around the mouth that was speaking to me (earth to Carrie, hello!). he was trying to make small talk with me. There was nothing small about that man nor our meeting. He said, "I likes wha' cho' wearin'" My foot went into my open mouth. I said something so lame, "Is that jacket leather?" He responded, "yes, it is" He was busy looking at me, up and down and kept saying, "yo' look'n good!" I complimented him, "you look good yourself." He was making me a bit uncomfortable the way he was staring at me, undressing me with his piercing eyes. He smiled again and that was the deciding factor for my meltdown. He had a gorgeous set of white teeth although I could smell cigarette smoke.

Connie and Tommy were sitting on the only sofa in the room deep in conversation. There was soft slow music on the radio. It was a popular song by Jerry Butler. His voice sounded so good, we both got carried away from his mood setting music. We began dancing the slow drag. I started singing along very softly, "He don't love you, like I love you, if he did he wouldn't break your heart." My knees were buckling under me. I looked up into his eyes. He pulled me even closer to him. The smell of his aftershave was so enticing. I got another smile from him when he saw me looking at him. It was then that I saw the dimples. My heart was pounding. I couldn't sing anymore. I forgot the tune. We continued to slow drag. There was so much heat that we generated from our bodies. His left hand slipped down my back and landed on my (oh God he was going to know that I didn't have a big bootie) butt. He touched me in such a way that I'd never been touched before. My head was resting on his shoulders. I could feel the pounding of his heart. He was so gentle yet masterful. I didn't want him to release me. He then touched my face with his left hand and caressed it lightly. I tried to keep my composure but I knew that he saw the longing yet frightened look on my face. I was breathing so hard, deeper and deeper almost out of control. I knew that I had better remain cool and calm as I had promised Connie. During those thoughts I felt his hand under my chin as he tilted my head ever so slightly – it was slow and deliberate. It felt like an eternity. I closed my eyes, I wanted it to happen and then – he kissed me on the mouth. I smiled as he was looking at me. He cupped my head on both sides. Again I felt his mouth on mine. I opened my lips a little. His tongue was so soft and tantalizing as it searched for mine. It was the longest and the sweetest kiss that a man, woman, boy or girl could ever experience. The music had stopped a long time ago. We were still dancing in a trance. We were brought back to reality. We kept looking at each other holding on to what seemed like a fleeting moment. The fact was he had been there for almost two hours and we never sat down.

Connie had gotten up to get Tommy a glass of cold water. She must have went in to see Muhmuh because I heard her call out, "Carrie Ann, is that you?" I answered, "Yes máme Muhmuh." (I was trying to get out of the habit of putting máme on to my responses). Connie and Tommy were walking toward the dining room where Muhmuh was cutting a piece of fresh baked pound cake that had been cooling on the cupboard. Connie beckoned for me and Joe Henry to follow them. He seemed a bit reluctant. He already knew who she was. I went over to her as she sat down at the dining table I gave her and kissed her on the cheek and a quick hug. She smiled at me then looked past me. Tommy did the introductions. "Muhmuh this is Joe Henry Mathis my friend." She was already taking a bite of the cake. Joe went over and shook her hand and told her that he had stopped by to see Connie and Tommy and that he also wanted to meet me, "Whew!" I was sweating bullets because I thought that she was going to go ballistic (although she had never before). She began talking about how she knew Joe Henry's family. She mentioned "meeting Mr. Mathis and the twin brothers."

Muhmuh was not about to go back to her room. I wondered if she had heard me breathing so loudly. She would have said something if she had suspected anything. It was getting late and time for the chickens to go to roost. Tommy planted a quick kiss on Connie's cheek in front of our grandmother. She seemed pleased that Connie was seeing him. Joe Henry was about to leave then turn around to face me. I had gone back to the corner where Muhmuh couldn't see me. He came over to where I was. He said, "I like you a lot, you are so pretty." Then he whispered, "you look like a beatnik." We both laughed. He added, "I'll call you later, I'll get your phone number from Tommy." He gave me a quick kiss square on the mouth. "Bye." My heart quickened as he left I felt so empty. He was outside talking to Tommy for a minute. He got into his souped up, pick-up truck. He started the motor then revved it three times. He reminded me of a wild stallion. He backed up so fast then like a bat out of hell he was gone, as he tooted the horn that sounded uuga! uuga! uuga! That was the first time that I had literally witnessed someone burn rubber. There was something so exciting about it.

I was still on cloud nine while I was regurgitating the evening with Connie. She told me in a playful tone, "girl, you are too fast, you need to cool your lily." I agree with her then I put on my ugly red coat then took off running to my house. The door was still unlocked. Deddy's car wasn't in the driveway yet so I left it unlocked for him.

Our house was cold and quiet except for the different sleeping snoring sounds that came from the three bedrooms. The excitement of the evening had left me ravenous. I could have eaten raw meat and that was about all that I found in the refrigerator. I had my chance earlier and I blew it. I found some dry cereal, and over ripened bananas and cold milk that was about to go bad (Lord I need energy give me strength). I felt a pang of guilt because I knew that God wouldn't find any pleasure from my behavior earlier with Joe Henry. I stopped eating and went into a trance for a while just thinking about him. I couldn't finish my cereal. The house was so dark…there was a hint of light from the street light through the window. I undressed without turning the lights on. I took off my size 32A bra. My tee shirt that I slept in was in my drawer. I must have put it on backwards. I felt like a bat in the night and my mission was accomplished. I found my hair rollers and clumsily rolled my hair up. I tied it up with my head rag. I sure didn't look like a beatnik anymore.

There was no need for reading my romance books because I had found the real thing. I inched quietly into the bed then under the cold covers. Bennie was already asleep. I said my prayers. I prayed that God would forgive me. I asked if Joe Henry would be a part of my life and – morning came again. Janie was such an early riser, no matter what day it was. Saturday were no exceptions. I got up and got into second gear because I had promised mother that I would help her do the ironing for Mrs. Knighton (the white lady who lived up the road from us). She had brought the clothes late yesterday. They had already been washed and starched. There were twelve men's shirts (her husbands') and a few little girls skirts and blouses. I had learned to iron my clothes a long time ago – "now why couldn't they?" I thought.

Mother said she "needed the extra money". Daddy didn't want his wife working for no body. They would start arguing about her taking another job with another white family in town. It was for only a half a day on Saturday morning until the afternoon. The Bailey family liked my mom and paid her for a full days work. They gave Mother a beautiful dining room table with twelve chairs that Mother repadded. She was given a full set of silverware. I think that most of the set was accidentally thrown in the trash by well meaning over zealous children. the dining set is still in existence.

Mother was getting ready to go to work Lottie was waiting to drive her. Mother found me and gave me instructions on doing the ironing and showed me where the coat hangers were. She warned me not to scorch the clothes. I asked, "Where is Janie?" Mother answered me as she was walking out of the front door and looking over her shoulder, "She's over at Muhmuh's looking after Gran." Mother was so pretty. She always strutted when she walked. She was in a hurry and moving fast. She must have been late for her job (she had always stressed the importance of being prompt). As children we all understood for the exception of Joyce, accepted what mother stood for and what she wanted from all of her children. Joyce would get a kick out of being a non-conformist. She took pride in being "just like my daddy." She had told me on many occasions, "I'm daddy's favorite." It appeared that it was true when we were growing up. He seemed to beam when she was telling jokes to amuse anybody who would listen. But on the other hand, he seemed so proud and stated, "I love all of ya'll the same."

The house was totally empty except for me and the mountain of clothes. I prepared them as I had been taught to lightly sprinkle them with water and roll each article tightly so that the moisture would remain in it until it was time for me to iron it. Mother had purchased an electric (no steam) iron. She had however saved one of the cast irons that she used to press our clothes with. I watched her as she would place two to three iron in the hearth inside a metal container to keep the black soot from getting on the iron. She used a "fire poker" to lift it out. She had a make shift ironing board and had pine straw to keep the bottom of the iron smooth (the starch would cake up on the sides and underneath the iron). We had come a long way baby and the cast iron was a friendly reminder to be thankful for what we had that was more simplified. I came out of my thoughts just in time to realize that I smelled something burning, no scorching a little. It was on the back side of Mr. Knighton's blue shirt. I became more careful not to drift off again or there would certainly be consequences. Mother would hear about it from Mrs. Knighton then I would have to hear the lecture again about, "when a task has begun, never stop until it's done, be the labor great or small do it well or not at all." Well quite frankly I didn't want to work but I needed the money and oh yes, "money don't grown on trees." There seemed to be colored folks saying for every subject that was being discussed.

My daddy's all time favorite was, "make do or do wid ou'" I didn't see myself doing without however I did have enough common sense to refrain from questioning his philosophy on life. I wanted so much more and became angry at what I was doing to earn such meager amounts. The pile of unironed clothes was becoming – "oh, I'm almost finished" I thought as I saw the bottom of the clothes basket. I began to smile. The radio was on low so I turned it up on high to drown out the quiet. It was an old floor model with a turn table that daddy had found on the side of the road. He brought it home and Uncle Brother (Aunt Gladys' husband) who was an electrician, fixed it. It served its purpose. I was able to get a station WMOX that played some rhythm and blues, spirituals, mostly country and western. I listened to it because that was the only clear station that we were able to get – it grew on me. I had to adapt because I loved music so much. I liked Hank Williams, Johnny Cash and Loretta Lynn.

As I was finishing the last article of clothes the phone rang. I turned the iron off and ran to answer it. I was hoping against hope that it would be Joe Henry. Well it wasn't it was for daddy. The man was calling him about a job. He sounded white with a distinct very different drawl and enunciation. He asked, "Is yo daddy at home?" I was careful not to say sir because it was getting tiring – instead of saying, "no sir mister Jack" I said, "He's not here, whom shall I say is calling?" (rather melodiously). There was a pause – "yo te him mister Jack Jimmerson ca'd" I was cracking up inside I almost giggled out loud. Regaining my composure I said very politely and proper, "I have a paper and a pen, please spell your name." Again a pause – he spelled M-I-S-T-E-R J-A-C-K J-I-M-M-E-R-S-O-N, my phone number is 555-2202." I paused, "I'll repeat it back to you." Enthusiastically I said, "that's Jack Jimmerson" and I repeated the phone number "is that correct?" (I refused to put sir at the end of the sentence). He answered with irritation mixed in with his southern drawl, "yo te' Tommie Lee I said to call me toni' and wha' is yo' name?" I could feel the hatred in his voice even on the telephone. It was his problem and I couldn't change him. So I answered him, "I'm Carrie Ann, I'm Mr. Tommie Lee Pearson's daughter. I'll tell him you called." I doubt if daddy got the job. I got something from it – I would respect a person when it was earned. I felt so proud of myself. I was on the verge of becoming a different person from being so passive and powerless when it boiled down to meeting problems straight on.

I didn't care about much of nothing except getting a follow up call from Joe Henry. It was midday. I thought I heard the phone ring. I ran to it and realized it was the radio. I need to get a grip on reality. I put the make shift ironing board away in the girls closet then folded the children's items neatly in the clothes basket.

The Knighton's house could be seen from my parent's house. They kept their lawn well manicured. There were flowers all around it. They had a paved driveway as much as I had loathed doing their ironing it was worst going to their house to take the finished product. I went to the side door then knocked on it after I had put the basket on the top step. I waited what seemed an hour. I could hear them talking inside. I knocked louder and called out, "Mrs. Knighton" I stepped back and looked to both sides. She finally opened the door – no hello kiss my grits – I thought, "what a homely woman." She stood about five feet eleven not fat just big boned. The frown on her face had frozen. It would probably crack if she had attempted to burst a smile. So, she didn't (smile). There was nothing feminine about her. Her reddish blond hair looked as if she had attempted a home perm and store bought dye that had gone bad. The hair just hung there not short not long (maybe that was why she had such a scowl look on her face). I couldn't understand what Mr. Knighton was thinking when he gave that creature his name and had the nerve to (yuk) lay with her. They had conjured up those two extremely dim witted overweight boy and girl that looked so much like her – Jimmy de cricket get me out of here. Still no greeting along with the non smiley face. It was one of the most uncomfortable moments in my life up until then. I thought, "wonder why you don't do your own ironing." I answered myself, "let the niggers do it as long as we can." She continued to stare at me. I was feeling so belittled then she finally spoke, "tell Cleo I'll have mo' ironing nex' week." She then put a whole one dollar bill and a twenty five cent piece in my hand (there wasn't a thank you see you later or kiss my ass ya'll come back now ya hear" Ouch! That hurt. I guess the golden rule wasn't applicable to the freight knights. I swore to myself that after that day I would never iron their clothes again.

The tears were welling up in my eyes. Then they streamed down my tired face – not just from the labor but I wasn't recognized nor was I appreciated for doing a good job. I was practically blinded by the tears and feeling sorry for myself. I wasn't ready for the cruel world – I came so close to being hit by a car that came off the roadway. It seemed as if it was done on purpose. I stopped crying because I needed to stay focused on staying alive. I looked back at the house of horror. There was someone in the window. I wasn't sure what those people were capable of doing. There was no where to hide so I ran as fast as my short legs would carry me.

It was late afternoon. Mother was already home from her day job. Mr. and Mrs. Bailey had driven her home because Deddy had made it clear that he didn't want just the husband driving his wife nowhere. I think that there was a tad bit of jealousy that wasn't provoked by mother. She just wanted to keep herself busy. She must have known that her babies were growing up and would eventually moving out. That was an unspoken hope that we all would get our education and find a good partner – no! husband or wife. There wasn't going to be no such thing as shacking up. It was perfectly understood that, "yo needs to be married befo you git in those watas." When that happened she would again be alone with Deddy.

My dad pulled up shortly in his pick up truck with my three brothers and my dads paid helper. They all began unloading the sand, bricks, lumber and nails. Scraps from the job site that he had completed. There were so many scrap piles that was filling up our huge yard all on the left side of our house. There was no clutter on the right side between our house and Muhmuh's house.

Daddy came in and sat with mother at the dining room table. He put the money that he had made in front of mother and she counted it. She already knew what bills that need to be paid and the amount that he had wasn't going to be enough. There were some disagreements, Deddy dug deeper in his pockets and found more money that he reluctantly placed on the table. Mother became somewhat satisfied. She freshened up then he drove her to the community grocery store. They had a running account there for years. There had been times that daddy couldn't work because of the weather or if business was slow at which times mother would use the money from her day jobs. The bickering would start again. One thing about those two people they never ever went to bed angry at each other. You do the math – eight wonderful children that they had brought to this earth.

It was getting late in the evening. There was excitement in the air. Lottie had just arrived home from a permanent job that she held with a prominent colored dentist, Dr. Cornigy. She was his assistant. She obviously was doing very well because he had just given her a raise and with her new found wealth she was able to purchased a used car and buy me some new store bought clothes. It was under the condition that I do more chores around the house. Lottie was like my second mom since she was the oldest and had proven herself to be responsible to all of us. She had been left in charge many times when our parents were away on errands. She looked and acted so much like mother almost like twins (I've told her how much she was appreciated). Although she may have resented all of the added responsibilities she never let it be known. There were many times that she could or should have been out exploring, playing or even resting, but she didn't. She cared for all of us so well. She would catch flack from Joyce who wanted to be the oldest with its lime light but she didn't want the accountability that it took for such a large family – I digress. It wasn't as hard as I've made it out to have been. We were actually raised to take care of each other. That's the reason that I accepted my duties to be a big sister to Willie and Janie.

I felt worn out but the prospect of getting two new outfits gave me renewed energy. I washed the breakfast dishes that had been standing in the kitchen sink all day. Lottie had stopped by Winn Dixie on the way home and bought all of the fixings for home made hamburgers. She had enough cooking space on the kitchen counter and the island that my dad had built for mother. Hunger had almost gotten the best of me. My mental list of things to do was growing. The moping and straightening up the living room I found a pile of sand on the floor in front of the couch where daddy had taken off his old Brogan (work shoes) and emptied all of the sandy contents on the floor. It was his ritual. Mother had given up long time ago on picking up after him. He was the king of the castle and we were the keepers of the castle, enough said! No back talk.

The bathroom was my last stop, I pondered, "were those outfits really worth all of this dang crap? Yup!" I tackled the sink that was so filthy with grime and grease from ten people constantly using it. The commode lid was…was, "okay I can do this." When I finally finished it was sparkling clean and smelled like pine oil. I was proud and I felt so good that it would be noticed and above all I would get paid.

I knew that Lottie would inspect the work that I'd completed. Oh no! I'd forgotten to polish the new furniture that she bought for the living room! She had also purchased tile flooring for the kitchen, dining room and living room. When I finally finished (for real) I sat back on the beautiful dusty rose colored sofa, the set had a small rocker and a big overstuffed (big wide arms) chair of the same color. There was a bonus electric wall clock on one wall. The edge was done in delicate laces in black and gold antique brass. On the opposite wall hung a large picture of a large orchid. It was framed beautifully and encased under glass. There were two matching end tables and one coffee table that the family's ceramic green frog was kept for years.

I didn't mind cleaning it because it was like being in a fairy tale compared to where we had lived before. We were no longer nomads.

It would bring me great pleasure to have a special young man visit me in that house that had been built by my daddy. What a princess I was in our home – then "supper is ready." Lottie summoned us as she had done so many times.

Everybody had the same hamburger, no supersized, have it your way – onions, jungle style with a coke, with fries – none of that – she had seasoned the ground beef and made thick patties, pan grilled twelve because there was always at least two people who wanted seconds. She had put mayonnaise and ketchup on each side of the burger buns. It was garnished with lettuce, tomatoes and onion slices. She had set the table for all of us. The colored tin tumblers all had two to three cubes of ice. Cherry Kool Aid had already been pored in all of the containers. The assembled hamburgers were on a platter in the middle of the table. There were some hot green and red fresh peppers for mother Lottie and Tommy (Boy Baby). Deddy liked home made pepper sauce or hot sauce. He sat at one end and mother at the opposite end of the large table. He had cleaned up real good and was ready to make his Saturday night escape. Mother asked the blessing, Deddy, "Rise Peter slay and eat." That verse was uttered throughout the many meals that we all had together.

I helped Lottie straighten up the kitchen. The phone didn't ring again except for a wrong number then uuga! uuga! uuga! I ran to the front door then out to the road. It had gotten dark and all that I could see was a disappearing glow of the fast moving vehicle front head lights. Connie was standing in their front yard. She must have heard the same phantom sound of the car or maybe it was a truck that we all had heard. We waved and we both went back inside.

My life seemed to have come to a screeching halt. Thanksgiving day had always been a special celebration for my family. Everything around me was changing or maybe it was I who didn't want to attend our yearly family Thanksgiving dinner that was to be held in town at Aunt Janie's house. Her oldest daughter (Daisy) had recently married and had moved to Indiana. The rest of her children were still living at home.

We arrived early and the feast was almost ready. The house had a tantalizing smell of cake that was still baking in the oven. The twenty eight pound turkey was being centered on an extra large platter then garnished with pickled crab apples, it complemented the beautifully brown bird. I soon forgot about being such a spoil sport because somebody (Janie) had told Deddy that I was acting mean to her and I heard him say to mother, "that girl had better straighten up and fly right, or else". Our Thanksgiving feast was a huge success. Our parents started planning for next year and it would be held out in the country at Mother and Deddy's house.

Georgia Mae and I did what we traditionally was expected to do. That may have been the reason that I had tried to get out of attending the gathering. She and I had the honor of washing all of the dadblasted dishes. We put up a good argument about why we shouldn't have to clean up all of the mess. It appeared that Aunt Janie had used practically all of the pots and pans in her kitchen. She had also used her fancy fine china, silverware and crystal glasses. We finished washing everything and put back into the china cabinet in about an hour – nothing was broken.

Later she and I found a quiet corner in her bedroom that she shared with Christine (her sister). They had a record player that played 45 RPM records. She put our favorite on – Johnny Ace – a popular tune was Pledging My Love. We began to sing along with it until Janie Ruth (my official spy) found us. We started talking in pig Latin. Georgia told me about her new boyfriend James Simms who had started calling her. We had to be ever so careful because Janie was trying to decipher our code.

We got permission from both our parents to walk to the neighborhood grocery store to get cokes. I was about to pop, I had eaten so much. We were walking real slow headed back to her house. The path that we took was short cut that all of the neighborhood kids would use. We were laughing about our latest ventures, her with her James and me with my Joe Henry. We didn't see or hear him coming (we called him the village idiot). He was riding his bike at break neck speed. He let out a blood curdling yell, "yeee haaa!" he was aiming his bike right at us. Georgia Mae flew to right and I to the left. There was a gulley on her side that was lined with medium sized rocks. Its banks sloped down approximately ten feet. There was a shallow stream that we had often played in the past. We both got up stunned and began to brush our selves off. It seemed that there weren't any broken bones only our spirit and pride. Georgia finally regained her composure then explained that Jonathan (the idiot) lived across the street from her. His grandma had taken he and his little sister in. Their mother had abandoned them five years ago. He was left to take care of his six year old sister. The experience drove him crazy. The authorities found out that he had been molesting his sister. The law was called and he was locked up in the nut house. Apparently he needed to go back. At one point someone had heard his grandma screaming for help. She was found tied up, he stood about six feet tall, he towered over her as he beat her unmercifully. The police came – although they took their time getting there because it was in a colored neighborhood. When they arrived they had their sirens on, Jonathan ran out of their back door. Their house was right next to the gulley upstream. The trees on both sides were so thick that the cops wouldn't or couldn't ever find him.

Becoming a woman did have its drawbacks. It appeared that my periods were very irregular – on two week – off two weeks. I thought I was going to die. My mother finally figured it out when she had to buy much more supplied of sanity napkins. I was looking so pale and not feeling like my usual self. The glee and laughter was slowly draining out of me. Mother pulled me aside and told me that I should have said something earlier. She was apparently uncomfortable to even have that conversation with me. She said, "I'm going to take you over to see Dr. Stodard," the family doctor.

I had heard Deddy tell mother that he would rather have a white doctor because he didn't want no negro doctor touching any of his daughters and she was included (whom he called Shorty, FYI).

My dad drove my mother and me to the doctor's office. He parked the old used Ford sedan that had the dullest grey paint job – it got us to where we needed to go – we had to walk about a block. The building was a medium sized wood framed building that had been freshly painted white and trimmed with brown around the windows and the door. I was eager to get this over with. As I was reaching for the door knob, mother called out softly, "not that door, Carrie." There was a sign on the door that I didn't see. In large letters it read, "Whites Only!" and under it another sign, "Colored in the back!" (as I write I'm finding it so difficult to hold the tears back). I turned to both my parents who were standing and waiting to lead me to the BACK DOOR. Mother had read the sign to daddy, he didn't blink smile or cry. He was like a blank canvas awaiting his superiors to outline who he was then paint the color that they had for him – colored – he had been taught and had became passive because he had to work for them to make a living for us.

Going back to the back door was like a slap in my face. On entering I noticed the nice waiting room to the right side of the entry way. There were a few whites sitting in the area that was so clean and inviting. They sat on a sofa and several comfortable overstuffed chairs. Magazines were strewn on a coffee table and end tables. There was the nicest live plant that loomed over the room in the far right corner. Just as I was about to step into what seemingly could have been a living room, we were intercepted by the white nurse/receptionist. Her voice was as cold and crisp as the white starched uniform that she wore. She said looking past us, "you kin wait in thar."We all turned to her as she pointed to another room that would be befitting for an animal (excuse me, to a person that is despised). There were about ten straight chairs with the wooden bottom. The small bare window made the room feel even colder. The walls were painted a sterile gray that was peeling. The ceiling had signs of an old water leak. The floor was tiled that needed replacing. We sat for what seemed like hours. I saw that all of the white patients in the real waiting were seen by the doctor.There were two others that had came in after us. They were about to be seen. I sat there and saw was what happening and I knew that I had better not say anything to upset their accepted way of life. My dad looked at his watch, he got up abruptly. He said, "ya'll com on!" he added, "I needs to go check ona job." My mother and I got up. She put her arms around my shoulder. "It's going to be alright" she saw the pain that I had experienced that day. Not white enough, not human enough, not good enough and above all not clean enough to be seen by a professional doctor. I wondered did he take the Hippocratic Oath to provide care to people who were in need of medical care. That incident was the deciding factor that would guide my life's path that I would eventually take.

Deddy drove around for a while without saying a word, his way of refocusing. We stopped to get something to eat. He wasn't in a hurry to check on any job. He did what he had to do to protect his family. Tasty Treat was a small hole in the wall that served the best burgers and barbeque beef sandwiches, their specialty, which we all ordered. The young waitress was very friendly to all of us and extremely friendly and familiar with Deddy. She called him by his name, Mr. Tommy Lee, real nice and smooth. They kept cracking jokes throughout the lunch. Mother was such a lady, she didn't say anything but her cordial smile was forced as she tried to stay in the conversation. I pretended that I didn't see what was happening. I loved coming to Tasty Treat. It was owned and operated by a colored couple, Mr. and Mrs. Lester Jackson. Apparently it was a successful business because it was always crowded. It was located in a strip mall that was surrounded by old homes. Some of which were so dilapidated they should have been condemned but they weren't. Families lived in them and for the most part, seemed content. Their children were constantly running in and out after school to buy a penny's worth of bubble gum or a jaw breaker (hard candy).

He also sold a nickels worth of ice cream cone. Occasionally he would sell fresh shaved ice that was flavored with either cherry or bubblegum (blue) flavor - snow cone. He had to stop working so much because of multiple medical problems. But that didn't stop him completely. What a jolly man. He was certainly suited for being a cook. He had a lot of experience of being a people person as well as monopolizing the best barbeque business in Meridian.

I remembered being in that place when I attended Weshler Jr. High School. After class adjourned I would sneak up the street as did most of my classmates. We got in line for the fast selling snow cones. Most of the time we got there when he sold his last one.

Mr. Jackson came over to our booth and he obviously recognized my dad. They shook hands. Deddy introduced mother and me. "How ya'll do'n?" He didn't seem to recognize me.

I looked at both my parents. I loved them both and respected their position in life. My daddy (player player) and my mother (the wife who didn't want to know the truth). There were so many life's lessons that I was forced to learn at my tender age.

Deddy drove us to Winn Dixie to get beef liver and rice. Mother got fresh fruit and a large head of cabbage for supper that night. She needed something from the drugstore down town Meridian. Deddy put all the groceries in the trunk then headed for the only drugstore in town that catered to the colored folk. She went in and came back shortly with a bottle of 'tonic.' "It'll make you feel better Carrie" she said as she handed it to me to read the label. She took it back because she would assure that I would take it.

We were parked across the street from Youngs Hotel and Beauty Parlor. Cousin Ruth Jones worked there. She was a beautician. She did our hair every two weeks (shampoo press and curl). I didn't see her in her booth. If she was anywhere close by we would have known it. The lady was so loud and talked so nasty. I genuinely enjoyed being in her company because she kept me in stitches. I had often wished that I had that kind of personality. She was quick to put people in their place. She would not have stood for the incident at the doctor's office.

Meridian was growing in so many ways yet some things remained the same. We were in the center of the colored area of downtown. All of the citizens of our persuasion that wanted to open up a business, here was the place to do it. There was always some drunken man all sprawled out on the sidewalk. Mother was looking out the window and saw such a person. She shook her head, "he must have had one too many." She continued, "I saw him come out of that place on the corner a minute ago." The man had staggered, reached for a lamp post but didn't quite make it. He fell hitting his forehead on the pavement. He wasn't moving. Someone from Joe Louis Café came running out calling for him. He kneeled next to the fallen man. A crowd was gathering around him. We heard a siren in about five minutes. Two people jumped out of the ambulance. They stabilized him then put him on the stretcher and took him to Matty Hearsy County Hospital.

Daddy turned to mother, "do you need anything else?" (he seemed content to drive her any place she wanted as she never learned to drive a car). She said, "no, thank you." They smiled at each other. As we were driving away I looked up to the second floor of the café. There were two couples near the window dancing to the loud music that filtered out to the street. They were intertwined so closely, their movements were sensual. How strange it was to have a dance floor over a café. There were Falstaff Beer neon lights in the window. My curiosity was getting the best of me about that place. I saw a young man come out of the main entrance. I couldn't see who it was but he looked so familiar the way he walked, it looked just like Joe Henry from the rear.

On the way home my thoughts were so intense on him. He had said that he liked me and would call me soon. That was several weeks ago. Mother broke my train of thoughts, "Carrie, how are you doing back there?" I answered, "I'm fine mother, can we stop and get an icee?" (a slush carbonated drink). Deddy heard my request. He stopped at the 24-hour store. He came back with three large containers for all of us.

The remaining days of our Thanksgiving vacation was slowly coming to a close. I had scheduled myself to work for a newly wedded white couple to babysit their four month old son. As a matter-of-fact, all of my babysitting jobs had to be pre-approved by mother. She would get their background information. They were either recommended by one of our relatives or word of mouth from another white family for whom we had worked for.

I did raise my eyebrow when I was informed of their marital status and already had a newborn. I knew that it would be impolite to ask questions. So I kept my mouth shut because I needed the money. There were so many things that I wanted to do with the money that I was saving. I planned to buy a small turn table and of course some of the latest records. My thoughts were interrupted by a car horn outside. It was too far for me to walk to their house so mother had the couple to pick me up and would bring me back afterwards. We got to their house that was fairly close to Aunt Gladys' house. They knew her because she had done some day work for the brides' mom.

Their home – modest – was wood framed. The yard was plain with a gravel driveway. Her mom and her boyfriend were sitting in their cluttered living room. I thought to myself, "this doesn't look as good as my parent's home." The shallow introductions were made. The mom and her man barely nodded as they continued to take sips of what smelled like scotch whiskey – it was morning people! – they were half cladded which didn't seem to matter to any of the party people that I was staring at them in amazement. The young couple could hardly keep their hands off of each other. Mom and her guest were getting frisky with each other also. I was awaiting instructions for the supposedly babysitting job. They must have forgotten that I was still in the kitchen and getting quite impatient.

I began looking around hoping to find a bathroom. The first door that I opened wasn't the bathroom but the couple's lions den. The groom was plunging so deep into her that neither of them realized that I had opened their door during their private moment it didn't seem to matter because I must have been invisible. She let out a yelp as if she was a wounded dog. I closed the door and thereafter I heard laughter from both of them. Was that my job, to observe that white man and his wife as they got it on? They came out holding hands as if nothing had happened. They got a drink from the half empty bottle on the coffee table. Mom and her man seemed to be getting busier on the couch then – yaaaah! – it was the cry from their forgotten infant. The bride went into another equally cluttered room as I followed behind her. I've never seen such a chubby, blue-eyed, white (very pale) baby in my life. He was so adorable and even tempered.

Mrs. Bride gave me my instructions quickly. I thought, "you want me to do what and where?" She wanted a miracle from me and I was fresh out. I didn't look like a dark version of Cinderella either. I needed the money – I nodded as if I was agreeing that it would be done. Starting with "Feed the baby then give him a bath. Clean the living room, clean the two (cluttered) rooms, clean the kitchen and the bathroom. There is two loads of clothes to be washed and the clothes line is out in the back yard." I thought, "Yeah right!"

They all left to run some errands and promised to be back by four o'clock. So my first and foremost responsibility was to that cute little fat kid. I made him comfortable and a full belly. I was getting so overwhelmed by the time that I had washed the dishes and was hanging out the first load of clothes.

The liquor had been left out and so was some loose change (probably to test me to see if I would steal it). I didn't take the change but I sure did hit that bottle several times. When I finished with it, I was on full and it was almost empty.

They returned back earlier than I had expected. Their cute kid was sound asleep in his crib safe and sound in his disheveled bedroom. They checked their bedroom and nothing had been touched. It remained in the same cluttered disarrayed state that they had left it in. I'm sure that they saw their liquor bottle was almost on empty. They had asked my mom if I could come and babysit and I did and then some. I was never asked to come back again. I've often wondered how that cute kid was doing. Oh, yes, I was paid three dollars, the amount that had been agreed upon. Not good yet not bad considering that they would have to go back to town to the package (liquor) store to replenish their supply.

As a child there was nothing no better than going to the walk in movie. All of the children in my family and our cousins would all get together to see who wanted to go. Generally it would be Lee and

Connie (my cousins) Bennie, James, Willie and me. We all had little odd jobs and had our own ten cents fare to the movie theatre. We were appalled when they raised the fare to 15¢ a person. How dare them. We had to walk about two miles to the city bus stop. We paid a token or 5¢ for the one way trip. Sometimes arrangements were made for my dad to pick us up after the movie if we needed him to.

We all paid up and headed to the back of the bus because that's what we were taught to do. On one afternoon it appeared that the bus was filled up with white passengers. Some of them had taken the back seats that were generally used by us colored. There were some empty seats next to a few white folks. I couldn't find a seat with my crew. So as I was about to sit next to – the driver almost veering into oncoming traffic. There was so much anger in his voice when he finally got the bus back on track. He barked out, "you don't sit there, you needs to go" – he was interrupted by a white man who saw my plight and the frightened look on my face. "I'll sit in another seat" as he arose and went past me – through me – he sat next to another white lady. They exchanged hellos and pleasantries. I said, "thank you" (I added sir). He didn't look my way or answer me – I was definitely invisible.

It looked like things had not gotten any better for us than when I was in the first grade and had to ride the city bus. I was so eager to be in school. I didn't want to miss any days out of that new venture of just being away from home. Many times we would see the bus as it was pulling away from the bus stop. We would all be running and calling out for the driver who saw and heard us. I believed that he purposely arrived earlier than what he was scheduled so that we would miss it.

One morning we arrived much earlier and got on without any incident. There were mostly school aged kids on it. We all knew the routine and to the back we went. The white kids were quite disruptive and were throwing spit balls at us. We had been instructed to not retaliate. There were two teen age girls seated in the middle section. They were taunting us saying, "nigger, nigger, can't git no bigger." It didn't make sense but it rhymed. One of the girls tripped as she was getting out of her seat to get off the bus. I smiled to myself. It served her right. "goody goody gumdrops" I thought. She had been wearing a beautiful silver charm bracelet that she'd been showing off and bragging to her friend. It was a birthday present from her daddy who was living with a new wife and children. I noticed that she didn't have it on after she picked up herself, her books and her pride off of the floor "tough titty" I thought to myself as we were getting off at our school stop. I noticed something shiny under the bus seat. It was her bracelet. I put it in the pocket of my jeans. I thought seriously about keeping it. I showed it to mother when I got home that evening. She told me to do the right thing and to return it to the rightful owner in the morning. It was burning a hole in my pocket as I got on the bus the next day. I heard her say to her friend how important that it was to her because of it having been a gift from her dad. I felt so sorry for her. As she was about to get off of the bus I went up to her and said, "I found your bracelet under the seat yesterday." I handed it to her and waited and waited (I'm still waiting for a 'thank you' or 'that's so nice of you' or 'kiss my ass!') She looked at me grabbed the bracelet out of my hand and turned her head away from me in a snobbish gesture. Then she brushed past me. What a loser. What a heavy duty lesson for a little girl to have to learn of hatred because of our different races the color of my skin. Mother said that I had done the right thing. She added, "There will be people in your life whether they be colored or white. They may or may not like you or respect you even if you do the right thing."

We were almost downtown Meridian. We would be seeing THE TEN COMMANDMENTS again and again. It was one of the reruns in the colored walk-in Star Theatre another regular was Rock Around the Clock and Imitation of Life. We dared not go to the Meridian Theatre – for whites only. It was owned and operated by the same man that owned the Star. The whites were privileged to have the new releases of movies each week. It was another "suck it up" we tried to make good of bad situations.

There were so much evidence of unfair practices that we were expected to endure. The philosophy of our parents were, "If it don't kill you, it will make you strong" well we all should have been either

Superman or Wonder Woman. We all were determined to withstand the many blows that we bore on a daily basis and sometimes multiple times in a day.

Finally in the movie. We all had popcorn, candy and soda. Of course we had to share it so that we all could have a taste of all the treats.

Upon exiting we made sure that we went to empty our bladders because of the crazy bus schedule and there were no public restrooms. I did as I was told. We discussed the movie as we had done so many times before. I became so thirsty because of all the salt in the popcorn and fresh peanuts in the shell. There was a water fountain outside of J.J. Newberry and Kress Department stores. The line had formed to get a drink of water. We were getting cold stares from some of those already waiting. We finally reached the fountain – there was a sign next to the fountain that read, "Whites Only." Another fountain right next to it was dirty and the water of course wasn't chilled. The sign under it was, "Colored" I heard a snicker from one of two white boys who saw it all. Oh the pang of humiliation and degradation. Such a let down feeling, that moment would go with me for a lifetime.

We had come out of the movie so elated about the film. Afterwards reality reared its ugly face and had taken most of the enthusiasm we had then left us all like deflated balloons. I wanted to know why were we being treated as we were. There was no real good answer. "It will get better some day Carrie Ann." I wanted better that day.

I tried to remain optimistic especially during my elementary school years. Things were improving somewhat. My first grade was held in an old run down school building which the color or lack thereof was the same as my parent's first house. It was built in the colored neighborhood in the over-crowded south end of Meridian. It was rightfully named Southside Elementary School. Frequently during the rainy season it became flooded. There were so many children who drowned during those down pours. Sawashee Creek would swell and spill over its banks in the large south side neighborhood. Their children would play in it, not knowing the depth and the undercurrents. They made do and played as any child who is curious would do. The Meridian Star (newspaper) would print on the back page accounts of the drowning. They would mention that it was a colored child. The city built a brand new state-of-the-art school that was relocated to higher grounds in the far yet I-can-still-see-It distance. The Sawashee Creek still became flooded and threatened to flood the new school. The city did their best for flood control because their intention was to keep the coloreds on their side of town.

Self determination was the name of my game at an early age. I wanted to gobble as much education that my tiny body and big head could hold. I wanted to do better than what Meridian had to offer. I hated the twangy slow southern drawl. So I practiced talking at a faster pace. My enunciation was so clear that it was to the point of me getting teased, "You thank yo' cute" my personal favorite, "Yo' try'n ta ta'k proper." Well, yes, and yes! And why not? I planned to be the best that I could and as soon as I could.

Since I wanted the fastest way to get out of the hell hole that I was so fortunate to be born in to. I would have to settle for and accept the present existence at that time. The term settling and accepting the worst were not applicable to me in the broader aspect of my plans.

I had to start from the bottom and without the proper education or even knowing the right person I was forced to become a faceless colored woman who knew where her place was. To cook in some white woman's kitchen; to clean up after her family; and to babysit children who were openly taught to hate me because I was not white.

Coming from the bottom and striving for much much higher grounds was my goal early on in life. Yes! I would to do the above mentioned however I was potentially much better than that and would have to pace myself and take things in stride to become the person that my parents had wanted from all of their children.

It had been about seven months since I had the encounter with Joe Henry. I was really struggling to maintain at least a "c" average while I attended Carver Jr. High. I wasn't pestering Connie as much to see if she had any word from my dream boy. She did know some twin boys from Harris High. Their names were Jerry and Perry. They were so cute. Mother allowed me to go on a double date. His name was Jerry who knew that my curfew was ten o'clock. We sat in the back seat of their car. I wasn't really into him and didn't care about how handsome he was. I didn't put out or melt in his arms so we got home before my curfew. He and I didn't see each other again. He later told Connie that I was too young for him. He was used to girls giving it up on their first date. I had control over my body and my mind.

Tragedy seemed to hit some families in droves. The Gathright family has seen its fair share of perils. My daddy came home one evening. He was to the point of tears – that's something that was rare about my father - we had seen several ambulances go by our house with their sirens blasting until they were well out of ear shot. My daddy said that there was a fire and that six children of different ages and two adults had burned up in the flames. He got so sick that he literally vomited. We were all crying because we knew the family very well. It was the family that Joyce had been engaged to marry their oldest son Robert who had been killed almost a year before this casualty from the flaming incident. Their remains were unidentifiable. It was the saddest closed casket funeral that any of us had ever witnessed.

Our church did as much as it could. There was a new house erected on the same property within months. Some of our members gathered at the new home to provide comfort. Connie and I rode with Mother and Deddy. The house was crawling with well wishers, standing room only. I ventured outside. There was an old truck parked in the yard away from the house. It was black and had been recently waxed. There was muddy clay dirt on its tires and partially on the sides of the fender skirts. The driver didn't get out. He had his head down, his hand was covering his face as if he was crying. I didn't recognize the truck or the driver. My heart went out to him, he had obviously came by to pay his respect to the grieving family. Their house continued to be swarmed with friends and family. Some of the people I had never met and some whom I'd forgotten. Connie seemed to have known most of the visitors. I found her as she was being her usual charming comical self. I pulled her to the side and asked her about the stranger that was still sitting in the black pick up truck. "Oh, that's Joe Henry" at which time Tommie came into their living room. He pulled Connie to the doorway. The crowd of people were so noisy. He was trying to talk above all the loud conversations and bouts of laughter that the hungry group of people that had came to socialize and eat. He said, "Joe Henry don't want to get out of his truck, he had too much to drink and his girl f…" He stopped short when he saw me trying to eavesdrop on his conversation. He knew how much that I wanted to see Joe Henry again.

My heart fell down to the floor. I felt so low as I spun around and hurried out the crowded doorway. Connie and Tommie were right on my heels as I ran down the sloping unfinished yard to where Joe Henry's truck was parked. I saw a dark skinned chubby girl talking to him and was leaving as I walked up to the driver's side. The girl got into another car parked behind Joe Henry. He was looking down and looked so sad. I called out his name with concern in my voice. He turned to look my way. The sun was still bright and was setting causing a glare. He was squinting and put his hand up to shade the sunshine from his light brown eyes (I got a better look at him in the daylight). His hair was coal black and curly. He managed a smile that grew bigger when he finally realized it was me. He said, "Hey Carrie I didn't know you wuz ou' heah" He seemed a bit jittery. He kept looking over his shoulder and looking at his watch. Then he looked at me. Connie and Tommie were too engrossed in their own conversation. Joe Henry asked if he could come to see me and asked for my phone number. It just so happened that I had a piece of paper and a pencil in my pocket book. I fumbled while trying to retrieve it. I began to tremble a bit. He didn't seem to notice or maybe that was what young girls did in the presence of a wild stallion. My handwriting was barely legible, my hands were shaking so badly. We both agreed that he could come over to my house on my fifteenth birthday, next week. He laughed and started the engine. He beckoned for Tommie to come to the driver's side. Politely I stepped back. They talked as he gunned the motor while it was still in park. They both laughed like two little boys. They had been friends since grade school. I was summoned back to the driver's side. He reached out the window, took my hands and kissed them. He winked at me and said, "I'll see ya nex' Sunday 'bout two o'clock." I asked him to please call me if there were changes of the plan. He promised he would. He backed the truck up like a mad man. There was smoke and screeching spinning tires when he was about to go forward. Uuga! uuga! uuga! and then he was gone. Poof! In a cloud of smoke.

I'm not sure how much longer that we stayed at the Gathrights' house. It was a well known fact that occasions such as that could bring strangers together. I found out later that the young girl was about my age and she had been seeing Joe Henry. It was suspected that she was pregnant by him. Well how dare she. I saw him first so I tried to rationalize that two trains can't run on one track. They must have been mistaken. Joe Henry wanted to be with me. He had told me so and I had to believe him. The person that they claimed to be his girlfriend was like a midget with bucked teeth and bulging eyes. I did notice one/two assets of hers, were her bigger than life tits. I had to put her and her tits out of my mind and concentrate on me.

My next problem besides being a nervous wreck was to get my parents permission that I could have company. They both knew that I had been a daughter that they were proud of. Well, that was easy, whew! I got the okay. The next week was the longest days and so many sleepless nights. I couldn't concentrate on reading. I burned a perfect would be pot of grits. My chores were half done. I was a basket case, again.

There I was, a fourteen year old girl about to reach what I considered a milestone for me. I was about to turn fifteen years old tomorrow and Joe Henry was supposed to come over and see me – it was too much – I had to get away. Since I couldn't drive and there weren't any drivers available I decided to take a walk in my favorite place since I was a child.

The woods were beckoning to me with all its multiple fragrances of honeysuckle (it actually had a drop of honey in its bloom. It had to be done ever so gentle to get the nectar sucked out). The dogwood trees were still in bloom also. I wasn't able to get any of its flowers but the aroma was enough. As I walked up through the woods I noticed the path that had once been so bare was becoming over grown with small unfamiliar bushes. The path was still etched in my mind. I could have walked it blind folded. A small garden snake slithered quickly to get out of my way.

I reached the summit of the once playground for me, my siblings and our cousins. I stopped to pick a handful of the colorful wild flowers. I finally found the makeshift tin sheet that we had used as a sleigh. We had hidden it the last time that we had played on the hill. There were some rusty areas on both sides. We used to keep it so shiny and smooth. I was about to chicken out as I looked down the steep hill. There was plenty of pine straw that mother nature had blanketed the sleigh path that we had etched out when we were much younger. I had gotten thirsty and the only water that was close by was down in the gulley between the two equally steep hills. I could hear the gurgling sound of the spring as if it was inviting me to have one more – the last – sip. Its water just appeared from out of the earth, out of nowhere. It trickled downward for about three to four feet then disappeared just as mysteriously underground. It was the perfect place for someone brave enough to ride down to drink from God's fountain. So that's what I had to do. It was fun and easy to maneuver the tin sleigh down hill. I got my thirst quenched and rested about five minutes. I looked up as I was about to head back realizing, "dog gone! That's some steep hill!" I'd done it in the past. I thought, I can do it now." I had the jagged tin sleigh in my left hand. I lunged up and lost my balance several times as I tried to lug the cumbersome sleigh so that I could put it back in our hiding place. My left hand was cut on it as I was grabbing a hold of a small seedling pine – it broke – I reached for a larger stronger tree to hoist myself upward.

The place that I had loved so much as a child seemed to be trying to end my life. At that time it would have been nice to have my siblings or cousins with me and all of what was happening would not have been…knowing my family, they would have laughed at my clumsiness. I had never fallen down the steep terrain and I refused to give in to it then.

I noticed my right palm was completely raw from the prickly pine bark. "Okay, I can do this." As I was still holding on to the sleigh I pulled myself up another two feet. It became tangled on a small bush that had some wild purple berries on it. I was halfway up the hill that became an obstacle course. My options were to continue to tug at the dead weight of the sleigh and risk falling down again to possible death. Or – the battle was over – I let the sleigh go and saw it as it splashed into the spring below. "That could have been me" I thought, but it wasn't. I looked upward, gathered my wits and my hidden strength and slowly pulled myself back up to where I had laid the bouquet of wild flowers. There were a few scratches on my legs which were superficial. My major injuries was my pride. One thing accomplished was to get my mind off of the upcoming day. It had turned out beautiful because I was still alive. And I wanted to give the flowers to my mom when she returned home that evening from shopping.

I went to our Sunday church services the next day which went on what seemed like forever. I got a few happy birthday wishes afterwards. I didn't feel any different being fifteen. There weren't any presents nor was there a cake. I had come to expect just that. I remembered when I was about nine years old. I thought maybe that year my family would all leap up out of their hiding places and shout, "Surprise!" That day never came. I looked high and low for a present that didn't exist and the only thing that I smelled baking in the over was corn bread. I never did let on to my parents that my little heart was shattered because of my disappointment.

Oh, I could pretend alright but I was a total train wreck inside. I smiled appropriately. I even giggled at nonsense things (forgive me, that was part of my normal character). I was watching the clock and had taken off my Sunday clothes and hung them neatly in the closet. I freshened up and put on casual wear (a skirt and a blouse). Mother and daddy went over to Muhmuh's as they generally did on Sunday afternoon. James and Willie went up to Aunt Gladys. All of the rest of the family had disappeared all for the exception of Janie. I think that it was planned that she stay and watch me/pester me. So be it. She was able to get my mind off of my unglued state of mind. She still had on her Sunday clothes. What an entertainer. She performed a new dance and sang off key. "Poison ivy, poison ivy." She started scratching all over – what a character. I laughed so hard and began to sing along with her – she wanted to do it herself so I had to be quiet.

Ring, ring, ring. She ran and beat me to it.·"hello, who's this?" She smiled, "Just a minute" (very loudly into the receiver) "Carrie, Carrie it's for you" as she handed the phone to me and smiled, "It's Joe Henry" My mouth was totally dry. I tried to swallow. I had to take a sip of water that I had in the living room. I took the receiver and had to literally walk Janie back to the sofa because she had plans to be all in my business. I smiled at her which usually calmed her down. She knew that I didn't mean her any harm.

It was three o'clock, I was a little irritated because he was late but I – "hello" my voice was somewhat raspy. I cleared it. Joe Henry said, "I'll be there in 'bout thirty minutes, I'm sorry I'm run'n late. I got car trouble." I answered dryly, "I thought maybe you had changed your mind. Are you okay?" He answered, "I jus' needs ta clean up agin at my brotha's house." Those thirty minutes turned into another hour. He arrived at four o'clock. Janie stayed to oversee.

I was so excited to see him when he came into our living room. He shook Janie's hand. She was all smiles practically flirting with him. I offered him water as he sat down in the middle of the sofa. Janie went and got him a big glass of ice water and added water to the ice that I had been munching on. Joe Henry had sat back, so relaxed – so I thought until I sat next to him – Janie excused herself as she had to go to the bathroom. At which time Joe Henry turned to me and pulled me over closer to him. He kissed me as he had when we first met. It seemed like a lifetime ago. I pulled away slightly and pointed to the doorway insinuating that my sister would be right back and furthermore my parents would be coming home soon. He smiled so broadly as if though there was a game going on. I scooted over to the far right of the sofa. He kept talking about his family and about school. He got up and moved right next to me. We both laughed, "Janie, Janie Ruth" we heard someone calling in the distance. It was Muhmuh next door. Janie heard it and took off running. The screen door slammed and we were finally alone. Joe Henry reached for me and I allowed him to kiss me which lingered until I was breathless. I stood up as did he. He pulled me to him. We blended so completely. The radio was playing a slow song. I got him to concentrate on dancing for a while. I was looking toward the screen door. There was liquor odor on his breath. He began to breath harder and holding me tighter. I was like a slippery eel that escaped out of his grasp. I thought, "what the hell." I moved in closer and wrapped my arms around his slender waist. He seemed to be in shock for a moment. He picked me up and spun me around and ever so gentle, I was back on my feet. He gave me another delicious kiss.

We both heard the voices of my parents as they were walking up to the front stoop. We sat down quickly. I wondered if we looked composed. Joe Henry certainly did. He got up with ease when Mother and Deddy came inside. I followed suit to introduce everybody, "Mother, Deddy, this is Joe Henry Mathis." I looked at him and said, "Joe these are my parents." He shook hands with my daddy which appeared to be a good firm handgrip. He ever put his hand over their clasped hand (how polite). "Please to meecha" each said. I looked into my dads face to see if there was any glimmer of truth to his response. All that I could see was, "I'm look'n at cho boy, don' cho dare hur' my daghdah" Well, that was pleasant enough I thought.

We sat down on the couch. Mother and daddy went back into the kitchen. She fixed him a plate of left overs from our Sunday dinner. She later joined him with a plate of her own at the dining room table. The TV was in the corner of the living room. I turned it on so that Deddy would have something else to stare at besides me and my date.

Joe Henry was so good at small talk. I was so jittery I couldn't really follow the conversation. Deddy asked Mother, "you got any desert?" I heard her as she got up to get Deddy some cake and ice cream. She came to the arched doorway to the living room and offered Joe Henry and I some desert. He answered in his nasal drawl, "naw thank you máme." I thought "now ain't that cute. Anybody else with that description I would have to hang them out to dry." Joe Henry wasn't shy at all. He seemed so at ease with my parents as if he had known them all of his life. He sat next to me and took my left hand which he held in his. He kept saying you have such small soft hands. Well I was a little person at least petite and well proportioned. He seemed to have gotten mesmerized with my hands. He kept bending my finger forward. I pulled it away somewhat annoyed and he took it back. He seemed so intense as he compared my hand size to his. He said after he had made an analysis "we b'long togetha." I wondered how he came to that conclusion. I didn't have a chance to ask him. Daddy let out one of his belches that sounded like he would rip his tonsils out. A minute later he began snoring so loudly while sitting in the large overstuffed chair. Mother had played out on the smaller rocking chair. I tried not to be embarrassed. I called out softly, "Deddy, Deddy" then a little bit louder. He awakened abruptly looking startled and dazed as he looked around trying to refocus. He had slobber (drool) running down the side of his mouth. Mother got up and said, "Tommie, get up, go to bed." He got up no question asked. Mother was about to head down the hallway, she turned and said, "Carrie your company can stay until ten o'clock." She added, "Good night ya'll". Janie came in skipping at that time she seemed out of breath from running from Muhmuh's. she came over and gave me and Joe Henry a hug, "night night" as she disappeared down the hallway. The rest of the family came in one right after the other just like clockwork and settled in for slumber.

Joe Henry was taking everything in with my family and still acting fascinated with the size of my hand. He finally said, "you a pretty girl you must have a boy friend." He must have known that I only had eyes for him since the time that we first met. I said, "no, I don't" I smiled as I got up to go to the bathroom. It sounded like some one was sawing wood especially from my parent's bedroom. Everybody was sound asleep snoring. Joe Henry was standing outside the bathroom door waiting his turn to use the toilet.

When he returned to the living room to join me again I had sat in the overstuffed wide armed chair. I gestured for him to have a seat on the couch across from me. He sat for a minute or two. We sat staring at each other. The small chit chat was no longer working for neither of us were responding appropriately to "was that a question?" or that must have been a statement?" The TV remained on and was drowning out our so called conversation. He patted the space next to him on the couch and said playfully, "Carrie come ova heah, I won't bite." I shook my head, "no" biting my bottom lie and looking up at the clock on the wall. I let out a fake yawn then stretched which only turned him on even more and determined that he was in charge. He got up and said, "okay, I'm coming ova dar' and sit wid cho'" He was like a gazelle, he sat on the right arm of the chair at which time I swiftly moved to the left arm of the chair. I thought that I would be safe. There was no where for me to hide as he reached for my hand and whispered, "Carrie, I wan' cho' so bad" He began kissing me first on the mouth ever so teasingly. He was smooth as he watched my expressions. I didn't know how to respond when he kissed my neck then my right ear lobe. I made a whimpering sound of pleasure as I closed my eyes for a second. I heard a noise coming from the hallway. I looked toward the doorway and saw my younger brother Willie as he was sleep walking to the bathroom. I motioned for Joe Henry to "shhh" he got up and turned the lamp off. I was still listening for Willie to return back to his room. He flushed the commode and he slept walked back to their room then shut the door. I breathed a sigh of relief. I remained perched on the arm of the chair. Joe Henry came over to me as smooth as silk. He began kissing me gently at first then so rough I could hardly breathe! I felt so weak. There was no fight or flight in me. I knew that it was at the point of no return. He gently yet masterfully removed my panties. I held up my arms to him and held him around his waist. He had obviously unzipped his pants. I was too afraid to open my eyes to look at the hard massive bulge that he was freeing. I was glad for the dimmed room because I would have been too ashamed that Joe Henry was touching me as I had never been touched before. I could only feel the heat of his penis as he tried to penetrate my unbroken hymen (I was still a virgin but not for long). I held my right hand over my mouth to keep from screaming as I held on with my left hand to keep me from falling. It was so painful yet more pleasure. I didn't know whether to laugh or cry so I did both. Joe Henry was still holding on to me. He kissed me then in a muffled voice he said, "I'm coming baby." Afterwards we embraced as we tried to catch our breath, still perched on the arm of the chair for a few minutes. He kept asking, "you a'ight?" I turned my head to the side so that he couldn't see my tortured face as I wept. He had zipped up and sat in the chair as he continued to caress me. He said, "Carrie yo' mine" It was a simple statement yet had so much authority and meaning. I was trying to get over the guilt that flooded my whole being as I was trying to retrieve the panties that were lost between the pillows of the chair. The room was spinning as I finally got up to go to the bathroom. Joe Henry said, "you betta hurry up n' get tha' shit out cho" most of it had ran down my legs. By the time that I had sat on the commode, I was so overcome with so many emotions and guilty feelings I noticed that there was a small amount of bleeding. I thought, "wow wee! happy birthday to me" although I was in so much pain I got a gift that I wanted to keep on getting and giving.

Joe Henry was still sitting in the easy chair when I returned. He had turned the lamp back on. I was about to sit on the arm of the chair. He gestured to me to sit on his lap. He held me in his arms for a few minutes. He said, "Carrie I do luv you" and that was good enough for me. That night I became Joe Henry's woman. I knew that he would be back when he finally kissed me goodnight. He was like an entirely different person as he got into his truck. I went out doors to see him off. He kept reaching for my hands as he said it again, "yo' my woman." That magic smile just sealed the deal. He turned on the ignition and basically glided out of the driveway then down the dark road. There weren't any screeching tires, just the head lights illuminating the night as he drove out of sight.

My excitement kept me awake for about an hour. I smiled as I was thinking that I must have been looking like a Georgia peach, so ripe and ready to be plucked. He had devoured my luscious juice that only I could give to him. I trailed off to sleep with a big smile on my face. If I had died that night, the undertaker would not have been able to remove that silly grin that was plastered on my face. I was as happy as a dead pig in the sunshine – as Deddy always said – that night I dreamt about the forbidden act that we had committed. His infectious smile was so thrilling when I could almost taste the sweetness of his breathtaking kisses. I awakened three times that night. Each time I replayed my life changing experience with the man that I loved.

I was so glad that our summer vacation was still in full force. I needed more time to sift through all of my thoughts. I had to be brought back down to earth several times after I finally crawled out of bed. My legs felt like rubber as I ran to the bathroom. "ouch, that hurt" I wanted to scream. I didn't expect to be so sore on my blooming flower. I drew up a hot tub of water with some dish washing liquid to make some bubbles. I had wanted to take a bath last night but it would have been too suspicious right after Joe Henry left. There was a new odor that was obviously from the semen that had been deposited and seemed to be still clinging to the inner walls of my too-too. That name was no longer appropriate, so from that day forward it became aka vagina (to Joe Henry it was his pussy).

Janie was right on time. As I was finishing getting my much needed bath I didn't feel filthy anymore as some of my classmates had described after making love for the first time. I'm sure that there was a glow on my face as I brushed past my little sister. She was a tad bit ticked at me because I didn't open the door as soon as she had knocked on the door as I had done in the past.

I smelled bacon cooking. The four older girls took turns cooking breakfast for a week. That was my week to wash the dishes. My daddy had left an hour earlier for a job out of town. Someone had obviously gotten up and fixed him breakfast, his usual hot cocoa and a bag lunch. My family usually had breakfast together. That morning we didn't. it was an opportunity for me to escape from being drilled and teased about my company last night. I was about to burst I probably would have blurted out the whole sorted wonderful exciting truth about my evening with Joe Henry. They would have seen the full story on my face.

My mom was already up and about. She was on the phone with my Aunt Carrie Mae. They were so close since their childhood. They both were equally humorous. I head my mother as she was cackling like a hen. She was so loud (laughing). It was a musical sound that made me feel happy that she was enjoying her life. They stayed on the phone most of the morning keeping each other amused. Janie was outside playing with the Smith children who were our cousins also. Their mother was cousin Martha, related to my mom. She was also very refined and seemingly happy. She was married to a Baptist preacher, Rev. Lloyd Smith. They were the parents of six children all of whom where well mannered. Their family had purchased the old house that we had moved from. The Reverend was remodeling the old structure, little by little. The last time I visited the old homestead I thought, "it still looks just as unfinished as when we left it." What it really needed was simply to slap a 'condemned' sign on it and tear it down and start from scratch. They did it their way.

It was about noon when I went to my mother's room. There wasn't any more laughter. She had talked so long on the phone until she had worn herself out. She was sound asleep with the receiver still in her hand resting in her lap. "mother," I said softly as I gently shook her shoulders. She awakened and realized what had happened – again. Her eyes were somewhat puffy. I thought maybe from sleeping too much. She got up, put her hand on my head as she replaced the receiver on the cradle. She put on her straw hat then went outside to her garden that she and Deddy had planted.

Mother seemed to have been in a world of her own. It was a great possibility that she was experiencing something that she couldn't share with her fifteen year old daughter. I had always wanted to be closer to my mom. She had her hands full with the eight children that were either grown and gone, teenagers and a youngon, "the baby" as Janie was referred to.

I saw myself as being lost in our woven tapestry. I didn't feel special or as privileged as the older children. my brothers had found favor with daddy as he took them under his wings training them to get out and work and how to become strong men as they were becoming. Boy Baby (Tommy Jr.) had already reached twenty-one. He had served in the army and was back home and was thinking about marrying his girlfriend, Jewel.

Those memories flooded my mind after I had straightened up my parent's bedroom. I began to pity myself as I had done in the past few months. My roller coaster ride took me so high then I went crashing to depths that I was then feeling after seeing my mother on her own roller coaster ride that she refused to allow anybody on. I sat down as I had often done since I was a little girl. I curled up on the chair in my parents room, closed my eyes and began sucking my tongue (some children had habits of thumb sucking). I was more aware of that bad habit that day than any other time in my life. I played with my ear lobe – I had to feel on something soft warm. I used to saddle up to my mom or dad and feel on their ear lobes until they became so irritated with me and my habit (it didn't work until I decided, no more). Apparently I was feeling the need for closeness and or there was something missing in my life and that act was a way for me to get fulfillment for the moment.

Mother came back inside shortly. She had picked some red and green tomatoes that she had tucked in her apron. She was complaining about the rabbit that she saw devouring the fruit of her labor. She seemed to be in better spirits. She still hadn't asked me about my date with Joe Henry last night. Before I talked with her I needed to straighten up and fly right (as my daddy had always said).

The phone rang several times. It was Joe Henry. He seemed so glad to hear from me, still concerned about my overall well being, "is you a'ight?" He was definitely a country boy but a very proud peacock. I loved the whole package. He asked, "when kin I see you agin?" I informed him "maybe this Saturday night." I remembered that there was a fish fry at my Sunday school teachers' house who just happened to live next door to us. I had promised her that I would help with the project that I had done on so many other occasions. I convinced him to come to the function so that I could show him off. He sounded reluctant but he finally agreed. He promised that he would get there as soon as he could get off from work and go over to his brothers apartment to get cleaned up (I figured that he would show up late).

He called me every day. He liked talking about my legs. He said they were so pretty. He mentioned all the hair that they had on them (hairy legs were fashionable in the south). He asked, "why don' cha wear a skirt to show off those legs?" I could hardly wait until Saturday.

I went next door to Ms. Verta Bells' house real early to get everything set up. It had started out sunny and had beautiful clouds in the sky. As evening approached the dark clouds began forming. The sky had flashes of lightening and heavy thunder that shook the old wood framed house. We had to hurry to bring in the barbeque grill inside. We opened up all the windows – it was an accident waiting to happen – we had to leave the fish outside in the cast iron pot, it was covered. As quick as the clouds, rain, thunder and lightening came, so it disappeared leaving the air quite muggy. There were a lot of hungry church people and a few other friends of friends, they came especially for the fried headless trout sandwiches that was sold for fifteen cents. The sodas were a nickel a bottle. We had hot dogs for ten cents. The barbeque had different prices depending on the order. We had basically sold most of the food when I heard a familiar sound…uuga! uuga! uuga! There were so many people who had came to help inside and outside. I made up an excuse that I was tired and was going home. I generally didn't like to go visiting at Ms. Verta Bell's house in the night because her house was on a steep hill and the only way to get there was up a treacherous stairway (I use the term loosely). Each step was so different from the last. Some were steep the others were shallow. The side rails were just as bad. They had seen their best days a long time ago. They had no lights to help guide those who were brave enough to venture up or down. There was a dim light on the front of the house, however.

Determined to go home, I stumbled down the rickety steps. I saw his truck parked midway between my house and Ms. Verta Bell's. Tommie G. was standing next to the drivers' side talking with Joe Henry who was smoking a cigarette. I approached the truck that could barely be seen in the stark darkness. There were several other cars that had parked down from the house. They were still trying to buy the rest of the food. I said my hellos, Tommie left shortly. He must have known what Joe Henry and I had done Sunday night, although he didn't say anything to me out of the ordinary. Joe told me to get in on the other side. I told him that my family was still at the fish fry. He promised that he wasn't going to do nothing wrong and I believed him. I got into the truck as instructed. He was on me like ugly on ape at which moment one of the parked car ignition was started and the lights flashed on us. Lottie was walking past the truck when the headlights of the parked car illuminated her shadow as it was pulling away. I was sitting so close to Joe Henry that we must have looked like Siamese twins. Their lights had definitely illuminated us as we were beginning to embark on another expedition. Lottie back tracked and said, "Carrie, mother wants you to come home now!" I was feeling so embarrassed. The headlights from the other car continued to shine on us. It had either stalled or the people were just being nosey. I wasn't in a position to argue that we weren't doing anything (in Joe Henry's parked truck that was hidden from view in pitch dark). We must have looked like deer on the road about to be run down by an oncoming car. Joe Henry reached across my exposed thighs, his hands brushed against them teasingly. He tried to open the passenger door. It was stuck but that gave him an opportunity to let his right elbow touch my breast. He quickly ran his hand to the once forbidden territory. I smiled to myself trying not to get too wrapped up in his smooth advances. He said, "I'll see ya' in a few minutes." I got out of the truck and stumbled over some overgrown shrubbery. Lottie was still standing there waiting for me. She was my beloved big sister, however, I wished that she would mind her own business. She gave her version of a sermon about my behavior, the same thing that mother would probably say to me. She said in a stern voice, "Carrie you hardly know that boy, and there you were parked and necking with him." I did so want her approval. It was important to me that she respected me as she had in the past. We arrived inside the living room. Mother was on the phone, the TV was tuned in to Lawrence Welk who was knee-deep in all of those bubbles and his champagne music. I sat down and watched the only thing that was on – how boring – I was still coming down from the high that Joe Henry had taken me to and then I saw headlights in our driveway coming closer to our house.

I looked out the window and saw that it was him getting out of the truck and was waving at me as I stood frozen in the window. I left the TV on. Lottie liked the show that was on. She was busy back in the kitchen. I went in and told her that I was going outside to get some fresh alr and talk with Joe Henry. She raiser her eyebrows as if she questioned my intentions. I became defiant and said, "it's hot in here." She was preparing part of our Sunday dinner as she had often done on Saturday nights. There was a delicious smelling peach cobbler that was bubbling over the side of the pan as it was turning a light golden brown. She also had a pot roast that she took out of the oven and was basting it. I didn't offer to help her that time. I told her that I would wash the dishes when she finished. She said, "Carrie..." She became distracted when one of the pots on top of the stove was boiling over the side. I made my escape at that point.

When I went outside, Joe Henry was already sitting in one of the old straight chairs that was kept outside. There was another one whose bottom was almost torn out. The front stoop (porch) light was attracting so many moths and those hard shelled bugs they were such a nuisance. They didn't bite but just annoying. I turned off the light. We could still hear Mr. Welk's bubbly melodies. I went over to stand next to the truck because the chair was not to be trusted. Joe Henry got up and stood in front of me. He looked me up and down and said, "I like tha' skir' cho have on." It was rather cute. It was a wide flare, yellow daisies on a black backdrop. My blouse was short sleeved pale yellow. I had on a pair of black sandals. I smiled and said, "thank y..." he planted one of his lingering kisses on my mouth before I could complete my polite response. I was about to finish and before I got anything else said, he had lifted me onto the fender of his truck. He stood in front of me causing my legs to spread and wrap around his upper back. He was holding me ever so gently on the small of my back. I began to squirm as I was about to slide off of the fender. He pressed his body against me and started his search under the convenient skirt. His right hand had found its way up my left inner thigh. I began to claw at his shoulder. He caressed me directly on the split. His hand was so warm and was a bit shaky as I started to moan his name, "Joe Henry, Joe..." He quickly pulled away when we heard Lottie answer mother, "She's outside with her company" Mother must have known that I was outside. I thought, why doesn't she come to see for herself? We dismounted from the fender. My skirt almost flew up over my head. I then realized the reason for the request for me to wear it. Lottie came to the front screen door. She said, "Carrie why don't ya'll come inside? Daddy will be here soon and he's gonna be mad." I said in a smart-alecky voice, "I'm not doing anything wrong, it's still too hot in there." She went back in the kitchen to finish up and I followed her. I fixed two tumblers of ice water. I handed one to Joe Henry and asked him to watch mine. I went to the bathroom and to check up on my family. Mother was in bed reading her bible. I went in to say good night. I hugged her then told her that Joe Henry and I were outside because it was too hot inside the house. She looked at her watch. I said, "He knows that I have curfew." She smiled at me and said, "I like the way you have your hair." It was a mess a few minutes ago. She was almost in lala land even as we spoke.

I tip-toed back outside where Joe Henry was sitting and waiting for me. He still had my water In his hand trying to keep the swarm of mosquitoes and gnats from diving into it. He was so handsome. I could see his face from the minute light from the street light. He handed me the water which I sat aside. I was thirsty for him and he knew it. He whispered, "are you sti' sor'?" I shook my head, "no" and we both laughed as he pulled me down to sit on his lap. I was facing forward as he began to ease his hand underneath my bra cup. He then squeezed my left nipple that was too tender to touch. I gestured that it was uncomfortable. His hand moved to the outside of my blouse while he cupped my extremely sensitive breast. "ah, that's somewhat better." The man was like an octopus and I was enjoying every moment of it. He pulled the crouch of my panties to the side. He lifted me up almost to a standing position. I balanced myself on both of his legs. He had unzipped and exposed that thang that I was still too shy and embarrassed to look at or touch. There was some discomfort when he finally penetrated, but oh the ecstasy that passed through my body as he repositioned my body and guided me to gyrate on him.

I saw the car lights as it slowed down near Muhmuh's house. It came to almost a complete stop as it turned into our driveway. Deddy jumped out of the car with us still within his view. Now, what's a girl to do? I could have stood up. My skirt would have fallen into place. I stlll had my panties on. Joe Henry quickly positioned me on his left leg. He picked up his tumbler of warm water that probably had all sorts of insects in it. I reached for mine careful not to dismount him or he would have certainly been exposed. Daddy brushed past us and mumbled, "e'ning'" Joe Henry asked, "how you do'n Mr. Pea'son?" There was no response from daddy as he slammed the screen door. I thought, "oh God, he's going inside to get his gun! I jumped up and it was as if we were synchronized. Joe Henry was on his feet and turned away from any possible onlookers. He packed that horse back in its pen. Deddy came to the door and turned the front porch (stoop) light on and said angrily, "Carrie, you and yo' comp'ny kin git in heah rat naw, tha's why we hav'a liv'n room." I went in right away and Joe Henry trailed behind me. Lottie was coming from the kitchen through the living room. She had just finished all of the preparations that she had intended to do that night. It wasn't quite ten o'clock. We kept the front porch light on. We heard daddy snoring almost immediately, his call of the wild. Joe Henry said playfully, "yo' daddy did say tha' he built dis liv'n room fo' yo' entertainment?" We both were so giddy and couldn't keep our hands off of each other. He came for a fish fry and stayed for dessert.

I was beginning to feel absolutely special being on someone's priority list. I was about to bubble over with the new sense of belonging and I didn't have to share him with a soul. It was mind boggling to know that with him we would be free to do as we pleased. It was the most exhilarating feeling that I had ever had until I awakened the next morning and found that I had fallen asleep in the overstuffed chair the night before. Joe Henry had left me there when we finished.

I hurried to the bathroom and found some old clothes in the closet and took off the flowered skirt and the blouse. I was met at the bathroom door by my daddy. I gave him one of my little girl hugs, afraid that he would smell the smoke in my hair. He had never been a very demonstrative person to any of us except for Joyce because she demanded the attention. And of course, Janie because she was the baby. I could never make someone love me. He was a tough nut to crack and I wasn't about to try to that morning.

Summer always seemed to go by so slowly, however the summer of 1960 went by as if it had been wound too tight or was it just me, out of control as a spinning top going in so many directions? I could hardly catch my breath. It was again time to register for the new school year. That was the time of hustle and bustle with buying new cloths. That school year I was getting new outfits as Lottie had promised me. I had a little cash saved back for frills such as jewelry, makeup, and other accessories. I planned to be styling especially the first day of school.

My parents were so frustrated with the failure of all of the different transportations that we had used to get to school over the years. Initially we had used the city bus with all the nigger haters. Then we had the contracted taxi cab drivers who picked us up at home. Then they would pick us up at school to take us back home. That became quite expensive for my parents. Later we went by the city unified school bus for one year. They stopped it when the officials found out that there were only a few of us riding it. A year later we rode with Mr. and Mrs. Wilson for a while. It just didn't work out. It was too much to ask of them, to have us all crowd into their car. My sister Joyce had gotten her drivers license and was put in charge one year for our transportation. We were late practically every day because she had to run back inside the house to change her freakin' outfit just because she could, just on GP and control issues.

Joyce met and married a young man whose name was Melvin Anderson. People had thought that she had married too soon after Robert's death and could be seen as a rebound. She didn't have enough time to elapse since the passing of her first love. She wouldn't be driving us to school again after her marriage.

How much torture should we endure each year just to get an education? One of our most daunting was with our cousin Martha's husband who was a Baptist preacher. Can you imagine slow…each morning he would pick us up in front of our house. His car would be parked on the (raceway) road. We risked getting run over each day by people who were in a hurry and we were like little bowling pins as we crossed the dangerous expressway. Once inside we had to listen to him brag about his big beautiful Buick, that it needed to be stretched out on the highway for it to perform. We drove 20-30 mph in a 50-55 mph zone. I wasn't too clear about his not driving any faster or God forbid to pull up into our driveway. He lasted for about three months. I could feel my parents' pain and anxiety. I'm sure that they didn't know that I was actually contemplating quitting school if I had to continue depending on the unorthodox modes of transportation another year.

James was our last resort. He saved the day for us weary travelers. He was a fantastic driver. Happiness can come in so many forms and our new driver was one for us all. I decided to stay in school.

I was beginning to have other struggles, to keep up my grades and of finishing school which was the ultimate goal. Joe Henry was beginning to be demanding of me whenever he visited, "Why are you wearing that slutty outfit?" he would ask. I rationalized that he loved me so much and just wanted me to look descent. I toned down the outfits and the makeup to almost dull and drab. I became active in school because I was in the tenth grade and would be graduating in two years. So close yet so far. Joe Henry had fallen so far behind. He said he was in the eleventh grade but I doubted it. He had been put in a special school that he hated and was playing hooky most of the time. He confided in me that his younger teachers would kiss him and they tried to get a date with him. I didn't question it because he was an extremely desirable young man. I didn't push him to elaborate on the subject, I didn't want to know. I only knew that I loved him more and more each time I saw him. It was an unconditional love.

I had the opportunity to go on a school field trip. I belonged to the Tri-Hi-Y an organization for young students. There were two large bus loads of us for the all day affair. I made the awful mistake to divulge the sorted details of my affair with Joe Henry to my closest friend, Barbara Cosby. She couldn't wait to blab to most of the student body and that included the (wanna be men) boys on the bus. They were acting more attentive to me than what they had ever done. They were trying to get me to kiss them. One of the boys exposed himself to me. That act was witnessed by a self-righteous bitch in the seat across the isle. I didn't tattle on the boy because I was afraid that it would get back to Joe Henry and for sure he would have beaten him to a pulp. The next day the school was buzzing that I had made out with the (exposed) boy. He didn't make it any better. He lied to make himself look like he was, "The Man." He was ecstatic but I knew that my reputation was ruined. I got through the next week. I no longer associated with Barbara and didn't want any more false friends. I hadn't done anything wrong and I felt so ashamed. I was so glad that the weekend finally came and I was going to see Joe Henry. He had called and sounded so cold. I had the feeling of looming doom that stayed with me. Maybe I was wrong about his voice. I was tripping because of the school trip.

It was getting colder in the evening. Joe Henry was sweating when he arrived at my house. I smelled stale liquor on his breath. He wasn't in his usual jovial mood. I kept asking, "what's wrong, why are you looking at me like that?" He didn't answer. He glared at me as he was about to walk away. He spun around and came back towards me with more hatred in his eyes than I had ever seen in whites so called because of the color of my skin. He still had on his work clothes that I had never seen. He was always so meticulously groomed when he visited. His nose looked like you could drive a Mack truck in each flared nostril. I thought somebody had better tell me what brought on his behavior. He finally said in a sneering voice, "I heer'd 'bout cho' and yo' boyfrien' ona bus, I though' cho waz bette'n dat." I was about to answer "what are y…?" I was in shock when he slapped me on the side of my face. It was so blunt that I actually saw red. I became still as I was feeling weak and about to pass out. He came closer to me. I thought he was going to console me. He said in a raised, angry, threatening voice, "bitch don' cho' eva, eva fuck wid me you heah me!? I wi' killya!" I was petrified and too scared to answer him. I stood there shaking like a leaf; hoping against hope that it was a nightmare, "I'll wake up in a minute." The sting on my face lingered until I quietly cried myself to sleep. I didn't want anyone to know the shame and hurt that I was feeling. Joe Henry had shown me the side of his personality that I didn't want to admit existed. I had fooled myself when

I saw him with the young girl at the Gathright's house. He was so cold to her, then she was dismissed. I made a pact with myself the next day I was so glad that it was Saturday. I didn't have to go to school. I promised myself that I would never be like my Aunt Tene who had been beaten so many times by her husband who was thirty years her senior. It was so humiliating to her. She would get smacked, she would run away and hide out. He would find her and promise her the world, he swore that it would never ever happen again. It was the liquor that made him do it. She found security in his empty words and in the house that they lived in (FYI when he died, he willed the house to his eight children, her stepchildren she had raised put her out of the house with nothing). I would never let some man treat me that way. What a weak woman my Aunt was. I felt so sorry for her. I thought, "I can't tell anybody about this, my family would have a fields day with the secret that I was forced to keep." I imagine my daddy would kill me if he knew what had happened although I knew that he didn't have killer instincts. The very idea that my mother would find out my secret was impossible to imagine. She would never allow me to see anybody again, especially that hateful bastard...I hated him. I was in a silent tug of war in my mind. One way or the other I was determined that I was going to be the winner. The phone rang, "Carrie it's for you." I said just as loudly, "tell whoever it is I'm not home!" Janie told the person on the line, "Carrie said she ain't home" That happened two more times that day. I was thinking how dare he call me as if nothing had happened. He was the judge and jury. He had no rights to slap me to punish me for no reason. He wasn't my daddy (who never laid hands on any of us in that manner).

My eyes were red and swollen for the next few days. I became a zombie just going through the motions. The phone calls had stopped. I had to confide in someone or I would explode. I talked with Connie finally who was so wrapped up in her own life being engaged to Tommie G. Their marriage was pending. I tried to pretend that I was happy for them. Any other time I would have been. I started to cry thinking that she would be more empathetic to what I was going through. She didn't want to hear me cry or see me shed any tears. She did however give me some words of wisdom that I didn't even want to hear. "I told you what kind of boy that Joe Henry is; he don't mean any girl or woman any good and you saw how he treated Matty Williams when she was telling him about his baby." I said, he would never be caught dead with a girl like her. I believed him because he said he had no reason to lie to me and because he loved me. Connie stopped typing and looked at me as she pointed to my face and said, "why is your left eye redder and puffier than your right eye? And you have a split lip." I began sobbing uncontrollably; to hear the honest truth but not yet willing to accept it. I didn't want to face my grandparents so I ran out of the house before they heard me.

I was living on fumes. I didn't feel that there was any reason for me to continue to live. I was tired of living and not ready for the Grim Reaper. God would never forgive me if I took my own life, at least that's what I had always been taught – that suicide was the unpardonable sin. That thought rolled off of my back like water off of a duck. I became angry with myself to ever entertain such a bizarre notion. I vowed that no man would ever make me take my own life. I must have hit rock bottom during my self loathing period. As much as I tried to get back into the swing of things I was constantly reminded that I still loved Joe Henry who just happened to appear over at Muhmuh's house to see Connie and Tommie. I saw him as he pulled up into their driveway, my heart jumped into my throat. It was all that I could do to keep from running over to him. I wanted to hold him, I craved to kiss him and – oh God he was back in his truck and leaving. I thought, "I must act fast." By the time I had reached the front screen door, he had already backed out of Muhmuh's driveway and into the road. I started to dash out to our yard because I knew he was like grease lightening. Something strange happened – he slowed down as he was giving a manual right hand turn signal into my parent's driveway. I stayed behind the closed screen door. I didn't want him to know just how anxious I was to see him. I ran to the girl's bedroom (my room). Janie was there playing with her dolls. I looked at her, she was such a happy child at eight years old as she should be. Her dolls had real hair and was the same complexion as she was. I became calmer and reflected back to my younger years when we were so poor that Christmas was only a grim reminder of just how bad off that we really were. I had written many letters to Santa Claus during the holidays asking for a doll with the same color complexion and hair texture as mine. Well I can say this, be careful for what you wish for because I did get a doll who was a shade darker than me. I don't know if it had been given to me as a prank by my parents or by Mrs. Annette who was the owner and operator of a small grocery store that we frequented. She had given a box of toys to my parents because she heard that we weren't going to have Christmas that year.

I was so excited that we had presents. It was wrapped in brown slightly used paper bag. No matter, I had a present. It was soft and I squeezed it in my little eager hands. I laid it down to see if it was going to say, "Mama" but it didn't. everybody was standing around, "open it Carrie." I undid the familiar ribbon (the one that I had worn in my hair to church) that was tied around it. I carefully removed the blue ribbon then tore the brown paper wrapping to expose the (hopefully little brown doll). It was the worst gift that I had ever and will ever receive. It was a foot long, grinning Aunt Jemima doll in all of her glory. She had on an old head rag (that was covering the hair) and her famous apron. The thing that I remembered the most was her menacing grin. I wanted to cry but my family was standing around waiting for a happy response, "Thank you Mother and Deddy" I said meekly. They explained that Santa had heard that I had wanted a brown doll so he left it over at Mrs. Annette's store and Deddy picked it up and brought it home for Christmas for me. I was such an eager gullible child but felt that the Santa story was not something that I wanted to hear.

The Aunt Jemima doll wouldn't die a natural death, however, I do think that she may have drowned in a steel drum on the side of our house where my mother caught rain water to wash our clothes. (hate is a bad thing; I'm glad that the doll wasn't human). Janie looked up at me. Her usual question was, "whatcha doin'?" I didn't answer her. She didn't realize it because she was so into her doll family. I told her to answer the door when Joe Henry knocked. We waited in the room quietly for several minutes and never got a knock at the door. I became irritated all over again. There was the sound of laughter from two male voices coming from the living room. It was Joe Henry and James sitting and talking and just shooting the breeze.

James had let Joe Henry into the house just as he was about to knock. James called out, "Carrie, you have company" almost melodiously. He had a fantastic baritone voice. I responded just as musically, "who is it?" that could have started the second world war. He said, "It's Joe Henry" teasingly I said, "In a minute, I'm on the phone." Janie kept looking at me then asked, "do you want me to keep him company until you're ready?" She was acting more grown up than I was. I got up abruptly and said, "no, you play with your dolls."

I went into the living room. James had left Joe Henry alone to use the phone that wasn't in use, "what a turd" I thought, he just blew me out of the water. Joe was sitting in the big overstuffed chair. I saw the back of his head as I came into the room and strolled past him without saying a word of greeting. I sat down on the sofa across from him. I looked at him and hoped that he could see the contempt and anger in my face. I squinted my eyes then rolled them while turning my head away from him. He took all of it in then burst out into an uncontrollable laugh, "yo looks so cute when yo angry." I tried to keep the sour look that usually worked on others but not on him. The scowl that I had was forced into a smile then I too was caught up in laughter. I couldn't stay mad at him.

It was early afternoon. Joe told me that he knew of a new place called The Dairy Queen that had recently opened and coloreds could buy hamburgers, fried and a malted milk shake. He explained how it was made. It sounded so delicious that I got my appetite back. Mother was walking through the living room to go to the kitchen for her usual big glass of ice water. I was so excited when I told her that I wanted to try out a shake. I promised her that we would be right back as soon as we ate. She looked at Joe Henry and said, "I'm trusting you with my daughter. She has a curfew to be back here by ten o'clock." Joe shook his head and said timidly, "I'll have huh back befo' den Mrs. Pea'son." I ran back to my room and got my ugly red car coat and trailed after Joe Henry to his truck. I warned him to go easy on the screeching tires, which he did until he was about a mile away then he let her rip. I was all smiles. I knew that he would take care of me.

When we arrived to the place that had just opened I was thrilled to be there with him and was famished since I hadn't eaten that much since our breakup. He moved me over closer to him. He was so strong. Although it was cold he wasn't wearing his jacket. He was flexing his muscles for me. The man was so full of himself. He must have known that I was taking in all of his displays to my heart that was filled with pride. He got out of the truck and told me, "wait heah." He went on one side of the stand and someone from inside motioned for him to go to the other side. There were two white couples on that side and about eight colored couples lined up – waiting patiently in the colored line. The whites were being served. Another car load of whites had come and was about to be served before they took the orders of the colored patrons. Hell hath no wrath as Joe Henry scorned. He went up to the window and said, "wha tha fuck do ya thank yo' do'n?" I thought maybe I should say something like I'm not hungry or simply get out and start running. I sat there motionless awaiting a response from the waitress. Joe Henry stood his ground with a wide stance and his arms folded. Most of the coloreds were walking away from the burger stand knowing that the cops would probably be there in minutes. Joe Henry said loudly, "I wants two of yo' burgers, two fries and two shakes!" He wasn't grinning and he was looking at them dead in their eyes. They must have known that he was not going to take anymore of their nigger shit – as I had heard him say so many times. He informed me again as he got back into the truck with burgers, fries and shakes. I was totally shaken but felt so proud that he had stood up to those bastards. The excitement had taken my appetite away. I couldn't finish my food so Joe Henry finished it for me. He was in rare form or maybe a bit tipsy.

It was eight fifteen as we were pulling away from the burger stand. We had eaten and talked about us. He reached under the seat at a stop sign and took a swig of whisky from a pint bottle. It was passed to me and I did the most natural thing and took two gulps that almost took my breathe away just to show him that I could handle it. In about three minutes I became so light headed and giddy. I moved so close to him. He must have known how much that I missed him. I touched his hair then his heavy perfect eyebrows. I knew that I had better not mess with those beautiful eyes so the mouth and nose had it. I outlined his top lip with my finger then gently his bottom. He allowed me to put my finger into his mouth and he sucked it like it was candy and then – and then we headed down the highway to God knows where. I was touching him in places that I had never explored with my hands. He got another sip of the strong liquor. He made his usual face that it was nasty to taste. I followed suite. There was also a small pistol hidden under the seat. I pretended not to see it. Oh Jesus! I wanted that man so badly! I was moaning uncontrollably as he kissed me and touched me. We had stopped in an unfamiliar area. We had driven for quite a while. I sobered up for a second, "we need to be back by ten Joe Henry." He answered, "we got pleni' time." It was so dark and the moon was in hiding. He had turned the lights off and was pulling his pants down. I did the same. It was as if we had never been apart. He positioned me on the seat with my head under the steering wheel. We didn't have a radio to drown out the barbaric sounds that we made since we were out of hearing distance so I thought. He moaned, "Carrie I missed you so much. I'm so sorry baby, please forgive me sweetheart." I answered as I was panting, "I missed you too Joe Henry and I forgive you." (It wasn't the speech that I had rehearsed). We were kissing as if we were two hungry animals. He mounted me and found the spot that caused so much ecstasy for both of us. I kept my eyes open that time because I didn't want anybody to walk up on us. I was at the point of screaming and clawing my nails into his back when an oncoming car light appeared. Joe Henry didn't see it or maybe he didn't want to see it. It came so close to where we were parked. It was then that I got up enough nerve to look at the joy stick that was giving me so much pleasure. I almost panicked when I saw and realized the length and the width of his penis as it plunged so deep inside of me. I started crying and clutching his naked bottom. He was so out of control as he yelled, "I'm coming Carrie, oh baby, I do love you so much." We cried together as we held each other as the waves of our emotions were freed.

Afterwards we began laughing uncontrollably. We talked later and it was then that I discovered that we were just a few yards beyond his house. I reached over to feel his pouch while he was backing the truck back into the main roadway. It was swelling again. I shook my head when I saw the smile on his handsome face. "No, Joe Henry I have to go home." We drove back nearly in silence. He slowed down when we were nearing my house. He began to sing, "-----my name is Joe Bailey, my nuts weighs forty-nine pounds, if you see any ladies who want some baby, tell them Joe Bailey's in town-----." He laughed so hard after his song. I didn't find any humor in it at all. It was insensitive and I should have told him so but I was only trying to please him and I didn't want to argue either. We were back on track and that was all that mattered.

It was late October. The air was crisp. There was evidence that the season was changing. The trees had a beautiful array of leaves of bright yellow, golden orange and burnt red. The woody areas were aligned with all of the brilliant arrangements as if to warn us to enjoy it now because winter would follow shortly with its frigid coldness. The woods would change to a bleak grey accompanied by the rainy season that made it more dreary. Not my favorite time of the year. Joe Henry saw me as much as my parents would allow. He was becoming impatient and demanding with me. He felt that he was being hindered from seeing me when he wanted and how long he wanted. He came over to visit me the last week of October. He was acting so jittery. I kept asking what was wrong. He just sat there for a few minutes holding and caressing my hand as he had done so many times. He finally broke the silence and said, "Carrie, I can' go on lak dis, I wants us to be together all da time." I looked at him in amazement. I shouldn't have been surprised because his brother Phillip was living with his girlfriend – Shirley Ann – he and his brother had typical sibling rivalry. Phillip had been on his own since he was fifteen years old when he broke away from the strong hold of Bigman who made all of his sons work out in the fields all day. He in turn pocketed all of the money. So Phillip one day while his daddy was lashing out at him verbally and with a belt, Phillip grabbed the belt and enough was enough. He left home and never regretted it because he became a responsible man who had good business sense. He made a way out of no way and was successful in all of his endeavors. Joe Henry wanted to follow in his footsteps. He had a lot to learn starting out with patience.

I didn't argue or say anything as I sat there dumbfounded. My mouth was moving but nothing was coming out of it. His argument was he was tired of school and his grades were proof of it. His next point was he wanted to be with me, "forever" and then he added, "I wants cho ta marry me." He wasn't asking, he was telling me. My mouth became so dry. I bolted up off of the couch. "Do you want some water?" I rushed out the room and stayed in the kitchen for a few minutes. I felt so pressured yet so loved. He sat with his head in his hands as if he had the weight of the world on his shoulders. I sat next to him and to my surprise there were tears running down his cheeks, something that he didn't like for me to see. His last pitch effort was to remind me that I too was unhappy with going to school and that my grades were spiraling downwards. I told him I needed some time to think. Then he asked, "will yo marry me? There is no time to think" He was so impatient with me, I knew if I didn't answer him he would walk out of my life forever and it frightened me that I would be alone. II continued to sit there with my mouth open, afraid to say yes and I dared not say no, he was waiting for a response. I began to talk, "Joe Henry we are too young to marry." He answered, "we will elope and dupe up our identity (I only had my birth certificate). We can cross the county line and get married as young as fifteen years old, we don't need no body to sign for us." He had an elaborate plan that he would cash in his savings bonds that he had since he was a little boy. He assured me that they must be worth thousands of dollars. He planned to continue to work at the service station washing cars (he got good tips) and pumping gas. He had to clean the wind shields and check the oil. I sat like a wide eyed drenched turkey, too dumb to come out of the rain. And then it started to make a lot of sense the more he talked. I piped in that I could get day work and babysit. I got my hopes up for a minute that I could put in an application at the Sock Mill. I let the idea go quickly because only white women especially those who were high school drop outs were hired. There had been several colored who had went in and put in an application. They had separate boxes for the completed forms – colored and white – no colored were hired.

We sat in a huddle for quite some time. We were so excited about our plans for the future that we didn't get it on as we generally did. Joe Henry's last bit of information to me was he was going to get his weekly salary of twenty two dollars on that coming Tuesday evening. He had plans to go down in the country to his mom's house and pack a bag. His off day was Wednesday and he had a lot of errands to run. He instructed me to start packing tonight and keep it hidden until Wednesday night, "I'll toot my horn lightly and you can walk down to the dark New Road and meet me." I wanted to argue but there was no saying no to that man when he made up his mind. He left there quietly that night.

There was a huge lump in my throat. I did what I was told and reasoned with myself that it was the right thing to do. Joe Henry assured me that he had great parents who wanted whatever he wanted. He had talked about what a good life that he and his family had and he wanted to share his life with me. He told me about the nice cars that his family had. He had an old Kaiser that he was fixing. His eyes would light up when he talked about his daddy's brand new Cadillac that he had paid cash for. "They gives me whateva I wan's" I fantasized that I was going to be like a princess when I married him and end up in the lap of luxury. We would be able to spend as much time with each other as we wanted. Maybe I would be able to get one of those cars that he had access to.

The more I thought about it the more real that it became to me. I was going to prove everybody wrong about Joe Henry. We were going to be just fine. I hated school, however, I knew of some folks (my daddy) who had made it just on street smarts. I was learning it and had a great teacher, my new soon to be husband. Wednesday night was looming over me, I was a nervous wreck. My mom was doting over me as usual. I told her and convinced her that it was probably my monthly. My whole family went to bed about nine thirty. The slumber sounds were evident that I wouldn't have any problems if I could get my stuff out of there quietly. I pulled the over-packed old suit case out of our closet where it had been hidden. I had a few other items stuffed in a plastic bag. I stood by the back door then I heard a car that was moving very slowly then the horn tooted. It wasn't the sound of his truck but I knew it was him. My knees were knocking, I swallowed hard. The plastic bag became entangled for a second as I dragged it behind me. The small suit case was made out of cardboard it too felt rather heavy. I was sweating bullets and crying as I looked back at the home that my daddy had built for his family. I thought about the love that my mom always had in her face. I knew she wouldn't approve of what I was doing but I felt compelled to be with the man that I loved and he loved me. I would miss my brothers and sisters but I had made a choice and that was to be Joe Henry's wife.

I was on the roadway headed towards an unfamiliar car. The headlights blinked, my heart quickened and I knew that it must be Joe Henry. He backed the car to where I was struggling with my bags. There was no traffic that night. I was afraid that someone who knew me would drive by and certainly inform my parents (maybe that was what I was hoping). Before I left my house I had pulled the cover over my pillow on my side of the bed. I made it look like a small body underneath it, just trying to stay warm.

Joe Henry was so elated when he got out to help me put the bags in the trunk, "It belongs to Phillip, my truck stopped on me." I was so glad because it was so cold, my teeth were chattering and that car had a good heater and a radio in it. He took off very slowly. I looked back and could see our front porch light fade until we were totally out of sight. Joe Henry reached under the seat and pulled out a pint of whiskey and said, "take some o' dist ta wam you up." I did just that and immediately felt warmth starting from my throat. I felt like a frozen chicken and soon the ice would be thawed out. I turned my attention to him because he wasn't too talkative. "Now what?" I asked. He didn't answer immediately. He was deep in his thoughts. Then finally when we were further down the road, he said, "I went to the bank and tried to get the bonds cashed out. They were in my older sisters name also. The bank teller had said they ain't mature." I was staring ahead at nothing in particular. I didn't want to light the short fuse so my words were chosen very carefully. I said, "I thought you had every thing planned?" He answered, "I did have e'ry thang figured out 'cept dis." He drove for about an hour. I said, "I should go back home but I locked the back door when I left." I began to weep silently and he wasn't able to console me. He stopped the car on another unfamiliar dirt road. He kept talking low and soothing assuring me that everything was going to be alright. He promised that he was going to take good care of me. He lit a cigarette (Salem). He handed me one. Anything to keep my mouth shut. We took a swig of from the ancient age bottle. It was so strong and mind numbing. We talked a little about our future together. All was better with the world when he pulled me over towards him. He didn't have to bring in the clowns or perform any magic tricks. I was always ready willing and able to response to what he needed and to my needs. He let me know that he was the master of his domain. Neither of us slept that night. The windows were steamed. As day was breaking I had to use the restroom real bad. Joe Henry opened the back door, "he'p yo' se'f" The red clay ground was frozen and so was my ass when I pulled down my panties. "aw that hurt." It was burning so badly I could tell that my (pussy) was swollen but if by any chance that he would want to tap it again – it would hurt so good.

I looked around as I was squatting. I knew that there was no snakes crawling about in that frigid weather only me trying to overcome myself and try to do better than what my parents expected of me. Suddenly I was conscious of Joe Henry who was close by and I knew that he was watching me. I felt so shame-faced (embarrassed). It took me longer than usual to empty my bladder because of all of the pain. I noticed that the urine stream flowed past a grayish white object that had the appearance of a small elongated balloon. There were several that had been strewn about on the ground. I heard foot steps and the sounds of cows mooing (and a bull). They were being herded by a white man in overalls and an old overcoat. He had an old dog that was doing most of the work of herding the cattle through the path they must have known. I tried to finish quickly and pull up my filthy smelly panties (I need a bath so badly). I was about to get back into the car. I noticed several empty Falstaff beer bottles on the ground. Someone had even dumped pint bottles of ancient age whiskey bottles along with multiple cigarette butts. Somebody had obviously been there before us and had thrown some party/picnic. I was too tired and sleepy to think about it, to try to figure it out. I would ask Joe Henry later. I wanted to cry so badly but instead I started giggling when Joe Henry finally got out of the car to relieve himself. I felt closer to him after that moment thinking this is our new beginning…it's what husbands and wives do.

He had run out of cigarettes and drinks. We laid on the back seat to finally get some sleep which was approximately one hour because we were awakened when a truck went past us then turned around to double back in our direction. Joe Henry sat up and gestured for me to stay down. He obviously knew the white people in the truck. His story was that he'd had too much to drink and couldn't go any further last night. He didn't want to kill himself or anybody else in a car accident. They agreed with him and said that they would be talking to Bigman that morning because they had asked him before to stay off of their private property. They pulled off slowly to make sure that Joe Henry got off of their land.

It was about nine o'clock Thursday morning. I was so thirsty and hungry. My pussy was throbbing – that's what Joe Henry called it, "tha' my pussy."

We drove past a small pond that was so beautiful. It still had some lingering fog that seemed so eerie. The water was so still and it mirrored the sky and the banks. There was so much serenity with the rustic scenery. Joe Henry had gone into his quiet mode. I asked, "where are we going?" He said, "we go'n to my house fo' a minute." I was still taking in the beauty on the right side of the narrow but paved road. He put his blinkers on for a left hand turn. I was sooo unprepared for what came next. It must have been that I was still asleep and having a nightmare, I would awaken soon and my prince charming would still be driving us to his parent's home. Well, I'm awake and he's turning into – he made a wrong turn – he continued to drive the car up the extremely rugged driveway then parked the car. He revved the motor at first then put the gear in drive and gunned the motor – spinning the wheels. There was so much noise, smoke and sand (I guess that's what's meant by raising sand). The house was shaking. I thought he would push it off its foundation. I sat there speechless. Two people came out of the house just as I as about to say, "Joe Henry what…" The house that he had bragged about could not be the one that I was seeing even with the cob webs still in my eyes. Apparently his parents had moved to that house (and I use the words loosely) when he as about two years old. Prior to that they had been living like nomads going from shack to shack that had been abandoned by other poor families. Their house was only a hop skip and a jump from the shack that my family had moved from when I was seven years old.

The Mathis family home was perched on pillars of old bricks and rocks that had been piled atop each other and mortar mix had cemented it for stability. The front of it had a faded redwood stain that someone had attempted to cover the thirsty splintering planks that held multiple rusty nails together (not a typo). The porch was railless that was about a six foot drop at the far end. The flooring were buckling planks that seemed to have been beckoning to those who dared walk across it to either get tripped or splinters in bare feet. There was a rippling effect from the front porch that could be felt by those inside the house and on the back porch that had almost separated from the house. I guesstimate that it was about 900 square feet. With the recent addition of a tiny bedroom and dining room that had their used Frigidaire. The tin roof held the heat in the summertime and the cold in the winter. One good thing, the house no longer leaked when it rained.

The white owner of the house had also allowed Joe's family to run electricity to the house. They were never billed because they had tapped into someone else's line. They had no running water thus no inside restroom. Their source of water was a spring across the road which supplied them for drinking, cooking, bird baths, whores baths, and Saturday night baths, wash water and water for their animals which included a yard full of chickens, four skinny pigs, two cows and a horse that had to be put out of its misery. Oh, there was also Joe's fathers pet, a duck named Drake. He was last seen waddling down to the pond and never to return. I'm so sure that he didn't drown either. He must have thought, "Fuck this, I'm out!"

So, that saying – a man's home is his castle – especially when he's seen such despair and not able to find a decent place for his family. He seemed satisfied that he was now sheltered from the elements. He didn't desire to have the finer things in life and he had passed on his family values to the man that I was sitting next to in front of their home (please get me a shovel because I'm getting knee deep in shit just thinking about going back to my yester years). Hell naw I would never live in a run down piece of shit like this ever again. they didn't have a phone either. "Who are those people?" I ask as the dark skinned older lady knocked on the car window. She halfway smiled at me exposing her two missing front teeth then quickly turned her attention to Joe Henry. He let down his window and said, "Muhdea, I want you to meet my girlfriend, we are going to get married." She nodded at me, "please ta mee'cha'" She stayed focused on Joe Henry. She said with a bit of irritation in her voice, "Joe Henry dis' gir's' parents wuz jus' hea' 'bout a hou' ago, they gwine call da poolese if'n yo' don' git hur bak thar!" They argued for a while. His father didn't say a word. He just shok his head as he stood on the rickety porch whistling an indistinguishable tune.

Joe Henry bolted out of the car slamming the door hard. He didn't say anything as he went inside behind his parents. He came back quickly with a fruit jar of hot coffee, a biscuit with a piece of smoked sausage. I took it gladly. I even remembered to say my blessings. I hoped I wouldn't get any germs from my filthy hands. I woofed down the snack so fast. I felt a little light headed. We shared the coffee as we drove the twelve miles back to Meridian. I was dozing when we past the turn off road to my parents house. "Where are we going?" I asked. He answered, "I have one mo' thang tha' migh' wok." I was beyond being tired. I went into a deep sleep and was awakened abruptly by Phillip in front of his apartment. He was the brother that Joe Henry was so close to. It was uncanny on how much they resembled each other. He knocked on my window. When I let it down he patted me on the back playfully then said in his drawl that they both had, "Carrie yo needs ta go back home to yo' fok's, yo' daddy's ou' look'n fo' you." He looked at Joe Henry who had gotten back in the car and had lit a cigarette that he'd bummed from Phillip. "You get dis gir back hom naw, yo hea' me, come back ova heah and we'll figar som'n ou'" I looked at Joe Henry who appeared to have had the last bit of air let out of his swollen head. There wasn't much to say. We eased back to my parent's house going less than the speed limit just like two wet hungry beat up dawgs with their tails tucked between their legs. Funerals could not have been any sadder than what we both were feeling. We had tried to do something that had failed, so we had to face the worse obstacle course and that was returning me back to my parents as damaged goods. My imagination was getting the best of me. I pictured them at home waiting with the police officer ready to handcuff Joe Henry. I just knew that my Muhmuh would be there wailing uncontrollably. The worse of all of my thoughts were my brothers and sisters would be outside waiting to point out how disappointed that they were. Most of all my baby sister would know that I had let her down for the first time.

It generally took about ten to fifteen minutes to drive from downtown Meridian to our house. That time it took seemingly one hour fifteen minutes. I didn't feel like the brave young woman with so many hopes and dreams as I had when I left the safety of my home last night. The only thing that I could claim was defeat and I was too weary to go on at that moment. I knew that I still loved Joe Henry as we clutched each others hands so tightly. I had to ask him to ease up on it – it hurt. He did then he smiled at me, "I love you Carrie, I still wants to marry you. We'll make it happen." I saw so much love and tenderness in his eyes, his face and in his strong hands that seemed to be begging for me not to give up on him. I gently squeezed his hand then reached over and touched his chest. I looked over at him. He must have seen the look of love and adoration that I had for him. Something that I wouldn't ever be able to give to another man.

We could see Muhmuh's house thank God there wasn't any fanfare in her yard. We past her house, I thought "now for the hard part." We pulled up into my parent's driveway. There weren't any police cars waiting to arrest us. Deddy's truck was gone. Muhmuh's car wasn't in her driveway either. Joe Henry pulled up to the house – the driveway had just been paved. The screen door opened just as I was about to get out of the car. Out came my mother and my little sister. She didn't have a switch or a belt or even a rope for punishment. The only thing she had for me was her beautiful smile and those beautiful delightful eyes that lit up when I appeared. She must have seen me for the first time as a young woman with a determination to grow up too soon.

Mother became more demonstrative that morning than I had ever seen. We wept in each others' arms. I gave Janie a hug. She said that she was sick but I think that she was playing hooky. She didn't look sick to me.

I asked my mom if we could talk later because I hadn't slept the night before. We both blushed. Her fair skin turned red and I felt hot all over. She made me breakfast of grits, bacon, eggs and jelly toast. She asked, "do you want some coffee?" I answered her, "Yes máme." She too was hungry but would not or could not eat anything until her sweet daughter, Carrie Ann was safe and sound.

Mother wanted to make everything right. She wanted to protect me from all of the gossip and also from my daddy. She had always stood her ground that he wouldn't be the one to punish their girls because it was too severe. I found out that he had just gone to work a few minutes before me and Joe Henry arrived. I didn't know what to expect from Deddy. He had always been okay with me but we didn't engage in lengthy conversations as he did with Joyce or Janie his baby.

Breakfast was perfect. I was so glad for the time with my mom. I'm sure that I wasn't making any sense as we talked because I was basically sleep walking. I almost fell out of my chair. Mother understood. I excused myself from the table. I went and got a quick bath. It washed away the funk but it couldn't cleanse the shame and humiliation that my family, especially my mother, was facing. She had made the bed that I had slept in so many times. The covers were turned down as she had so often done whenever I was sick or hurt. She had removed the pillow that I had left the night before to fool everybody to think that

I was all tucked in and asleep. Now who was the fool? The feeling of remorse overcame me when I noticed that there were clean fresh smelling sheets on my bed (they had been line dried). Mother cared for me and the rest of my siblings – her children.

I didn't say my prayers as I generally did before going to bed. I was afraid to close my eyes for fear that God wouldn't allow me to awaken again. the tears were welling up in my eyes. My mother and Janie sat on the side of the bed. It was comforting for me to have them present. I turned my back to them as I sobbed silently. Mother put her hand on my shoulder. I turned over and gave her a hug. Janie was somewhat subdued but was able to refocus mother's attention to her because she was sick. She forced a very dry, "cough, cough, cough" You had to give her an "A" for effort. Mother had tears in her eyes yet she was laughing and so did I. With all said and done, I went to sleep safe and sound with mother watching over me.

I slept all day and that Thursday night after it had gotten dark. I heard the voices of most of my family. The table was being set. There was a different fragrance wafting from the kitchen. Was I in a dream? My thoughts came pouring back to me, "no, it's not a dream." I got up to use the bathroom. The whole episode of Wednesday night came flooding my mind especially when I tried to urinate. I was so swollen on my p- - - -. Knock, knock, knock. Who else could it be? I thought. Janie said, "Carrie supper's ready, come eat with us." Overcome with so much guilt and remorse, I answered in a meek voice, "I'm not hungry." I drew another tub of hot water. I was able to soak for about 20 minutes in Epsom salt water while my family ate their evening meal much quieter than usual. My mother was coming out of the girls room just as I was about to dart across the hall in hopes that nobody would see me. She said, "I put your supper on the dresser with some iced tea." It was so hard to eat and cry, so I did both. The phone rang. I heard my sister say it's Joe Henry again. I pretended that I was asleep when she knocked on the door and then entered. She took my plate and left the glass of tea. She went back to the phone and said, "She's still asleep. Maybe you can call her in the morning" Just the mere mention of his name gave me chill bumps. I was too washed out to talk to him, yet, I could feel the longing that would eventually get the best of me.

Mother came to the door, "Carrie I'm going to keep you out of school tomorrow. We'll talk then." I answered, "Thanks mother." I was feeling too shame faced to look at her. It would be a while before I would be able to look her in the eyes. I slept another eight hours until I heard mother say good bye to the rest of her children going to school the next morning. I felt a new found freedom that I had never experienced. No school for me today and it's Friday. I yawned and smiled to myself. I started to think of so many things that I could do that day. My thoughts were broken by the sound of a truck that had pulled up in our driveway. It was my daddy. It wasn't usual for him to come home during the day except on Saturday. He was alone. He must have forgotten something. Mother had been on the phone about ten minutes probably with Aunt Carrie Mae. I heard a light tap on the door and before I could say anything, there stood both my parents in the doorway. My first thought was "were they planning to beat the hell out of me since there were no witnesses?"

Mother stood in front of daddy who had the most solemn face that I could ever remember. "Carrie put your clothes on and come in the living room" my mother said sadly. I got dressed quicker than lickety split. I didn't even take time to comb my hair because it wouldn't matter when I would be found later hanging from the big pine tree in front of our house (my mind was really screwing with me). The phone rang as I was walking down the hallway. It was more like the Last Mile. Mother answered it. "She's not able to talk now, you can call back later." Mother looked at me and didn't say who was on the phone. I went past her to get my dose of medicine. There were four judges and no jurors when I got to the living room. I didn't get any eye contact from any of them – or was it me? Muhmuh and Gran sat on the couch with their arms folded (I needed a hug). The Grim Reaper was about to have his day. Deddy came out of the kitchen with a big jar of ice water. He sat in the big overstuffed arm chair (if he only knew). Mother took a seat in the small rocker. They all must have planned that whole trial scene. Someone had brought the straight chair from outside. Deddy said roughly, "sit down Carrie." I wanted to grab another chair from the dining room that had been padded (for my sore bottom) but that wasn't the time for my comfort. I sat down and waited and waited. Muhmuh was crying softly. Gran just sat there shaking his bald head. My dad finally spoke up after clearing his throat because he knew that he was the man of the house and was in charge, "Carrie wha' cho done wuz wrong, I can' have no daghdah o'mines do wha' cho don an' jus wáz back hea' and thank eva thang iz a'ight. You iz now a grown woman cuz yo took tha' step. I heer'd cho wans ta git married so me and Shoty wi' do was'sen eva hit takes so'z yo'l be happy" at which time Muhmuh went into second gear with the "boo hoo, boo hoo, boo hoo, Cleo she's just a baby." She stopped short and turned to me, "Carrie Ann are you pregnant?" Surprised I stammered a pitiful, "no máme" no time to be impolite. She thought about it, "You don't know if you're pregnant from the other night though?" Was that a question or a statement? I answered, "no máme Muhmuh I couldn't be pregnant." The room felt quiet because none of my judges wanted me to elaborate on my rationale for my not being pregnant. They wouldn't want to know that no baby nor sperm could have survived the extreme, fiery fucking that me and Joe Henry had done that night.

That was not the time to smile knowingly as if I had swallowed a canary so I kept staring at my folded hands that I was wringing constantly. They needed to know that I was sorry for what I'd done. My mother asked, "what are you planning to do about your schooling Carrie Ann?" She became misty eyed, her voice was trembling at which time I decided to let them know how I felt about Joe Henry and what we had planned to do Wednesday night during our failed elopement. "He still wants to marry me. We don't have a ring and we still love each other. I will talk with him later when he calls back." Everybody seemed to be relieved. There were no objections. Nobody spoke up and said, "Hell naw, you ain't gonna marry nobody!" I waited and it never came. No siree bob tail. They talked and it was finally decided that I would quit school and go on with my marriage after me and Joe Henry ironed out all of the details. Mother said that she would sign whatever documents that was needed.

My grandfather was squirming in his seat. I'm sure that he was thinking that his church members wouldn't think too well of him if they knew that one of his grandchildren had defiled herself. My grandmother was obviously on the verge of a nervous breakdown. She was chewing her tongue so fast (a nervous habit) because she would have to explain to her Women's Society/Club at church that her namesake had made a fool of her and she would no longer be able to keep her official position that she had held for so long. My daddy said that all he wanted was what was best for all of his children and I'm sure that he didn't want to compare notes with his sister – Aunt Janie – who had made it clear that her children were better than his. She had often bragged unmercifully whenever she could when their mom – Grandmaw – was present. She didn't care what either of her kids said, she loved us all dearly. Last but not least was my mom who wanted things better for me. Everybody had their reason but nobody ever said, "no," absolutely not, nah uh, natha, knet – no means no.

I waited by the phone then finally Joe Henry did call that evening of my trial. I felt like a fox in a hen house, an outsider. I had reached the highest of highs then plummeted to the lowest of lows. Joe Henry was trying to appease me that everything was going to be alright. I didn't want to hear it. I just wanted to die. It seemed that all was lost. My parents wanted me out of their house. I couldn't face my classmates and forget about my church family. Joe heard the desperation in my voice, "I'll be right there." He hung up and in the next few minutes he was outside. I must have looked like a rag doll (poh lil' thang). I ran out to his truck that he'd been working on all day. He got out and reached for my hand, pulled me towards him then lifted me up in his strong arms. We were smiling at each other and just knew. He kissed my forehead because of the certain audience from my house and over at Muhmuh's house. We walked hand in hand to my house. Joe Henry said, "I wan's to tak wid yo' daddy and Mama." They were sitting in the living room as well as Janie. Lottie was back in the kitchen straightening up the supper dishes. I attempted to brush my tangled hair with my fingers but to no avail. It looked like a mop and needed the nine yards of wash, press and curl but it would have to wait. I wasn't sure about what Joe Henry was going to say to my parents. He wasn't known for diplomacy in the past. He went over to daddy who was sitting on the chair where it all began. He put out his hand to daddy and they shook hands. The normal formalities followed. Joe Henry cleared his throat, his voice was still cracking but he continued. He looked at my dad then to my mom, "Mr. and Mrs. Pea'son, I wants to ask your permission for Carrie's hand in marriage." He didn't wait for a response (we both knew that it was wrong about what we had done but we were in love). He told them "I'm gwin'e wok hard ta provide fo' Carrie." He took my hand then we waited for a response. Deddy cleared his throat as he had often done before talking. He then had the opportunity to let us know how he was feeling and the sermon began. It was right to the point basically the same that he had told me earlier, then it was over. My daddy gave Joe Henry permission to marry me. It was going to be a simply ceremony, at which time both my parents should have put up a fight and just said, "no, Carrie, you are too young" but they didn't.

Everybody was under the assumption that I was pregnant and no amount of denial would change their minds. My cousin by marriage (Josephine) asked me over to her house. Her and her husband (Mr. Wilson) – he had been my fifth grade teacher in school and it was the proper thing to call him – not cousin Little Brother – as my family called him. They were well respected people of the community. She was the principal of East End/Carver Jr. High School. They wanted to talk me out of going through with the crazy idea of marriage and the big question popped up again, "are you pregnant?" I tuned her out after she asked that. How dare those people who thought that we wouldn't make it a whole year. She had doubts about Joe Henry. She had heard that he wasn't from a good family. My rationale was no family was perfect. I became defensive and tired of people meddling. Out of all the people I spoke with – I didn't see one truly happy couple including my parents, my grandparents and the Wilson's. I was bound and determined to show them that although I was fifteen I would make it work (I knew, there was no I in We). We were determined to make it work.

Joe Henry and I went to the court house in the middle of November. We were accompanied by both our mothers so that they could sign to give their permission for us to marry. His mother was so sweet to me and my mom. I had good feelings about Joe's background after actually meeting with her and spending that time observing them interacting with each other and with me and my mom. After getting the papers signed Gran agreed to perform the marriage ceremonies for $10.00, his flat fee for everybody. The marriage certificate cost fifteen dollars. I offered to help pay for it with some of the money that I had earned babysitting. Joe Henry wouldn't hear of it. His mom paid for it.

Mother took me shopping for a dress for my wedding. We went to Learners Shop on 5th Street. I was looking for a simple white dress. Mother said, "white dresses are for virgins." I thought, "oh, for crying out loud, how old fashioned." She finally found an inexpensive light blue wool form-fitting dress on sale and a small white pill box hat with a small veil. I already had a fairly new pair of pumps that Lottie had bought me already. Joe Henry called me when we got home and he was just as giddy as I was. He had just bought a new suit for our wedding that was slated for Saturday evening.

It was November 19, 1960. It had gotten as cold as a well diggers ass. The clock on the living room wall was ticking louder and louder. Daddy turned the heater up because my teeth were chattering. My hands were cold and shaking. I had forgotten to eat. I was so excited and yet I was afraid that Joe Henry would jilt me. He would be so proud of me when/if he arrived. I had on my new dress and hat with a surprise gift of pearl earrings and a single string necklace. I felt so pretty. My waistline was so tiny but I felt my family were staring at me as if I would blow up like a balloon right before their eyes. The TV remained on. Our one channel didn't offer a wide variety on Saturday evenings only Lawrence Welk which my mom enjoyed.

Grand and Muhmuh came over and they both took a seat. We waited for the groom to arrive. When he finally arrived one hour late, he had the heavy odor of hard liquor on his breath and of course the smell of the cigarette smoke that filtered in on him into the living room. My sisters – Lottie, Janie and Bennie – were present. Willie, James and Connie were present also.

We signed all of the necessary papers that Muhmuh had prepared for Gran. He stood up and told us to join hands (Joe Henry and I were so nervous our hands were literally shaking). We said our marriage vows to each other and with my family as witnesses. I listened to every word that Gran had said and I answered him truthfully. I would take this man to be my lawful wedded husband: In sickness and in health; for richer or for poorer till death do us part. There wasn't a ring; there weren't any objections only a fifteen year old girl and her seventeen year old man, "For what God has joined together let no man put asunder." (I think they should add 'no woman' also). He added, "you may kiss the bride." Joe Henry in the presence of my family gave me a puny kiss on the mouth – not one of his famous juicy kisses. He was so nervous, I planned to collect it later. There wasn't a reception. There were only half ass well wishes afterwards.

My clothes were all packed including that dang red car coat. My mom told me to follow her to her bedroom. She was fumbling for words on how to be a good wife. I eased the pressure off of her by telling her that I had many examples on being a good person. She and Muhmuh had been my guide. She cried as she held me, "I want you to be happy, Carrie. Remember you can always come home if you need to." She added, "I forgot to buy you a nice negligee." She then pulled out one of her new gowns. "This is yours." She also gave me a flannel gown and smiled, "if you need it later."

I went back through the living room. Deddy was still sitting in the rocker at which time I realized that he had his back to us throughout the whole ceremonies – except for when Gran had asked, "who gives this woman?" Deddy said, "I do" then he sat in the swivel rocker and wouldn't look at me.

He got up with mothers urging him when we were leaving out the front door. He hugged me and shook Joe Henry's hand then he looked away – maybe he felt tearful or angry at me. All I knew was, "I'm out of here."

We drove away as Mr. and Mrs. Joe Henry Mathis. I took his name and gladly. It had started to rain and the road was practically iced over. We drove slowly just trying to take in what we had just done. We began laughing and I finally got my juicy heart felt kiss from my husband.

I was so hungry and thirsty. Joe pulled out a fifth of liquor from under his seat. He gave me a swig and said that he was going to find a place for us to eat. Everything was closed at nine o'clock. He decided that he wanted to go over to Phillip's juke joint. The usual crowd was there either drunk or getting there. Shirley Ann was behind the counter because she had so much people skills. We announced our new marital status and neither of them were phased.

Joe Henry wanted to introduce me to everybody that he knew. It was as if we (I) was invisible. They were so drunk. The only person that they wanted to see there was Joe Henry. I got a soda and potato chips and sat with Shirley Ann. I noticed my groom had slurred speech and had fallen over several times. Finally Shirley Ann fixed me a burger reluctantly. I didn't want to be so sick that I wouldn't be able to consummate our first night as man and wife. I began to feel nauseated so I ran to the back of the café to the restroom. I couldn't get the door open because something was on the floor. I heard muffled moaning. It sounded like a woman's voice then a male voice joined in and drowned hers out. Curiosity and my sick stomach got the best of me. I felt for the light switch on the wall inside then flicked it on. There to my surprise on the nasty bathroom floor was a huge butt naked man and a very nice looking dark skinned woman. They both were so drunk neither of them realized that I was there for their grand finale. Shirley Ann came to the door where I stood in shock. She shook her head and put her hand on my shoulder and said, "Carrie meet your new brother-in-law, Billy. And that is his girlfriend, Banana Pudding." Shirley Ann was able to get them out of their stupor long enough for them to dress and get back out to the party animals. The juke box was blasting an unrecognizable blues. All of the small tables were jammed packed with couples. My queasiness had subsided. Joe Henry found me and was trying to stay on his feet. Phillip asked, "wahr ya'll sta'n ta nigh'?" I told him that we had planned to honeymoon in the Youngs

Hotel downtown Meridian. He answered, "I don' know tha' place cos' a lots of money." We stayed another ten minutes for Joe Henry to say his goodbyes. I got in the truck and tried to look happy. The two brothers were standing outside the café. Joe was about 3-4 inches taller than Phillip. I just noticed his new garb. He looked so handsome in his wedding clothes that consisted of a tweed greenish brown jacket, slacks to match. He wore a shirt and tie and a hanky in the pocket. That was the first time that I'd seen him in dress attire. To set the whole outfit off he had on a brown derby with a small feather on the rim. His shoes had a spit shine you could see your face in them. Wow! What a man! I got those longing feelings again just looking at him.

I let the window down and got his attention. He put his hand on Phillip's shoulder, shook his hand and they did the half hug that men do.

Everybody in the neighborhood must have known that Joe Henry wasn't a shy man as he got in his truck, gunned the motor until it shook the windows (I thought they would break). We went spinning side to side down the street. He excited me to no end.

We arrived at Youngs Hotel safe and sound. Both of us went to the front desk to get a room. We had never slept together in a bed so the night promised to be fantastic. He was given a list of different prices for rooms and their accommodations. He hit the ceiling. He acted as if they had purposely set those prices when they saw us coming, we had been warned. He said, "who da he' do ya thank you is?" His fist was clenched. I thought he was going to clock the man who was backing away from the counter with his hands up. I told Joe Henry, "let's go, we'll find something else." That 'something else' was right across the street. It was a flea bag. He became more human once we got back out to the truck. All I wanted to do was make love to my new husband and make love to him for the rest of my life. He kept calling me "Mrs. Mathis, my wife." He remembered part of our vows, "you will love, honor and obey me, right Carrie?" I answered without hesitation, "Yes, Joe Henry, that's what I promised I would do."

We both knew that we had run out of options. I suggested that we find one of our spots where we had parked and made love. He wouldn't hear of it. He sobered up and we were going in the direction of The House.

He awakened his mom who was sleeping on the couch in the front room which pinch hit for a bedroom, a sitting room that had a full size bed and a long dilapidated (springs were sprung) sofa – for sitting and sleeping. It should have been set outside and set on fire. His father was sitting up with a fresh cup of coffee and the wood burning heater was ablaze. It felt so warm and inviting.

Joe went to another room and called his parents to follow him. They went obediently like two trained dogs. His mother came back with a big grin on her face, "ya'll kin tak Bigmans bed fo' a whi' ti' ya'll kin fin yo' own place." Bigman came back in the room and sat down. I didn't like the way he was glaring at me. Joe Henry took it all in stride. The welcome wagon had long gone and in its place there sat an old resentful person who reeked of hatred. I don't know what Joe Henry or his mom had threatened or promised him but he reluctantly went and slept in another room next to the front room (there was no door or curtain between our two rooms).

We both had sobered up but not enough for me when I needed to freshen up and use the bathroom. We were trying to wait until we heard Bigman snoring which he finally did (after all of that coffee he drank). "I got to pee" I said. Joe Henry got up and found a large tin can. "Use dis" he said and he handed me a wet wash rag. "we can use dis when we finish." Thinking to myself I remembered the vows that I had just promised – for richer or for poorer. When I finished I noticed that he had already crawled into our honeymoon bed. The fire in the wood burning heater was just right at first then it became too hot. Our body heated up so much till I had to kick the heavy covers off. I was exposed to whomever that needed to walk through the front room. Joe told me several times to be quiet. It was as if he was asking me to stop breathing. He was so excited too and kept saying, "You my wife, I love you Carrie." We went to sleep wrapped so tightly locked into each others' arms.

Bigman had gotten up early the next morning and built another fire. He sat at the far end of the couch slurping loudly another cup of coffee and a pipe that finally was producing enough smoke to choke a mule. I sat up in (his bed) bed. I said brightly, "good morning, thank you for allowing me to stay here!" He looked at me with a blank face and just nodded. He took another loud slurp then continued to puff on his pipe. There was no, "you are welcome, I hate you or go fuck yourself." I was as welcomed in his house as a fox in a henhouse. I awakened Joe Henry who was – sounded like sawing wood – snoring so loudly. I would learn many things about him but meanwhile I needed to get up and use the toilet. Bigman wasn't about to budge from the couch. He just sat there staring ahead. I heard a young child cry out, "Daddy!" Bigman got up and rushed into the side room and came back with a cute little boy who was the spitting image of Phillip. It was his son whose name was Grady (Gregory). He was about three years old. He whined a lot. There was no pleasing him. He was the worse spoiled brat that I had ever seen. Bigman had taken him under his wings – the same as with my husband – poh child!

I took that opportunity to get up and put on some clothes that Joe Henry had just brought in from the truck. I was making up the lumpy bed and noticed there was a huge pool of blood on the sheets. How embarrassing. It needed to be cleaned up. Let me guess? There wasn't a washing machine either. I told Joe Henry that I didn't come prepared with sanitary napkins and was almost in tears I said, "I need to clean up that mess."

It was Sunday morning and Joe Henry's family was slowing arising. They were putting on their everyday clothes. I asked, "do you all go to church?" That wasn't a good subject obviously. Joe Henry told me to leave it alone and that's what I did.

Joe hadn't told me anything about any of the people in his family who all lived in his parent's small house. There were other children awakening and trickling into the front room to get warm. Mammie Dell, Joe's older niece who wasn't shy and quite boisterous (Loud). She came in and sat on the side of the bed where Joe Henry had crawled back into. Mammie's nickname was Boot. She and Joe Henry seemed to be so close. She said loudly as she slapped him on the back, "Git up from dar boy!" she laughed and started coughing and hacking because of her smoking. He answered her, "you go ta he' " They both laughed. He introduced me as his wife, "Carrie dis heah is Boot. She take you to da sto' fo' those thangs you needs." Boot had a little girl she was carrying on her hip. She was about two years old. I looked at the little girl (Frannie) then at Boot. There must have been some mistake that she had brought the wrong child home from the hospital. They were as different as night and day or black and white. I knew that it would have been impolite to inquire about who was the daddy. Well goodness gracious alive she was a beautiful child. Boot's oldest girl finally came out. Her name was Easter Mae (nickname Duntley). Now she looked just like Boot. I didn't have to wonder about what race that that child belonged to. Last but not least, in crawled the cutest little nine month old chubby baby girl. She had brown skin and big brown eyes that lit up when someone took the time to pick her up and hold her. She was Billy's baby, Jan. He had taken her from her mother Louise aka Banana Pudding. She had a houseful of children and she wasn't taking good care of Jan. she didn't put up a fight when the baby was taken. Jan looked a tad bit lost and out of place. She seemed to be in everybody's way. I picked her up and hugged her. She seemed to thrive on the least bit of attention that Bill should have been giving her. Joe Henry snapped at me, "put that little monkey baby down." He tried to pretend that he was teasing but I could feel the dislike that he had for that child. That was the last of the Mathis clan that lived at The House except for the phantom twin.

Joe Henry was out numbered by his family. They all agreed, "no mo sleep'n yo' life away, you needs ta git up." They all treated him like a super star. I had hopes that I too would be loved as he was.

He showed me where everything was. Here is some newspaper. I thought good I can read it while using the toilet. It may take my mind off of all the stench that was wafting from under the wooden seat. He waited outside the door because I was afraid of their mangy, flea-bitten dog who was more afraid of me. He was scratching so much – almost constantly. His skin was raw. Gloom and doom was about to overtake me. I had chosen to live in the squalor that Joe Henry was used to. I repeated to myself, "for better for worst; for richer for poorer" Lord, was I going to be tested on all of those vows and all at once? So wherever thou goeth, I will go. He showed me how to crumble the newspaper to make it softer, "to clean yo' beautiful yellow ass." We laughed when I came out. He planted one of his luscious kisses on my mouth. I started to complain that I needed to brush my teeth, wash up and go to the store to get those pads. He said, "I don have no mo' money. We use it all las' nigh'" He ran his hand in both front pockets and pulled out the liner. He pulled out his wallet. He came up with zero.

I followed him back into THE HOUSE, his mom (Missy) had already put fresh linen on the bed. She was humming off key an off beat tune. She looked at both of us and smiled. She said, "I'm gwine fix sump t'eat a'fa Mammie Dell comes back from da' sto'" She looked at me, "you kin go wid huh if'n you needs sump'n." she was a mind reader or maybe she had seen Joe Henry with his empty pocket syndrome. He was about to ask her and she reached down into her bosom and pulled out a wad of money. She peeled off a few dollar bills and handed it to him and laughed, "boy, I want dis heah money back naw you heah me?" Joe Henry nodded his head and hugged his mom. He put it on his running account. I could tell that he was a loving person and would be a good husband to me because of the way he treated his mother. ■

Chapter III

Beginning of Married Life

I WAS QUICKLY learning to adapt to a simpler life style because I was so in love with Joe Henry. He seemed to like having me with him. I joined forces with his family to spoil him rotten. What ever his heart desired that was what I was willing to give him. If he said jump I would ask how high and when.

He was commuting the twelve miles from Clarkdale to Meridian every day. I got up every morning about four thirty and made his lunch and prepared a light breakfast. He looked so handsome in his dark blue uniform that Mr. Wade Willouby provided for him. It even had his name engraved on the pocket. He liked his job and his boss, and he was getting small raises frequently. He knew how to wash the vehicles, he did the gas fill ups, cleaned the windows, checked the oil – if needed, he changed the oil. He was learning to do a lot of things mechanics were trained to do. Mr. Wades' business was booming because everybody like Joe Henry's charismatic personality no matter how brass he was to them. He began coming home dog tired. He would just lie there across the bed with his grease-stained clothes. I found out that I was supposed to do our wash because Mammie Dell (Boot) said so. Missy had been tending to his clothes until I was set straight.

On wash days, I toted the buckets of water from the spring across the road to the back yard. We used a big wash pot made of cast iron. I had to build a fire around it to boil the grease and grime out of Joe's work clothes. Missy allowed me to use her scrub board that aided in getting the dirt plus the skin off of my tender knuckles. Missy had some homemade bar soap that only added to the tenderness of my hands (my hands had began to resemble my grandma's hands). I chose to buy Oxygon bar soap that was a little less harsh. I hung all of our clothes on the line to dry. Then would begin the task of ironing all of his clothes – Bigman did everything he could to trip me up at every corner. He would unplug the iron while I was hanging up a shirt in the same room. He watched every move that I made. I was a nervous wreck; however, careful not to disrespect him. Missy would say, "don' pay Bigman no neva mine" she explained that he and Joe Henry was real close and Bigun didn't want to give up his baby boy.

On weekends he had began having Joe Henry to drive him to town to get his weekly drunk on (Saturday Nite Special). I found that I was spending more time with Missy (her name was Armonia Mathis) she said that she named herself when she was about six years old it was their family's tradition, prior to that they called her Edie Cah) than with my new husband. At first he would find time for us to steal away to go fishing or take long walks in the woods behind the house at which time we would renew our love making and I would let it all hang out. I had so much tension built up inside of me.

I was closely monitored on the amount of food that I ate, also, Mammie Dell informed me that Joe Henry had stopped giving her money to pay for the food that I was eating. I was also asked to buy supplies that I needed to wash our clothes. I made sure that I helped around the house such as washing the dishes which was a task in itself. Again, I had to tote the water from the spring. It had to be heated on their apartment sized stove. Bigman didn't want me using up the butane gas because it was too expensive. The rinse water was left cold in another dish pan. I had been warned several times to make sure that all of the dishes were cleaned or they would have to be cleaned again. Bigman would make spot checks when he thought that I wasn't looking. It was a miracle that I was able to get those glasses and mason jars spotless because the drying towel had been used by Missy for wiping her hands and for removing hot items out of the oven. I'd even seen her wiping sweat off her face with the same towel.

I knew that I was losing a battle and weight because my clothes were fitting me looser. I was limited in eating portions that I had been so used to eating at my parents home. Missy hated to cook so I volunteered to help. It worked out better when I helped with the cleaning and the dishes. I was able to help the family in other areas also. Boot and I would go down to the pond and harvest the large collard greens leaves. The stalks had been planted by the owners of the pond side trailer. We went to gather the greens when their cars weren't parked in their driveway. Boot encouraged me to hurry up as she also picked the greens and was looking over her shoulders as a look out. We picked as many greens as we could put in a croaker sack. I followed her further on up the road to an old house that was occupied by a huge big boned colored woman in her twenty's and two (about the size that she was) teen aged boys. The woman's (Monk) husband had beaten her. She said, "fo' tha las' time, I wi' ki' him if'n he coms back heah" Her two boys stayed close by as if on the ready to protect their mom. Boot changed the subject back to the reason for our visit, and that was to get some vegetables from their garden. Monk said, "take as much as you wants we aint gwine needs any oh'it. Weez leav'n" Boot showed me how to dig up the sweet potatoes. We got so many and a few of the cucumbers. The watermelons weren't doing well at all. I wondered who was going to carry all of those heavy bags. Boot did because she was strong and had been raised with all of those boys, she had to survive. She bragged about herself. She stood about six feet one inch tall. She was a wide track but not fat, just big boned. She laughed, "I kin beat up any man including yo puny husban'. I wuz raised up wid aw'those boys soz I hads to be strong." With that she flung the sack of potatoes over her shoulders, "com'on lil scrawny gir'" She teased me. I followed her back to The House to drop off all of the food we had stolen (gathered) and begged for. "We haves one mo' stop to make Miss Mathis" (she called me that or Miss Carrie). I was tired but I didn't argue because I had to carry my load to pay for my keep as far as being in their family. We walked up the roadway not too far from The House to a fenced area that had a sign that read 'Private Property. Keep Out. Enter at Your Own Risk.' She stepped through the barbed wire fence just like going through a doorway. She turned and pulled the wire so that I could pass through. My hair got tangled in it. And so did my back. She, "shhh, you gotta be quiet." She untangled me. I didn't want her to see that I didn't want to be there stealing. But the small inner most part of me knew that I had to survive. She held on to the sack and told me to keep my head down. "don' run into tha sták cuz the owner will know we git'n some of thay co'n," she added, "if'n they ketchus ova' heah they migh' star' shoot'n." She gathered most of the ears of corn. We came out of the field with 'nuff fo' dinah tanigh'"

At The House I got a bite of leftover spaghetti from last night's supper. I washed it down with water. The refrigerator was basically empty. The light no longer shined because Bigman had unscrewed it. "So's it woudn't use that much 'lectwicity." He heard the refrigerator door open and he came to the doorway with irritation in his voice he said, "clos da doe, you needs ta lurn." So much for getting a cold glass of water. I was trying to get some ice to go into the warm water that sat in the water bucket – Missy was in the room and saw what he had done. She called me to the side, "Bigman don' mean yo no hum. Hez still not use ta you and hez fight'n you soz you wont take away hiz son." I looked at her in disbelief. She needed to talk with the source of the problem. Although I could tell that she was on my side she said in no uncertain terms, "Joe Henry don gots him a fin gir' from a good famly. I nos yo' grandma. She wuz niz ta my boys."

Bigman told the story about the Christmas that he had bought a toy that cost a lot of money for Joe Henry that nobody else in Meridian had ever seen. The whole family seemed to get a kick out of the fact that Joe Henry had been spoiled on Christmas as his brothers just sat there and watched as if they didn't matter. They all played it off that he was the last (baby brother) that they would ever have.

Missy was ever so eager to fill me in on one of her secrets that she made me promise that I would never tell anybody (until now). She waited until everybody was away from The House. The only interruption that we had was the onslaught of flies and mosquitoes. She came closer to me and said, "you know, Joe Henry wuz not tha las chil'. I wuz prenan' wid..." she continued as she looked around, "I wuz five or six months along when we mov'did to this heah house." She lowered her head and fidgeted with her folded hands refusing to look me in the eye. She said, "Bigman wuz act'n as nutty as a fru' cake. He wuz git'n so drunk 'n trea'n me and tha chullen sum'n fierce. I coul'n stan' it no mo'. I did'n want anotha' chi'o hiz..." She thought for a while as she anguished over information that had been bottled up and eating at her soul. She said that she drank some turpentine that she had bought. She waited until Alain and T-Bone were visiting so that Alain could help her if things got out of hand. After drinking ample amounts she waited "out on da garrey. Bigman wuz in da house spraw'ed ou' on da flo'. I wuz as sic asa dawg when da lil baby boy came out on da flo of da garrey. It wuz mov'n and jirk'n fo a lil' whi'. It shook one mo' time then hit musta died." She was in tears. It was the first time that I had seen her crying. I know that what she had done must have been her last resort. She allowed me to put my arms around her. I knew that her family meant so much to her and enough was enough. She didn't tell me what had happened to the fetus as far as its resting place. There are some things that is best left unspoken. She did admonish me that me and Joe Henry didn't need any children until he changed his ways. She knew her son and his capabilities. He's just like his daddy. She was afraid that Bigman would kill her even then if he ever found out what she had done to his baby. She seemed to get relief in talking with me because she knew that I wouldn't judge her. The only thing that I could do was to bear the secret. What a burden it has been. Joe Henry would never know that his mom had aborted his little brother.

Joe Henry had another older brother who was a paternal twin to Billy. They called him Bobby. He stayed out of site. He was not known for his social skills. Although he was out of sight, he wasn't out of mind. He had the strongest body odor that soap and water couldn't wash off. Deodorant didn't help either. Missy said it was because he had a nervous problem. She said that he had been in a car accident that left him mentally retarded (challenged). Muhmuh had remembered him as being mentally unstable even as a child. He wasn't able to learn so he was left behind in grade school until he was pulled out of school by his parents. It was a losing battle.

He had the look of someone who had been tortured. His eyes were so crossed. Bobby's speech and vocabulary were less than a first grader. He spoke with such effort and the southern drawl was more pronounced than the rest of the family.

I didn't meet Bobby for some time after my first nights at The House. He made it his business to stay hidden. Curiosity got the best of me. I pestered Missy to introduce me to him, "oh, he' come 'round, jus' don' cho push him." I made it my business to be where he didn't want me to be. He would rush out without even looking at me. One thing I knew was he loved listening to music on his radio that played sometimes (most of the time it was on the blink). My family had a radio such as his. I had fiddled with it when it stopped working. I fixed his radio while he was away from The House. He warmed up to me somewhat but not for long. He was in and out of severe mood swings his family had accepted his behavior. His outbursts could only be compared to that of a caged animal. He would yell and use profanity which I was becoming accustomed to and from all of the other older family members. Everybody was either known as a 'soma bitch' or 'niggah' and please let me not forget 'you bastard cho'. Add a little southern twang and that added a whole new flavor to it. I had to listen carefully because there was a language barrier. I cared enough to try to break the code.

After living there with my new family I figured it out what everybody else knew. Bobby hated Bigman (and I wonder why). He emphatically refused to be in the same room with him – so I wasn't alone – it must have been all of those years of unresolved resentment against Bigman for making him feel like an outsider – like the way I was feeling. Bobby wasn't one of his favorites. You see Bigman seemed to like darker skinned people. Bobby and Billy were fair skinned (I was fairest of them all). Missy was darker than any of her family. Bigman's terms of endearment for her was, 'my black bitch' or 'you ol' black woman'. She must have gotten used to it. She would answer with a chuckle,

"Bigman is as crazy as a road lizard. I don' pay him no nev'a min'". She had a way of putting things in their proper perspective.

Bigman knew when it was time to cool it ever since he came home from a drunken night out with Joe Henry. He was cursing and using language that even I had never heard of. His loud screaming was so intimidating to me and embarrassing. He lashed out filthy phrases that was best being said in their house since there were no neighbors within hearing distance two miles both ways. Sometimes he could see people who weren't really there. He would swing out at the illusion and shout out, "oh! Go kiss a monkey's pussy" and then he would yell out loudly and tearfully, "God damn you!" I was so afraid to be there in The House. There was nowhere to run – nowhere to hide. He came out of the front room waving a pistol and began pointing it at Missy. She put her hand on her hips and shook her head then pointed her finger in his face. She shouted, "Bigman you pu' tha' damn gun dow' fo' you hur' somebody." He turned away from her then started the same scenario with Bobby who had turned a bright red hue. He was standing in the kitchen/dining area having a cup of coffee – his favorite pastime – Even drunk, Bigman should have known better (I guess he musta forgot). Bobby slammed his coffee cup down so hard that the coffee and glass went flying in all directions. He swirled around and hit Bigman square on his chin with his massive fist. Well, that kinda sobered him up enough to know that he'd met his match. Bobby quickly grabbed the gun from his stunned father. Everybody in The House scattered like scared rats trying to save their dear lives. I was hemmed into a corner and couldn't escape because it all had happened so suddenly. Bobby yelled loudly, his voice seemed to have been cracking as he shoved his dazed father onto the couch, "you sid dow' now! Wha' cho' gwine do' bout hit?" Bigman didn't move because Bobby still had the gun and didn't make empty threats. Bigman's eyes were always big but they were bulging and his mouth open with nothing coming out. He was speechless. Bobby turned around and picked up an old manual/pedal style sewing machine over his head and pitched it across the room. He wasn't aiming at anyone in particular, just angry and frustrated with his dad. He said, "I'm sick o' dis shit!" He hurried out of the back door slamming it so hard that it jarred the whole house. Well, I knew what side my bread was buttered on and for sure I wouldn't try to make Bobby mad at me. Bigman sobered up for the rest of the evening. Missy got the gun and hid it (there weren't too many hiding places except in her apron pocket that seemed to always have a bulge).

I really did begin to look like a race horse from being starved. Joe Henry told me that I needed to get some sun because I was getting pale (pallor and anemic). I was always cold and stayed hungry. I asked Boot if she knew any white people that needed me to do day work so that I could help buy groceries. My pride wouldn't allow me to ask for help from my parents. Joe Henry would have a hissy fit, "I'm tak'n care o' you" he would say, but he wasn't. I had to do something quick or otherwise starve to death. Let's see now – the vows were 'in sickness and in health, till death us do part.'

I found a half a days work with Ms. Iva Murray, a hairdresser who had been recommended by Ms. Sweet. Ms. Iva lived with her husband, Mr. Witt. She made me breakfast when we arrived at their house. I can still smell the bacon and hear the sizzling of two eggs being fried in the bacon drippings. She made me some toast and coffee. I didn't know just how hungry that I was until I gobbled it down so fast. She observed me wolfing down my food and by the looks of my race horse thin face and the frailness of my body – she knew – she said, "Carrie, you kin help yo' sef' to mo food in tha ice box." She had two customers that morning in her little beauty shop a few steps away from their house. I helped myself to a sandwich and found the energy to do my job. It was so good to be able to earn a little money. Their home was nothing to write home about. As a matter of fact, the furniture was so old and had a musty odor throughout the house. Highway 45 ran so close to her front yard the dust was constantly settling on the furniture. I attempted to clean everything that she had on her list of things to do. She seemed happy with the thorough cleaning under the circumstances. It was good to see that she did appreciate me. She paid me in full $1.50, the amount that we had agreed upon. It was just enough for me to buy me a loaf of light bread, a pound of bologna and a small jar of mayonnaise. The community grocery store was right next door. Before I left her house she asked if I could come back next week but in the meanwhile she wanted me to help her daughter tomorrow. I was so excited for the ability to be able to get out the house to work and get paid. Things were going to get better.

I had met her daughter earlier that morning. She had recently married. They seemed like a lovely couple, just as happy as two peas in a pod. Jan was absolutely pretty with dark shiny hair that flowed down her back. Her husband was as handsome as he could be. I wished them well and truly meant it.

Ms. Iva followed me out of her house. She was looking at me kind of strange. I must have looked like a living corpse. She asked, "you wanna see my garden?" I thought, "no," but answered, "yes." She showed me her tomatoes and collard greens. She even had corn growing on a ½ acre of land. "Here you kin have this bag, now pick as much as you want." She said in her nasal southern drawl. I thought those tomatoes would certainly go well on my bologna sandwiches. She was playfully irritated with me, "Carrie, tha' aint enough; fill tha bag up". So she took it from me and began cramming all sorts of fresh vegetables into the bag. She put my tomatoes in a smaller bag.

She waited out in the car while I did my little shopping. I had about 25 cents left. She took me back to The House. I could see the disappointment as she drove into the driveway. She stated, "Yo gonna be jus' fine Carrie, I kin te' by the way you carry yo' sef'". As she backed out to the roadway she said over her shoulder, "I'll seeya early in da mon'n." I waved and said, "thanks Mrs. Iva." She was definitely on my good list for good people.

I put my groceries away and handed Missy the fresh vegetables. I showed her where I had put my sandwich fixings. I didn't want to put my name on it. Bigman was sober and was within watching distance as he whistled a tune that was driving me f------ crazy. I said (trying to break the wall of ice), "Bigman, help yourself to make a sandwich." He didn't answer. Missy came over to me and smiled, "you don good Miss Carrie." She started fussing, "I don' know why Joe Henry ain't do'n lak he 'spose ta by you." I didn't answer her because I didn't know what to say. I helped her prepare supper which was (more) "baghettiz" greens and fried chicken which she smothered it to make a gravy and a big skillet of corn bread. All were Bigman's favorites especially the chicken, pot liquor and corn bread.

I had been eased onto the older couch (not fit for a human to sit on) that was at the lower end of the kitchen (I say this because the flooring was slanted). There was a wood burning heater but it was seldomly used except for the family taking a bath during the winter months. There was a round tin wash tube that was used for the baths, and also used when they killed and butchered any edible farm animal. I wished that they would build a fire that night…I was so cold.

Joe Henry didn't come home last night. He sent word by Boot who worked for Mrs. Sweet (the owner of The House). She allowed the family to get message from those members who lived in town. He wasn't coming home again tonight. I've never been in a hailstorm before. It was the most frightening sound like as if it was a train traveling across their tin roof. It lasted for about five minutes. There was no one to run to or to comfort me. Only the old musty couch that had more spring that sprung each time I laid on it. I cried as I tried to sleep but it was so cold in the open makeshift room. Someone had taken the quilt that I had been using. There was a pile of clothes at the foot of the couch. I kept layering my clothes and still my teeth were chattering. The door to the front room where Bigman slept was closed. I could hear the wood in the heater as it burned making its crackling sounds. It would occasionally give off a popping sound as Bigman would poke the fire and add more wood. I got up to use the slop jar (potty) actually it was a large tin can that had once had contents of oil sausage. Some of the fluid spilled on to the wooden floor that sloped downward. The knots in the planks allowed most of the urine to drain to under the house. The rest was found frozen in an icy stream the next morning. Missy heard me get up. She came and piled two home made quilts on my shivering little body. They were not pretty not by a long shot. There was no pride to the maker of those quilts. They were simply scraps of old clothes pieced together randomly (no pattern needed). She had placed a middle layer of cotton batting. The bottom was either an old sheet or a thin blanket. It served its purpose – no frills – I was warmer. Missy had came to my rescues once again. she cared about her family and I had become a part of her family. "thanks, Mi..." I said for the first time – "...Muhdea." She looked at me with pity in her eyes. "Carrie, I knos you love Joe Henry, but cho' deserve betten' dis." She was right, I did and it would get better, but when?

I got up early the next morning before the family gathered in the upper kitchen area for breakfast that was being prepared by Muhdea. I thought that I would have a sandwich before I left and I didn't want to see Bigman's ugly mug as he guarded the food that would be served for breakfast. I thought as I looked at him he must have been a handsome man in his younger day. Muhdea must have seen some qualities in him that was now hidden from everybody. Whatever he had then was completely gone and in its place was an old bitter possessive old man with an attitude against me. I wanted to teach him a lesson that I was above all of the hate and aggressive behavior that he had displayed against me. I opened up the Frigidaire as I was about to get me a bite before I left for work. Most of the bologna had been eaten. The mayo was still in tact. There was a couple of sliced of bread that remained. I stood there shaking and frozen in my tracks with the door open, as if it all would return if I left the door open – I – wanted – to – SCREAM – Muhdea came in and noticed that someone had eaten practically everything that I had bought the day before. She turned around and found Bigman as he was eating his rice, eggs, bacon and a cup of coffee. Generally speaking I would have a plate of rice with margarine and a cup of coffee. He would eat all of the bacon or sausage. Now he had gone too far. Muhdea knew who the culprit was who had either ate it or fed it to the chickens. She came back and said, "He gwine buy you smo'". She took money out of her secret hiding place and insisted that I take the $1.50. I had just finished eating when I heard the car horn being tooted out front. I found my little red jacket – although I was skinnier it seemed to have shrunk. I must have been still growing? I told Muhdea that I'd be back by twelve.

Ms. Iva was so refreshing. She was in her usual happy-go-lucky frame of mind. We drove past her house about five miles down highway 45. She turned into a driveway, the house looked like a manufactured, "we started it, you finish it" type of home. She got out and knocked on the front door then went back to the back. She told me to wait in the front which was so different from the norms of white folks. There weren't any cars parked out front so her son-in-law must have gone to work already. After about ten minutes she appeared at the front door with a person who looked as old as she did. Her eyes were redden, there was a shiner on her left eye. She wore an old terry cloth house coat. There was a baby in her arms squalling to the top of his little lungs. She looked at me then to her mother, "it's probably not a good time for her to be here" she said almost apologetically. Her husband Joe (also) had just left and he was supposed to have been coming right back. "He went to git the baby some milk (I thought maybe a bottle for him too). Ms. Iva asked, "Ya'll been fighting agin?" she answered, "Yassum" at which time she broke down and wept. Three small children came into the almost empty living room. Their ages ranged from approximately five, four and three years old. The living room had a long sofa and some old toys strewn all over. I thought, I can clean this up in about thirty minutes. Judy, who was so different from the other daughter. She would never be able to enter a beauty contest no matter how much make up she put on to fix up her face. She was beyond homely and furthermore the poh child was about six months pregnant. She had just found out that her husband had another woman. He was planning on leaving her to be with another pregnant woman. I had enough on my plate with my screwed up life with the backwoods family. I asked, "Where do you want me to start?" and why would I ask such a crazy question? She brought out some Tide washing powder and some Purex. She pulled out a laundry bag of whites, coloreds and a bag of towels. I finished washing and hanging out all of the laundry by one o'clock. The clouds started forming there was thunder and lightening. I started taking in the dry clothes. Ms. Iva had left to go get something from her shop. When she came back she said, "I can help finish this." She had a large paper bag – I wondered, did she have more veggies? She said, "this is fo you." She took out a beautiful metallic blue jacket that felt like it was lined with down. It was hooded. It was the most gorgeous coat that I'd ever seen. She said, "Try it on Carrie." It fitted me so well that I could even grow into it. I usually didn't like to show so much emotion to people that I worked for. She saw that I was having problems with expressing myself especially since she must have known that there was a dividing line that I had been taught (I didn't like it but it was there). She took the first step to break down some of the barrier. She came over and hugged me. Her face was so full of joy and so was mine as tears flowed down my face and I returned the embrace. She whispered, "you needs ta take better care of yo' sef'" I thanked her over and over again as I continued to cry. It was good to get rid of that old ugly red car coat. Her daughter came over to me. She said, "Thanks fo' tha he'p Carrie." She gave me three dollars that we had already agreed upon. I was so happy. I had four dollars and fifty cents. I didn't stop at the grocery store that time.

We arrived at The House about one thirty. Joe Henry was there to my surprise. Phillip had brought him home and had just left. Joe was lying on the couch that I had been sleeping on. I could smell the stale liquor on his breath. His eyes were blood shot and out of focus. I went outside to regain my composure. As I was leaving Bigman was coming in and went past me, "Whar is Joe Henry?" I couldn't remember my vows anymore because my husband had basically abandoned me at The House for a whole week. I went back inside and he was sitting on the arm of the couch and wouldn't make eye contact with me. I went over to where I kept my packed suitcase. I looked in it then closed the latch in an angry manner. He got up and jumped in my face, "Naw wha' cho' thank you do'n?" I looked up at his unshaven face, the eyes that had lost their lust for me and the mouth that sneered hateful things to me. I thought I could do better than this. I answered him as my voice trembled as I tried to fight back the flow of the tears that were about to burst. I answered him, "You've left me with your parents. I'm not married to them, I'm married to you but not for long." He came in closer to my face as he hovered over me. His face so distorted. He asked in a loud voice, "Wha' cho gwine do 'bout it?" I said as I was backing away, "I'm going home..." and before I could finish he slapped me so hard I went sprawling down to the floor. I could taste the blood from my bleeding lip. A little bit closer I would have hit my head on that damn sewing machine. I couldn't get up quick enough because I was dazed. He stood over me, "Bitch you aint go'n no whar yos my wife. Yo'll leave heah in a body bag." Bigman stood there taking it all in with a look of pleasure and nodding his head 'yes'. Muhdea saw that Joe Henry was about to go for something in his pocket. She cried out, "Joe Henry naw." Bobby had taken as much as he could. He came over and got in his brothers face and playfully with a smile on his face he said, "Joe Henry naw gimme dat." I was in a state of shock. Muhdea came over to me and literally lifted me up off of the floor. She too was extremely strong – "Carrie, he jus' drunk, hit gwine be a'ight." Bigman slithered out of the room as if saddened that I wasn't dead. Again I had cheated the jaws of death. My hopes were to reach a ripe old age of thirty six and have children. I didn't see neither of those things in my future.

Joe Henry slept it off for the most part of the day on Bigman's bed. Everybody tip toed around him. When he finally awakened he was looking around as if though he was disoriented. He got up and went past me like I was a ghost. He found his mother and began playing with her. I heard him say, "Muhdea I needs another loan." She got so angry – something that I hadn't seen since I came to The House. She said loudly and with conviction, "Joe Henry you is dead wron' and Gods gwine punish you fo' wha' cho do'n ta yo' wife. You say you loves huh bu' cho aint act'n lak it. I'ms shame tha I sign up fo' ya'll to marry. Eithea you tre' huh righ' o le' huh go home. She been try'n to earn money wrk'n in white folks ki'chen, you ain't no good huzban ta huh, I did'n raise you lak tha'!" He broke down and cried like a baby. "I los' my job Muhdea." He held out his hands toward me and I went to him. I was so lonely for him. He said, "Com'mon I needs ta go to tha sto'" He got the keys to his fathers' prize possession and drove to the store.

We went inside the store as he held my hand he said, "I don' have no money. How much cho got? Give it ta me, I'll give it back when I git anotha job." He bought a few nabs and a big bottle of antiseptic. They wouldn't sell beer to him because Ms. Sweet had ordered them not to. He had become notorious for his bad behavior because of the liquor. We all had problems and mine was I needed him to make passionate love to me. We hadn't been with each other for a long time. We stopped along the side of a dirt road. He wasn't acting the same. He seemed so distant only going through the motions as he opened the pack of nabs and antiseptic bottle. He took a swallow from it and made a face of displeasure then started coughing uncontrollably. I thought that he was going to pass out – he didn't. He was looking at me, but not with the longing that I had become so used to. He asked, "are you wid me o' agins' me?" I said timidly, "I'll always be with you Joe Henry but you need to treat me better than what you have been." I could see that I had pushed the wrong button again but then his attitude changed suddenly. "Carrie I'm sorry, please forgive me. I wuz feel'n so bad 'bout loos'n my job tha' I took it ou' on you. Do you sti' love me?" I was talking to a man that I didn't know but I felt I had better give him the right answer. I said, "Yes," then he insisted on knowing how much. I opened up my arms as wide as they could go and said, "This much." He said, "Tha' aint enough" which shattered my thoughts and reasoning for loving him. I didn't dare let him see the disappointment in my face because it may have turned out lethal so I took a little of the antiseptic to numb my brain and my reasoning. It took away the ragged edges. He started the car and went down another dirt road that the neighbors had been using the side of the road to dump their trash. He stopped and took several gulps of the antiseptic he reached in his wallet and took out a round gold package. I asked, "What is that?" He said, "it's a rubber, I don' wan' ta git cho' pregna'" It was all so mechanical and uncomfortable. I wasn't feeling the love that we had before. Something was terribly wrong. Where was my love? A couple of days went by and he and Bigman were getting closer. Bigman had found work for him over at Ms. Sweet and Mr. Lucus. He told me that he hated those people, as a matter of fact he said that he hated practically everybody. He added, "I do love yo' mommy but I can't stand yo' daddy." He said whatever was on his mind no matter who it hurt. I stayed quiet to keep the peace.

Everything was lovely the next week until I got the worst itch on my vagina. I noticed that he would have bouts of scratching himself in the groin area also. I summed it up to be bed bugs that were mentioned in my childhood prayers. I told Joe Henry who seemed to take it all in stride. We went to town and the druggist recommended a special liquid for both of us to kill the crabs. It worked. Joe Henry said that, "they probably came from the public toilets." Hmmmm!

Thanksgiving had passed without the familiar family gathering because Joe Henry wanted to spend it with his family. I got to meet his older sister Alain and her husband T.Bone Barfield. What a pair. They brought their favorite doggie – Hard Times – he limped. He had so many ailments. He lived to be fifteen years old.

I liked Alain right off the bat and the feelings were mutual. They could never do me no wrong. Muhdea boiled a large hen and made her rendition of dressing, Mammie Dell baked a sweet potato pie. I thought, "Where's the cake?" They didn't go overboard for Turkey Day as my parents always did and the last time that we had a gathering at Aunt Janie's I was complaining so much. Maybe I would be able to go over to my parent's home for Christmas dinner.

Joe Henry had started staying with 'my brother Phillip', "I'm try'n to find a betta job." Christmas came and it would have been our first Christmas together. Joe Henry remained in town and there was no one at The House who would give me a lift to my mom's house. I felt so low I would have settled for the Aunt Jemima doll again. I longed to see my mother and daddy. I didn't want to eat the bland food that Muhdea would prepare. I just wanted the traditional fanfare that my family had. I cried so hard as I went walking down to the pond. Little Easter Mae – Duntley – was always by my side. I welcomed her company. The fish were nibbling but not biting. It was getting dark and I didn't like being in the woods so late. I saw a car as it pulled up to The House. Could it be? Yes! It be! It was my – I ran so fast to the driveway. It was my grandmother's car and she had brought my dear mother down to see me. We stood outside in the cold holding on to each other. They both said that I looked thin but looked good. I gazed into their familiar faces I had let them down so badly. I lied and said I was doing fine and so was Joe Henry whom I expected to come home later tonight. My voice sort of trailed off and I'm sure that they could see through my lies. They were also able to see Bigman in his hateful glory. He excused himself so abruptly as if they were scum. They were both dressed so charming and Christmassy. Both donned a holiday corsage, two very beautiful colored women who were filled with the joys of the holiday and both loved me and I could never go back. I made my bed then and now I have 'a couch' I thought. They didn't stay too long. It was apparent they were not welcome and the conversation was not conducive to try to keep skipping down the memory lane. Before they left mother gave me a pair of pearl earrings that had ruby rhinestones that encircled it and some of my favorite cologne, To A Wild Rose. I put some on before they left then put all of my gifts inside of my packed suitcase because I didn't want it to be destroyed by my nemesis who kept up with my every move. I looked out of the window. I wanted to call out to them as I saw them slowly drive past the pond, "Please wait for me, I'm sorry I made a mistake." I wanted to run after them but I didn't because Joe Henry's warning was still etched in my brain. I didn't want to die.

I stayed so busy to help ease the loneliness and to keep down the urge to call a cab, or call somebody to come and get me. I continued to help Ms. Iva. She told me about another family who needed someone to do some day work. I agreed and they came by to pick me up on that Monday morning early January 1961. It was a middle aged white couple who barely spoke to me when I got inside their car. It was about six o'clock in the morning. I told them that I didn't have time to eat breakfast. The just looked at each other and neither of them answered me. Upon arrival to their home, she told me to go through the back door. I knew the drill, but it was getting to be a bitter pill to continue to swallow. She had a long laundry list of things that she expected me to do including: wash the dishes, mop the kitchen, the hallway and the bathroom, clean up the living room and dining room. She gave me instruction and supplies to clean the filthy bathroom. I started to move with ease until about nine o'clock I had gotten so hungry and felt light headed. I saw that there was leftovers where she and her husband had eaten breakfast earlier. I said with determination in my voice, "Ms. Brown, I'm so hungry and I need a glass of water." She looked at me as if I had asked for her first born child. There was some grits that was still in the pot on the stove that had gotten cold. She found a disposable aluminum pie pan which she put the cold grits on with a piece of dry light bread. She ran some tap water into an old tin can and shoved it on the table towards me as if though I was a dog. I felt the lowest of the lows – I didn't and couldn't eat the food or drink out of a tin can, "I'm not an animal" I thought as I got up, gathered my jacket. I said abruptly, "I need to go home. Will you drive me home now?" She seemed stunned of my abruptness. She offered to pay me for the time that I had worked there. I figured that the lesson that I had received was payment enough. I had to start somewhere. I deserved better than that.

Joe Henry's birthday was on January 17th. He had turned eighteen years old. He was scheduled to enlist in the army so he came down to The House to get some clean clothes and brought some to be washed. He said, "I'm sti' look'n fo a job." I took the dirty pile of clothes. Muhdea was ironing him some pants. I looked wearily at the task at hand. How dirty his shirt were as if he had been sleeping with pigs. His pants were even worse. There was a dried blood stain on the fly of his beige pants. I began seeing red. I couldn't think straight. My imagination got the best of me as I confronted him with my suspicions. He said with irritation, "Gir' don' cho sta' in on me I don' know whar tha came from. Wha' cho' tryin' ta say? I gots too much on my mine to worry 'bout cho'" I backed down and began preparing to wash the clothes. Muhdea insisted that she would do it. He got cleaned up, shaved, his shoes were shined. He took off in a huff in Phillip's car that he had borrowed again.

Loneliness was my best friend that was overcoming me. I was still able to stay above ground but had lost the lust for life, no pep in my step. I found out through the grapevine that Ms. Sweet had found out what had happened to me. She made life a living hell for that white couple. Nobody was going to mistreat her "niggahs" so I thought. That couple was also living on Ms. Sweet's property. They soon moved out or was evicted. Justice was finally served to a certain degree. That gave me a little hope and a reason to jump back on the bandwagon of life. I began buying cosmetics to fix up my face. Boot even offered to fix my hair after I had washed it. She burned my hair and scalp that I looked like a plucked chicken. I made sure that that was the first and last time that she would ever come anywhere near my head with a hot comb and curlers. I continued to stay on her good side because she would let me ride with her when she went to town. One Saturday we even went by Phillip's. I thought that I would be able to see Joe Henry. He had just left, or so I was told.

Joe Henry came home that same night. He asked me why I was up in town earlier. He made it clear that he didn't want me asking anyone about his whereabouts. I made sure that I was in close proximity of Bobby or Muhdea because I wasn't sure what his short temper would make him do. I seemed to be the brunt of his anger. I felt trapped at his mom's house. He didn't want me there yet he dared me to leave. So I became as invisible as I possibly could whenever he was in one of his foul moods.

He finally received the paper from the army draft that he wasn't a good candidate because of his asthma. He didn't seem disappointed that he wouldn't have to serve our country. He wasn't used to being disciplined and wasn't able to focus on anything except himself and his own gratification. It would have been a challenge for him. I saw relief in his face. His mom on the other hand wanted him to be drafted so that he would become a strong man who would be proud of his accomplishments in getting a higher education and could easily get a loan to buy a house. Mr. Lucus really did want to see him succeed. On the flip side of the coin was Bigman who only saw the negatives in life. His beloved baby boy would be away from him for too long. He was delighted with the news and he didn't try to hide it. When Joe Henry read the results I must have shown my disappointment. I had so many high hopes. The bubble was burst. Shortly afterwards I could tell that he was getting into one of his moods without any provocation from me. He wouldn't talk with me. He made sure that I saw him interacting with all of his family. It hurt me so much to be totally ignored by the man that I continued to love unconditionally. He and Bigman were whispering as they planned a trip to Meridian. Bigman wanted him to drive his prized Cadillac. They took it down to the pond close to the sandy shoreline where they washed and polished it. What a beautiful car. Muhdea was finishing up her never ending chores. She sat and talked with me while the boys were, 'being boys.' I asked her about the car. She said that Bigman had a good year of share cropping. When he got paid, he went and bought the car of his dreams – he paid cash for it – I looked around at the shack that they (and I) were living in. he could have bought a nice home for his family and a brand new Ford or Chevy for about the same amount that he had paid for the big Cadillac. "Share cropping don't pay that much, does it?" I asked. She didn't have any answers for me. All I knew was Bigman had a brand new car and they were living in that shack rent free. I wondered if there had been some hanky panky and walla! Joe Henry said that the beautiful daughter of Mammie Dell was half white).

The Cadillac was as shiny as a new penny and was like a mirror. It looked so out of place parked next to the old eyesore shack. Muhdea didn't seem to mind. She had settled for what she had and didn't seem to want anymore. It didn't take Joe Henry and Bigman but just a few minutes to jump sharp. Little did they know that I too was getting cleaned up and looking cute in my cheap rags but 'looking good' after I made myself up. I was standing next to the car waiting for them with my pocket book, my jacket and my wavering confidence. They were both shocked when I said, "I'm going too!" I was more surprised when neither of them said no. I climbed into the back seat; they sat up front.

The ride to town was so quiet and boring. They talked with each other. I tried to horn in several times but received icy responses. They had their windows down and that didn't help my hearing. The cold wind was blowing in my face and ears. It was so harsh and loud. My hooded jacket came in handy. I knew what they were trying to do to me and they should have been ashamed of themselves. We stopped at The Three Miles Inn that sold hard liquor. It was illegal to sell liquor in Meridian. There were some people who knew the sheriff and with a little hush money they would look the other way. You could buy and sell practically anything your heart desired. Joe Henry drove up to a building that had a window with a sliding partition for coloreds. The whites were allowed inside. He bought a pint of Ancient Age whiskey. Bigman took the bottle and gulped a large amount. He past it over to Joe Henry who did the same and he made a face that said, that was nasty. He handed the bottle back to me. I would show them how it was supposed to be done. I did – and in a few minutes I was drunker than a skunk. I had to hurl as soon as we got over to Phillip's Café (Bigman called him Joe Louis because he looked like the colored boxing champion in that era. He was also built like him). Bigman was acting like an entirely different person especially with Shirley Ann. He was extremely playful with her. He had her to sit on his lap (ewe). His hand were all over her ass. It was embarrassing. I didn't enjoy myself at all because I was being ignored. I still felt alone in a crowd of people who didn't know me. Joe Henry didn't seem to care about me anymore. He was acting flirtatious with some of the women in the café. He became angry when I asked him who was the woman that he had put his hand playfully on her butt. He answered, "you mus' be see'n thangs." I got back inside the car and fell asleep. I don't know what time that we got back home. I do know that when I awakened I was lying on the sofa fully dressed with a quilt over me. Joe Henry and Bigman had gotten up early to go to work with Mr. Lucus.

That next Saturday night was seemingly like the previous one. The Bopsy twins had gotten paid. They did, however, do something a tad bit different. They waited to see me go to my little living quarters to spruce up. That's when I heard the car take off. The tires were screeching as they burned rubber. I heard the loud 'yeehaw' from Bigman. That was the last straw. I waited up all night. They didn't return until the next evening. They were both drunker than I had ever seen them. Since it was so cold I had on my flannel gown that my mother had given me to wear when a negligee wouldn't do. They came into the kitchen. Bigman demanded that Muhdea get up to "fix sum'p t'eat." Joe Henry looked at me then looked away as if he was disgusted with me. I could feel my blood boil as I ran up to him. He was too quick for me to land my hand across his arrogant face. I turned away and said as I was about to put on some clothes. "I'm not going to take this anymore." Bigman came over to my area of the room. Joe Henry stood there with a smirk on his face that I wanted to scratch off. His dad said angrily, "What tha fuck you thank yo's do'n?" He stood between me and Joe Henry at which time he began yelling at me, "You needs ta git the hell outa my house bitch, you ain't welcome heah and you nevah wi'be." He grabbed my shoulder length hair that was standing up all over my head and began yanking it so hard I thought he would scalp me. It was hurting so badly. I tried to get away from him. I heard Muhdea yell out "Bigman stop!" there was no stopping him. I grabbed the broom that had been propped against the back door. I started popping him on his ugly effen head as hard as I could. The more I hit him the tighter the grip on my hair. We were literally going around in a circle. Neither one of us would let up. I finally heard Joe Henry say, "Daddy naw!" Bobby came in and grabbed for Bigman who had shoved me to the side. I broke my fall by grabbing a hold of the door knob. I kept my eyes on him as he broke free from Bobby's strong grip. The man must have snapped when I stood up to him and in his house. He ran to his bed in the front room where he had obviously had hidden another pistol. I saw him as he was aiming at me. I heard it as he pulled the trigger, "POW." The bullet came so close to hitting me in the head. The wall splintered. I heard a commotion in the room as Bobby had been the one to push Bigman just as he shot the gun aiming at me. Muhdea was coming over to where I was trying to put on my clothes. She said, as if it was an order, "Carrie you gotta leave naw." She stood between me and that ferocious animal. I didn't have time to think because there was still a such a shuffle in the front room. He said as Bobby was pinning him down, "God damn dat bitch!" fight or flight? I chose the latter. I dashed out the door. There was an old pair of shoes on the back porch that Muhdea kept there so that they could air out. They were so big on my feet. There was no time to go and get my own.

Bigman must have gotten the upper hand on Bobby with Joe Henry's help. I wasn't in any position to ask questions about who was helping whom. Feet don't fail me now! (see Prologue) I ran until I came to the field of corn that looked so familiar. I wound up at an old shack that Monk and her two heavy weight boys had moved to. Her husband George was there as he lurked in the next room. He was old enough to be Monk's father. I felt naked as he kept staring and undressing me with his bloodshot eyes. I thought he could probably get the program on if given a half a chance. I began to feel just as unsafe in their house as I did out in the woods. Monk reassured me "He ain't gwine ha'm you." He had beat her fat ass up, I thought to myself but I had to trust her.

I heard the familiar sound of Bigman's car as it was going back and forth in front of Monk's and George's house. They must have doubled back to the house when I had escaped in the woods. Knock, knock, knock. George got up from his bed in the back room. He had on a filthy looking long johns. He had put on his dirty tattered pants which he held up with his left hand. He had a rifle in his right hand. I heard it as he had cocked it and was ready to fire it at anyone who would dare fuck with him or his family. The room remained dimly lit from an oil lamp that Monk had next to her bed in the front room. She had helped me get out of the wet clay ridden flannel gown. It had began to dry and caked up. She gave me one of her old dresses that she could no longer fit into. It hung loosely on my frail body. She had made me some hot tea and warmed up some leftovers from their supper. I felt so grateful for her kindness. I had to try to forget about the stench that was wafting from her and her husband's body (they needed to wash their asses). I almost chocked when I heard the second knock on their front door. It was louder and more insistent. It was Mammie Dell and Joe Henry. I ran and hid in the back room when Mammie asked loudly, "George, have ya'll seen Carrie? She's Joe Henry's wife." George answered, "naw, we ain't see'd huh." Mammie continued. "She lef' ta night, we rill wurry 'bout huh." It was about day break when Boot came back alone. She knocked and said, "Miss Carrie, I knows you in dar. Com'mon out, ain't nobody gwine hu'cho. Com'mon naw. Daddy's is dead to da worl" I got up off of the couch and looked out the window that was so filthy I could hardly see through it. One of the panes was missing and was covered with taped on cardboard. Monk had gotten up and was standing behind me. I knew who it was because of the strong odor that was emitting from down under. I turned and told her that I was going back with Boot. She went and got me an old coat and an old pair of shoes. I thanked them both. George had came in and was about to plant a tobacco stained kiss on my check but I was too quick for him. Instead I ducked then reached out my hand to him and shook it with a firm grip. I apologized to them for putting them in harms way.

Joe Henry was out in the yard, back at The House. He had been crying. I got out of the Cadillac and he ran over to me and swooped me up in his arms. I was taken by surprise because I didn't know what kind of greeting that I would receive. He said, "I've pack everything o' mine and loaded it up in da old Buick" – an old car that he had insisted upon buying – He had said, "it's a steal Carrie you will love hit" He and his father had worked on it and got it running. It was big and heavy when he turned the ignition it had sounded like it needed more work on it. He said, "it's da manafol" Whatever it was it was loud and sounded awful.

I went inside through the backway where Muhdea was found up and at 'em. She came over and hugged me, "I know'd cho be a'ight" I shook my head and said, "I'm not alright but I know that I've got to get out of here." She told me that Joe Henry and Bigman had had a big fight last night when they came back from the woods. As she talked I was putting on my clothes from the suitcase that was already packed to go. "I'm so sorry ta see you go." She kept busy and was trying hard not to break down. She went over to the stove to stir the rice – that was a staple in their household – she began to sing her favorite song, 'oh mary don't don't you weep don't you moan oh mary want you sing yo' song' I knew I would miss her and her off tuned song. She had became a positive force in my life.

I got all of my worldly belongings in the little old suitcase, said my good byes to all that mattered, hoped that that mean ass old man would get his. It would be in God's hands and in his time. I looked for Bobby who was obviously somewhere hiding. Muhdea said she would tell him what I had said, "Thanks Muhdea, I love you."

We drove away in silence except for the noise made by the manifold. When we got near Monk and George's house Joe Henry turned to me and said, "I don' trus' tha' George I bet cho he tried to git him som las' nigh' did'n he?" I could tell that he wasn't kidding by the way that his chin curved in and up. His eyes squinted even smaller than their usual size. His voice was even different than when he was playing, it sent chill bumps up and down my spine. I tried to play it off but he became more irritated. I said, "What was I supposed to have done, was I expected to sit at your moms house and allow you and your father to kill me? I'm sure that it wouldn't matter because the law doesn't care about a nigger woman." I corrected myself, "They wouldn't care if a colored man killed a colored woman or another colored person." I added "I'm sure that Mr. Lucus would make sure that you or your family would never have to stay in jail for committing any crime." He seemed shocked that I had figured out some of the things that he had kept hidden from me. Time would tell.

We pulled up in front of the Henderson Hotel and Grill. He said without getting any response from me, "We gwine stay heah till we kin' git us a apartmen'" I asked, "What will we do for money?" Most of the money that I had made working on day jobs had been borrowed or he took it.

I found that he had gotten money from Muhdea and he said that Bigman had given him a loan. Now if they were fist fighting last night how could he get a loan from someone who didn't want me alive? (hmmm). We went in to register for a single room. It was owned and operated by a colored couple. The wife seemed to have been doing most of the work. She was a pretty, fair skin woman whose smile just lit up the area that she was in. she seemed to be just happy to be here on this earth. On the other hand there sat her husband who must have weighed a good 450 to 500 pounds. He sat behind their cash register to rake in the dough. They had a houseful of children. I wondered "but how?" I'm sure he had the how when and where. We were shown to our room (closet) with a bunk bed only. We had to share a bathroom down the hall. I tried not to drink too much fluids. The other patrons in the hotel were either hookers with their john's or semi homeless peoples. We were obviously going backward. We stayed in the hotel for two nights – too many – the food was so greasy. I wondered how toast could have oil dripping from it. Maybe that was how Mr. Henderson had gotten so fat. I was told to either stay in the room or sit downstairs with Mrs. Henderson during the day while Joe Henry tried to get another job or get his old job back with Mr. Wade. He came to the room while I was napping. He began looking under the bed and looked suspiciously around the room. I didn't say anything but my face was a dead give-away. He said, "Jus kidd'n" His face had projected something else. He then became overly happy, ecstatic that he had found us an apartment. He said, "I go' us a good dea' in the project and I go' some furniture tha's brand new." I said, "I thought we both would shop for what ever we needed together." He didn't hear me. He continued in his excited voice, "Oh you gwine rilly lov dis com'mon be happy!"

We went over to the east end projects, not too far from Phillip's place. It was a worn down area for coloreds. Our new address was B1, Reese Courts. As we got out of the car he said, "Itz reel niz" Going upstairs was like going to the gas chamber. The paint was institutional green and was peeling off all of the walls. The stairs I must say was steady and it did have a rail. We got to the head of the stairs. The fumes from the small apartment sized stove were unbearable. The manager was with us to give us a grand tour. Joe Henry had already been there and was grinning from ear to ear – tah dah! A small kitchen with opened shelved so that you could see the bugs as they crawled over the dishes. There was a small pantry area for groceries. He opened the apt size refrigerator that sounded like it was on its last leg. The rubber sealer was missing. I opened it and a few of its occupants scurried for a hiding place. The small freezer compartment was totally caked up with a mass of ice. It would need defrosting at least twice a week. The roaches had found a haven inside it, away from the gas fumes from the gas chamber.

We continued the grand tour of our first home. Joe Henry grabbed my hands and said, "Carrie, you gwine love dis I promise." The manager led us to the living room – my heart sunk when I saw it. Joe

Henry seemed as proud as a little boy who had just given his mom a wet frog and beamed, "it's a present for you!" I tried to put on a happy face in which I should have won a gold medal for my performance. "This is great" as my voice trailed off. He said, "I knowed cho' loved red" I said "I do" but that was maroon/burgundy. I touched it and it was the hardest pleather/plastic that needed so much padding. I could feel the springs in the looooong sofa. There was an arm chair to match (there wouldn't be any hanky panky on it because when you sat on it, you were literally stuck to it). The set came with two side tables that were double tiered (may I add that the edges were like a sword). It would cut you if you bumped into it. The loooooong coffee table was the same workmanship!

"I tol'd cho I wuz gwine git cho a home" and so he did. I wish with all my heart and soul that I could say The End, but I can't.

"Oh, I forgot! Let's take you to your bedroom." (the man was actually getting off on my expressions of disappointment). It was an average size room with a small closet. Joe Henry had already set up the used bedroom set. The bed sat so close to the floor, that one of us would need to crawl to get in it. There was even a spread that looked very used. I found a positive: we had a bathroom with running hot and cold water, a commode that flushed. I tried it and it did. He was right it was a wonderful place. I was happy again to be with my handsome husband. He got his job back with Mr. Wade. Our rent was thirty two dollars a month. Joe Henry's salary was now twenty six dollars a week. We needed so many things such as a dinette set, dishes, pots and pans – household items.

Chapter IV

On Our Own

It didn't take long for me to settle into city living. I was only too glad to finally escape from the person who was trying to break me and Joe Henry up. I thought back on several occasions how he (Bigman) would rub it in like salt on an open wound. He said when he knew that I was listening, "Joe Henry wuz so crazy 'bout dat lil gir' when he wuz even in da firs grade" The whole family would get a kick out of it and agreed with him how Joe Henry loved him some Cassy Gipson. I got so lost in my thoughts that seemed to be consuming me. One of my neighbors in my building had warned me that Joe Henry had been seen on numerous occasions over on 49th Avenue and that was where Cassy lived. She continued "and he been ridin that woman around in yo' cah'" I interrupted her, "I don't have a car." She said with annoyance in her voice, "you gotta speak up fo' yo'sef. What's in eva dats hiz is yoz." I didn't want to believe Laura Lee who had gotten married at the tender age of thirteen and was now pregnant with her third child. Her husband was about two years older than she which meant that he was fifteen years old when they got married. He was at home most of the time and mine was gone most of the weekends. He would however come home during the week after he got off from work, ready to eat, fuck and go to sleep. We didn't have a TV or a record player. The only entertainment we had was an old radio. I would spend most of my days visiting with Laura Lee after I had finished with cleaning and doing the wash by hand. In between visiting her I made sure that I had a good meal that Joe Henry liked. Laura Lee teased me that I was spoiling him and that whatever I started he would expect it to continued. I argued that I took my vows seriously including 'honor and obey." She ran into her apartment (#B2) when one of her baby's had awakened. She seemed so positive and happy. She had it going on. Her husband had a motorcycle that they both loved to ride on it together. At night I heard the sounds of them making love even through the thick walls of concrete.

Joe Henry was still capable of getting my eye balls to roll back in my head when he decided he wanted to be with me. I felt that there was something missing in my life. Most of the things that I had loved so much were no longer available to me, my family, my church, clothes and last but not least – me.

After observing Laura Lee I began to get a crazy notion that I wanted to have a baby. There was another incident that got my maternal juices flowing after I had gone down to Phillip's place and had a few beers with Shirley Ann. Joe Henry had played yet another Casper act on me on Friday night. He didn't come home at all on Saturday night. So I dressed up in a little black dress then I walked down to see my in-laws about four blocks away. My hair was done up in a French roll and bangs. My make up was nice I spent a little time trying to get with the program. I was too wound up thinking about Joe Henry. I worried that maybe he had had an accident. Maybe he was in the hospital. I was certainly a basket case. I walked outside to cool off. There were several women standing around a young woman who was rather pretty. She was about five feet six inches and a medium frame. She was holding and showing off a beautiful baby boy (dressed in blue) who was about two to three months old. On closer look he was absolutely gorgeous. He was getting so much attention. I felt so shy but was compelled to join in on the ooohs! and aaahs! I went over and did my baby talk to him and he responded to me by smiling widely. I held out my hands in gesture, "may I hold him?" She looked at me and all the other women became so quiet when she allowed it. I held him close to me. I asked permission to kiss him, she said, "Yes" somewhat reluctantly. I said out loud and I'm sure that everybody heard me, "I want a baby like this." Phillip and Shirley Ann came out to where we were standing and took the baby boy (Peter) out of my arms and handed him back to his mom. It was extremely quiet there standing in front of the café. The baby's momma (I got her name before she left) was Thelma Hackmon – I walked back and spent yet another night alone on a Saturday night. Joe Henry came home early Sunday morning. My premonitions were right – he had been out and became "sick as a dog and went to da hospital." If I questioned him I would surely get an ass whipping so I waited. When he came home from work that Monday evening I was ready for him because I knew that he would not have had a drink after work. I told him about what I was feeling and about him going out and leaving me alone. He really seemed to listen more attentive when I told him about my trip down to his brothers place and seeing such a beautiful baby boy. I blurted out, "I wish we had a child." He snapped, "Well we don' nee' no God damn baby and you needs ta sta' away from dow'naw, I'll take yo' thar when I go!"

The next upcoming weekend which was Friday night, he picked a fight with me about nothing. He threw a tantrum and slammed out of the apartment (raised the roof off of hell so to speak). I didn't go down to Phillip's since he had already warned me and he probably had his buddies looking out for him. I put on my glad rags to go up the street a ½ block away where there was always a crowd of people going in and out of the house. There were fifteen children that had been fathered by one man. The man of the house sold moonshine out of his house. The children was a good cover-up whenever there was a raid. He would hide the white lightening in the most unlikely places (in baby's bottles). It had been said that he had held out on the cops cut so they had to shake him up to get him to cooperate. I wanted to be around people just for socialization. Laura Lee wasn't anywhere to be found. I could see the illegal liquor house on the hill from my apartment. I walked over and to my surprise there sat my first grade teacher, Ms. Smith who was enjoying the booze and also the company of a smooth talking young man. Oh, he was like fine silk. He talked a big game about what his daddy had. He was dressed to the gill, Mr. Smoothie (Lavalle Hockenhull) was homeless but not for long. Mrs. Smith had plans for him. He was trying his best to amuse both of us. A young girl and an older woman. He saw that I was alone so he bought me a shot of the moonshine – it was so strong I could have died because I was breathless for about a minute – "I gotta go!" I heard the loud rattle of a car with manifold problems. I left in a hurry. Their house was on a steep hill. The flight of stairs didn't have railing and the steps were steep. I had to hurry. Mr. Smooth followed after me, "will I see you again?" I said, "it's too dangerous my husband is going to come looking for me." He threw both of his hand up. I got home just as Joc Henry was pulling up (how strange). I told him that I had come down to talk with Laura Lee. He looked at me and the garb that I had on. He opened the door and pulled me into the apartment, up the stairs and to our bedroom. Although I had been drinking I could smell the extremely heavy liquor fumes on his breath. It was mixed with the sour odor of vomitus. He opened up his huge hand and slapped me on the side of my face. The blow sent me hurdling on to our bed. He quickly leaped on the bed and straddled me pinning both my arms where I couldn't fight or grab his nuts. His knees were digging into my arms. I was kicking but not enough strength to get him off of me. I was screaming to the top of my lungs. The hands that had held me, caressed me, loved me, was choking me as he screamed, "You God damn bitch, who you been wid?" His hands tightened as I tried to beg and scream, "Please Joe Henry I've not been with anybody." My voice was muffled. He said, "Yo' ly'n ta me!" My screams were cut off. I felt my eyes bulging. My air supply was totally cut off and his voice was fading. All that was left was redness. I thought I must be dying as I stopped struggling. He must have thought so too because I had gone limp. He jumped up. Was it divine intervention or was he just tired? Whatever it was I will never know, I got up and went crying out of the room. I slept on the couch that Satan had sent. I would talk with him the next day. He offered to take me out to my mothers house that afternoon.

My eye was slightly red. There were bruises around my neck and some scratches. I put on a scarf and hoped that no one would notice.

My sister Joyce lived in the same projects with her new husband. Their apartment was A-1 – a half a block from me. It was so good to see everybody including Joyce who asked, "Carrie, are you alright?" I answered in a slightly hoarse voice, "Yes, I'm fine. I'm fixing up the apartment real nice, you all need to come over and see it." Joe Henry had barely spoken to my family as he rushed over to talk with Tommie Gathright and Connie. There was so much tension in the air you could cut it with a knife. Everybody was standing around the kitchen island waiting for an opportunity to tell me something. I began talking about my urges to have a baby. I told them about the baby that I had held, how cute he was. I told them the mother's name was Thelma Hackmon. My mother came over to me and held my hands, she said sadly, "Carrie that's Joe Henry's baby" How much more hurt could I endure? I was totally devastated. My whole world was crashing around me as I cried in front of Mother and all of my sisters. I still tried to take up for Joe Henry's short comings. I literally slithered back out of the house when Joe Henry came to escort me back to his car. He was being such a gentleman when he opened the door for me as my family looked on. A few days later I confronted him about what someone had told me. He vehemently denied it. How dare they tell lies on me. "I don know if'n dat woman is a man o' a woman." With that he forbade me to go back over to Laura Lee's house because he felt that she was the one to fill my head with those lies. I didn't go back over there. I would talk to her out of the opened window of my kitchen. I was so lonely and was being alienated from everybody that mattered even getting back in church. He was definitely against that, "You aint gwine go ta no chu'ch cuz all they gwine do is take yo' money and fill yo' head up wid a bunch a lies." I didn't know who to believe because he was so convincing especially when he held me and made me feel like putty when he looked at me. He made love to me just the way I loved it. I refused to dwell on anything that people were saying about him. It couldn't be true. I excused his behavior, it was because of his father who had spoiled him. He had to grow up too fast when we got married. It was a lot to put on him. I would help him as much as I could in hopes that he would change.

I wanted to help ease some of the burden on Joe Henry and it would also make me feel good about myself. We could work together and get ahead. I needed new clothes because my old outfits were becoming worn and in disrepair. Joe Henry had bought himself new shirts and slacks. He was even sporting a name brand new pair of shoes. He said that someone was selling men's clothes off a truck at a bargain that he couldn't pass up. I bought it hook, line and sinker. I told him that mother had a few things for me that a white woman had given her. He threw one of his worst tantrums. He sneered, "Nobody's gwine give my wife nut'n I tolt cho I kin take car o' you. All ya'll thank yo' better'n me and my family." He hissed as he got up in my face, "you got diamons up n' down yo' back huh? Yo' rilly ain't shit!" I braced myself because his face and chin had that horrible frightening look that he got just before he would strike me. I was backing away. He jumped over to where I was cringing as I held my hands up to the front of my face to block the horrible blows that was becoming a pattern. I screamed out, "Joe Henry noooo please don't." He grabbed both my forearms and said as he shook me so violently my teeth rattled, "You don' fuck wid me no mo' you heah' me?" Tears were streaming down my face as I said, "Okay, Joe I understand." But I really didn't understand any of it, not even my staying with him and taking his shit. I thought, "I've got to get out of this." I began to come up with a plan, "maybe I'll see if any of my folks knew some white folks who would hire me for house work or babysitting, yes, that's what I would do. Joe Henry left not too long after he had showed his ass. He had on his new clothes. He had bathed, shaved and put on some new cologne. He didn't say a word to me as he went past me (through me) and by the look on his puss he dared me to say a thing to him. He slammed the door so hard that one of the panes shattered. He would have to replace it. I left the broken glass on the floor.

I'll show him as I gathered my wits. I no longer had any pride and that had been one of my characteristics. Self loathing was deposited in its place. I tried to pray but I felt that God would not hear me or answer anything from me because I had certainly turned my back on him. I did it anyway. Lord please forgive me; have mercy upon me. That afternoon was dragging by. I felt so lonely. I had no one to turn to. Knock, knock, knock. I thought that maybe it was one of the neighborhood kids trying to sell something. I went to answer it and to my surprise – there stood my beautiful oldest sister. God did answer prayers and he was right on time. We hugged and I cried for joy but she was a bit distracted. We settled in (on the couch and chair from hell). She wasn't the least bit interested in my furniture as I apologized to her. I told her about some of my marital problems. It was nothing that I couldn't handle. I asked her to ask around for a job for me. She said that she wound. She looked as if she had the other half of the world on her shoulders. She said, "Carrie, I have something to tell you (as if thought she was apologizing about something that she had done) I'm pregnant." She explained, "Although I'm not married, I'm going to keep it." I respected and loved her so much. I didn't see how she would think that I could feel any different about her and of course she would keep her baby. She and the baby's father were planning on getting married. I was overjoyed about the baby and her pending marriage. She was going to be an excellent mother. I thanked God for that afternoon with my sister. We both needed it.

Two weeks passed since Lottie's visit. She came again bearing more news. She said Auntee knew of a white family who was desperate to find someone to work as a full time maid and a babysitter. I was simply ecstatic. The lady had asked if we could arrange a meeting for the interview at their house to see if I would be suited for the job. I got the address and directions. Joe Henry was reluctant at first because (who's going to cook for him?). There were so many reasons that he wanted me to stay home. I finally convinced him – we – need – the – money. We didn't have enough for groceries sometimes when he went on his weekend trips.

He drove me there and parked and waited in the car as I went to the side door. I knocked and Mrs. Shalles came to the door. There was a little girl who was clinging to her moms legs whom she introduced as Linda. She was four years old. She was as frightened as I was. Her two older boys were Teven and Micky. They were both boys that any parent could be proud of. Her two year old child was sound asleep in the nursery. I went in and got the grand tour. What a beautiful home. She showed me to all four bedrooms, a den, kitchen with a nook. The living/dining rooms wouldn't need daily cleaning. She told me what she wanted done on a daily basis and then she asked if I had ever done that kind of work. I said, "Yes!" (God forgive me because I've never had to do everything). She wanted me to start early Monday morning at seven o'clock until five o'clock in the evening. "I need you for a half a day on Saturday also. I'll start you out with $19.00 a week" she said. Before she could finish I blurted out with enthusiasm, "I'll take it!" I was beaming with happiness. She finally cracked a smile also. I floated to the car and back home. I knew that it wasn't much but it was a start.

I started out working for the Shalles family with high hopes. The kids were manageable. At first the house chores were basic. Each day there were more responsibilities such as washing windows, stripping the wax off of the oversized den tiled floors. She rented a machine. It was as big as I was. It got away from me several times. Mrs. Shalles saw that I couldn't manage that task so she hired a young colored man who I was acquainted with from Phillip's place. She was so pleased with his work that she paid him twice as much as what she paid me for one week. I was loosing a battle that I should not have been fighting. Things definitely hadn't changed since I was growing up at home. She seemed to want me to be the scapegoat when her children misbehaved or when she and Mr. Shalles had a spat or if it was raining and she wanted sunshine. I would catch it. I was the one that she would take out her frustrations. I began to wonder which house that was the most hostile – mine or hers.

I would get there early enough to cook breakfast for the children, help them get dressed then off to school they went. Except for the youngest child would follow me as if I was his mommy while his biological mom slept the day away (it didn't help those large bags under her eyes). I would do the wash daily and fold them after they were dried. The laundry area was out on the back porch. Some days it would be freezing cold as a well diggers ass. In the summer it would be as hot as a pu- - - with the pox. I would be wringing wet from the sweltering humid weather.

She came out there to check on me frequently. She gave me such a look of disgust after looking at the towels that I had neatly folded. She yelled as she undid the job that I had just completed, "I want it done like this" as she showed me how to fold them so that the designs could be seen by her guest when they used their bathrooms. She continued as she stood in the doorway with her arms folded, "I don't want them in this house until they are done right." I figured that she had had a fight with the mister or that she was on the rag. I said, "Yes máme Mrs. Shalles." (I needed to work and I did what I had to do). I redid them all and hurried to complete my other never ending chores. She watched me as I swept the kitchen floor. She snatched the broom from me and said angrily, "Carrie, that is not how you're supposed to sweep. You're making too much dust. This is how it's done" as she gave me instructions. She slowly belittled and whittled away at my soul. There was no pleasing her but I wasn't a quitter. There were no other jobs available in Meridian for an uneducated colored girl because I had looked.

I cook all three of their meals and served them. Afterwards I had to hand wash the dishes (and her nasty bloody silk panties). Most of the time there wouldn't be any leftovers because all of the food was dished up and was placed on the table. They seemed to love the food that was prepared and devoured most of it. The leftovers were eaten by me or their pet cocker spaniel. Mr. Shalle was well aware of his wife's behavior and he tried to compensate by paying me a little extra and, "shh – don't tell Mrs. Shalle" he added, "thank you for doing such a good job. I hope that you will continue to work for us."

I babysat quite a few times on Saturday nights. It kept me from being so lonely at home alone. Plus I got paid an extra three dollars a night.

I had finally been convinced that Joe Henry was tipping out on me. I saw him one night with a woman in his car. He said it wasn't him, it wasn't his car and that I was crazy. Oh well!

I began to buy new clothes and fix my self up and seemed to have attracted several young men who would approach me and ask me, "is yo' huzban married?" I never could understand the question so there was never a response from me. I needed to be noticed and wanted. I was so hungry for my husband who was never there for me. When he was at home he was either too tired or too angry. I didn't feel desirable anymore. It was about that time that I met a young man who was working as a helper in the projects. He looked so much like Joe Henry, it was uncanny, although he had a better grade of hair and his muscles were more defined. What a hunk! He invited me to a party in the west end projects. It was on that Saturday night after Joe Henry did his routine Casper act. I took a bus to the party. The place was crawling with high school students and older men. Practically everybody was drunk or getting there. I didn't stay too long, just long enough to get me some kisses and to see what Johnny Boy was all about. "He was hot!" I had a hard time convincing him that I had to go or it would be my life or death situation. He wouldn't allow me to go until I promised him that I would see him again. "Somewhere, so that we could put out the fire that had been ignited in both of us." I felt that I wanted to be with him yet I was still delusional that I desired to salvage my marriage. It didn't take but a little coaxing and I agreed. We agreed to a rendezvous on Saturday night while I babysat. He knew the area because he had done some odd jobs in the vicinity.

That Sunday morning Joe Henry insisted that we go down in the country to see his family. It was the first time that we had gone back there since that awful fight with Bigman. It was as if though nothing had happened. Muhdea and I did what we liked to do best and that was talk about "those two niggahs" as she so eloquently put it. She said that she wanted to come up to town and see the apartment but Bigman wouldn't bring her. "Tha man is so hateful" she said as she studied her hands (as if they had the answer to her problem). She continued as she lowered her voice, "sometimes I wish he wuz dead" I wasn't shocked. I looked at her when she finally had the courage to look me in the eye. I said, "Me too" but I couldn't tell her my wishes wasn't just for Bigman; it was for her beloved son also.

Muhdea stayed busy during our visits. She was pulling old clothes ('damn rags') out of the wardrobe. She was muttering a few of her choice cuss words. She took off in a hurry when she heard the sizzle of the fire as her greens were boiling over on the top of the stove.

It felt like old times, I missed her so much. We were interrupted by one of the kids screaming frantically. Duntley had skinned her knee. She was such a tomboy like her mama. I stayed over in the corner that I used to claim as my space while Muhdea proficiently multi-tasked. I couldn't find a place to sit. There were some envelopes in a pile on the shelf of the wardrobe. One that caught my eye that had been addressed to Joe Henry Mathis. The return address was from Matty William. I knew her name and remembered seeing her at Tommy Gathrights' parents' house. There was no turning back. My instinct was right when I saw the proof with my own eyes in a black and white Polaroid snapshot. It fell to the floor when I picked the envelope up. My curiosity had peaked to its capacity. It didn't make sense as I tried to read the scribbled penmanship. She wrote, "Joe Henry, I love you, and you said you loved me too. Here is the last picture that we took together. We were so happy together. I'll wait for you. Love, Matty." I was feeling frantic. Joe Henry had told me that he would never be caught dead with a woman who looked like that yet, there they were on the photo, she was looking up at him in adoration. He had a grin on his face and his hand rested on her more than ample breast. I stood there shaking. I reread the letter as I was shaking my head, "this can't be true" I thought. I found a place to sit on the old couch. Muhdea found me in a trance. "How could he?" I asked out loud and not really addressing anyone. She asked, "Wha' cho' look'n at Miss Carrie?" I handed her the envelope which had a recent date stamped on it. She took it and put on her specks (that had masking tape to hold them together). "Lordy mercy dis is a cry'n shame. I tolt Joe Henry dis letta' wuz heah. I'm so sorry you had to see dis." I got up and didn't say a word. I wondered how much degradation should I have to endure. Joe Henry and Bigman had taken off to God only knew where. The old rocker on the front porch was uncomfortable but it gave me solace as I began to map out my life. It was quiet out on the garrey (front porch).

Muhdea probably wanted to give me some time and space. There were no tears as I contemplated on how I was going to get revenge. The only thing that broke the silence were the birds as they flew about so freely. I could almost taste it. Oh, he's going to pay and it will be soon!

Billy came out and broke my spell. I'm sure that Muhdea had informed him of what had happened and what I had found in the envelope. He started making jokes and it was good to break the ice. I joined him in a good belly laugh. He had me cracking up. What a clown. He actually could have been a comedian. Then he got serious. He said, "Joe Henry don' got hiz sef' a pretty youn' wife naw look wha' he don' did" (he had the thickest drawl but not as bad as his twin brother Bobby). He obviously wanted to fuel the furnace and so he did. "You needs a betta man like me." I looked at him and laughed because he wasn't my cup of tea and he must have been kidding – he wasn't – and we both knew it. Although I flirted back and forth with Bill. One thing that he got credit for was getting my mind off of the murder that I wanted to commit. My marriage vows were out of the window as of that day. "I'll show him. That bastard wasn't going to get away with what he had done to me and the way that he had continued to lie to cover his filthy tracks."

Vengeance is mine saith the Lord but on the other hand, God helps those who help themselves. I knew that it wasn't right but it was the only thing that I could focus on to keep from killing myself or him.

He was convinced that everything was just fine after he swore to God that he had never talked to "tha' ly'n bitch" after she had got herself pregnant. Anyway, that picture was old. He wanted me to believe him. I looked at him then through him. He had a strange look on his face. He must have known that he was dealing with someone who had had enough and was about over the edge. He hugged me but didn't get a response from me. I was like a stiff corpse with a fire cracker up my ass just waiting to be lit and explode. He settled into his new routine with me close by so that he could monitor my every move for the exception of when I was working.

That Monday I was hell bent on settling a score with my Mr. Cheater. "Hello! Johnny, I'll be baby sitting this Saturday night, be here by nine when the kids are asleep." He said "I'll be there baby." I gave him the phone number just in case he couldn't make it. "Oh, I'll be there, I can hardly wait." He said with enthusiasm.

Joe Henry was getting antsy since he hadn't been out on the prowl for a while. He was more than happy for me to stay over and babysit. He piped in, "I'll go down and keep Phillip comp'ny." I glared at him and thought whatever is good for the goose is good for the gander.

He drove me to work that Saturday morning. I jumped out of the car and literally ran up the driveway to the house without saying goodbye or even look at him. He stayed there for a while with the motor still running. He took off faster than usual. Ms. Shalle met me at the door and asked what was all of the noise that Joe Henry had made when he took off. She reminded me that it was a quiet neighborhood that she and her family lived in. she pointed out that "You people may keep up a lot of noise where you live but it wasn't going to be tolerated here." She added, "I'm going to speak with Mr. Shalles when he comes home this evening." I didn't hear a word that she said, it went right over my head. I was as nervous as a hooker in a church on Sunday morning. I had never been with another man other than Joe. I thought about all of the lies and the women that he had been with and would probably be with tonight. That just drove the nail straight into the coffin.

I had the hardest time getting those hyperactive kids to settle down to go to bed, especially Linda who tried every trick in the book. She finally gave in after several bedtime stories, trips to the bathroom, 'I need a snack' or 'there's something in my closet.' She wore herself and me out. I kept a close lookout at their long driveway. He was almost halfway to the house when I looked out the last time. His tall slender body moved swiftly but not running (that wasn't a good thing for a colored man to do in a white neighborhood especially after dark). I got his attention and pointed to a grassy area in the huge back yard, away from the patio lights. I said, "I'll be back." I went in and grabbed an old blanket and went through the children's bedroom. They all were sound asleep including the baby boy John. What a sweet child he was. The TV remained on in the den. I was so excited when I rushed out to meet my new lover. I wished that I could say that IT was the best that I had ever had – it was not! I was so uncomfortable even on the grass with all the small pebbles that the children had thrown at each other. The blanket didn't help any either. It was over before I could get started and I wasn't about to try for seconds. I lied and said, "mmm mmm good!" One lie on top of another. There wasn't any remorse or regrets for what I did with Johnny. We made plans for another rendezvous. He called me several times. I didn't want to see him again. there wasn't any sparks or chemistry. He finally gave up. The taste of getting even with Joe Henry hadn't been quenched. I received an extra five dollars that night when Mr. Shalles drove me home to the apartment. Joe Henry was just pulling up as I was getting out of the car. He didn't say a word to me and neither did I to him.

That next Saturday night Joe Henry was nowhere to be found. I got dressed and walked up to the neighbor's house with the white lightening. Lavalle was there and was looking soooo good. There were definite sparks between us. He was so smooth. He came up behind me while I was paying for the moonshine shot. He touched my shoulder and bent over and kissed the back of my neck, it gave me goose bumps. It was still twilight so we sat inside the house till it got dark. He seemed to have known all of the right buttons to push for a quick response from me. He had a room that he had rented from Mrs. Smith across the street and she didn't allow him to have any female visitors, I wondered why?. He had an old Cadillac that he bragged about constantly. It was a gift from his father who was living up north. He bragged about all of the money that he had. I thought, "Daddy needs to get you a house or an apartment." I wondered if it was some kind of inborn thing that men or boys had to stretch the truth to compensate for their inadequacies that they had be it of their mine, body or soul. I wasn't mature enough to figure out what made me tick so I would have to contemplate their plights later. Lavalle and I really rocked his car that night as it stayed parked out on the street a half a block from my apartment.

It seemed that most of the good times happened during the weekends. I listened to a song on the radio by Shirley and Lee. It was very popular – come on baby let the good times roll. Boy! Did I need to dance off some of the frustration that I was experiencing. The closest place that I could get to without a car was down to my brother-in-law's joint. What did I have to loose? My life was worth a plug nickel. I did what I had to do and joined the party people. Phillip didn't want to serve me beer, but my running buddy didn't mind. Shirley Ann was always on time as she sneaked me beer at no cost to me. She ever took money out of the cash register to pay herself since she didn't get a salary. I think Phillip knew what she was doing. They seemed to have a good relationship. There was no evidence of any physical abuse. She could out talk, out dance and had a "let's get this party started" attitude at all time. So I stuck close to her. She always seemed to know how to handle Joe Henry if he got out of line. I didn't want to question their relationship. When I got there the party hadn't jumped off like I knew that it would. I must have had a 'come and get me' look on my face because that's exactly what was happening. Phillip was out in front as a look out because if Joe Henry had found me flirting with all of his crony's I wouldn't be here telling this story today.

The last person that I expected to show up would be Bigman. Boot even came along with Billy. They had came by the apartment and "no" I wasn't at home and neither was Joe Henry. Phillip played it off real cool but I figured that he knew where Joe Henry and his old lady was. In about fifteen to twenty minutes of his family's visit, in walked Joe Henry. He didn't seem surprised to see me there and his family. Shirley Ann and I continued our dance revue. Everybody was applauding and going wild about the exotic jitterbug dance steps that we performed. I was in dance heaven. The music stopped abruptly. Joe Henry had unplugged the juke box. He didn't want people (especially men) gawking at me. Everybody seemed to be enjoying the floor show including Phillip. I walked back to the restroom and he followed me in before I could latch the door. He asked, "Wha' tha' God damn hell you thank yo' do'n dow' heah?" I answered him as I tried to keep my voice steady, "I came here to see Shirley Ann and Phillip." He backed off a little as he squinted his eyes and said, "You don' have ta move lak tha', lak som slut." I answered him firmly, "I'm a woman, not one of your sluts that you've had illegitimate babies by." He didn't say anything else to my surprise. He went to find his father. They left in the Cadillac for a minute (one hour). They were both smashed when they returned. Neither of them could walk straight and they both tried to out curse the other. It was suggested that we (Joe and I) ride down to the country and spend the night. Bigman wanted his precious son with him. Boot drove. Joe Henry sat up front with his daddy. I sat in the back and insisted that I sit next to the window just in case that I got sick during the trip back to The House. There were two of the older kids sound asleep on the back seat (Duntley and Grady). Bill got in and sat in the middle and I climbed in behind him. Halfway down the highway I heard snoring from Bigman and Joe Henry. I was seated behind Mammie Dell. I felt that she was watching me as I tried to keep a conversation up with her. I found it very hard to do when someone's hand was fondling my legs, my neck, my ears. He was like an octopus. I wasn't drunk and didn't want to make a scene. Bill kept trying to ram his hand up my dress as he took over the conversation. I gave up, laid my head on the back seat and thought, "What the hell, let's see what big brother got." He didn't have no magic touch but he was a forbidden fruit that I wanted to partake. I was so excited and totally afire when we go to the house. Surprisingly Bigman said, "ya'll kin take my bed fo' tanite." Joe Henry was so drunk that he had to be carried in and went to bed with all of his clothes on. Muhdea stripped off his shoes. I saw Bigman as he staggered into the kitchen area to sleep on the couch that I used to sleep on. Muhdea and Boot went to their room. I turned the light out and stripped down to my bra and panties and got into bed next to my husband. I was almost asleep when I felt something touch my foot and shake it. When I opened my eyes, there he was hovering over the foot of the bed. I thought it was a nightmare but it wasn't. it was Bill, totally naked. He refused to go away. The evil person within me said again, "what the hell. Joe Henry had really tied one on. I shook him and he continued to snore, oblivious to any thing that should have mattered and sacred to out marriage vows. Bill continued to stand at the foot of the bed awaiting something that was so forbidden to anyone except for me and Joe Henry. He was literally begging that I join him. I whispered "somebody's going to find out." He pleaded in a lower voice, "Carrie, I wan' cho' I nee' cho naw, nobody gwine know." I hesitated then got up to join him to the side room only a few feet from where my husband slept. His twin brother Bobby was in the bed next to Bill's. we both must have had a death wish or the need to be banned out of our families. I crept out of the bed that squeaked so loudly because the mattress was on coiled springs. Each movement produced sounds that was amplified by the quiet of the night. Some of the sounds were muffled by the different chorus of intermittent snoring from ten people that were crammed into such a small space. I got to the foot of the bed and was climbing over when Bill lifted me over the old iron foot board. He carried me to his bed. There was no door to his room because of the crammed furniture. His bed was within view of where Joe Henry was turning over to grab some covers. We watched him as he went back into a stupor. The window was opened to get a breeze. There were more noises from the squawking tree frogs and the crickets added to the nightly melody. I got in between the sheet as Bill followed. He was so clumsy. Each movement was like an untamed hungry bear whose hands were mauling me. He kissed me so hard that my tongue was numb. He obviously hadn't been told that he didn't have the kissing technique down pack. His mouth covered mine and all I could feel were his teeth – he seemed angry or maybe that was his style. There may have been some sibling rivalries and he probably wanted to defile something that his brother had. There was no doubt in my mind that love had nothing to do with the act that we both allowed to happen against the person (who slept) whom we both had very mixed emotions for. He opened his mouth again, it seemed that he would devour my face. I turned my head so that he could get through. He was making animal like noises that I couldn't get him to be quiet. I wondered for what? I didn't feel a thing. He hadn't been blessed with the tools that Joe Henry had nor did he have the skills. He was sound asleep before I climbed out of his bed. I do regret one thing- I didn't get my jollies on. I felt only anger. It will never happen again. Revenge is sweet. I felt that when Joe Henry would be beating me again about "who you been fuk'n?" at least he would have a reason to wonder. I went to sleep and woke up refreshed.

His back was turned to me. I looked at the back of his head. It seemed that the snoring was getting louder with each breath. I kicked him in the back of his leg. He awakened startled and dazed. "Wha' wha'?" I asked, "What's wrong? You must be having a nightmare." He turned over and was facing me. The snoring stopped as I was falling asleep my thoughts were, "you mean mother fucker, I'm turning into someone like you."

Mrs. Shalle's family was planning a vacation trip to Tampa, Florida. I felt so excited for them that they would make the trip across country in their station wagon. They would be traveling with another couple who also had four children. they obviously had made the trip before and decided they needed household help (maids) to accompany them. "Wow! I would get to go to Florida!" When Joe Henry was informed he was all for it. I would be away for two weeks and get a bonus of ten dollars per week. I would have almost sixty dollars when I returned back home. I knew how to budget and make it stretch a long way and hopefully Joe Henry would see how valuable that I could be.

The other family hired my cousin Gloria G. I was so glad that she was the one who would be my roommate. She seemed happy that I would share the responsibilities.

We encountered the usual problems of coloreds traveling in the southern states. We weren't allowed to go inside the restaurants with the family when they stopped nor could we use the restrooms. The kids didn't understand nor did they like what was happening. Mrs. Shalle just took it in stride. "That's the way things are" she drawled. They had to make different pit stops for us and they brought us food to go from the restaurants after they had eaten.

We arrived at the rental property late in the evening. I was so tired and wanted to rest but that wasn't what I was hired for and Mrs. Shalle made it perfectly clear when she basically blew a fuse in the presence of everyone, "This is my vacation and you are here to take care of us." She said in a shrilled higher pitch tone than usual. She slammed out of the room. The McPhearson couple stood there looking at each other probably wishing that they had thought that whole thing through. She ran hot and cold. I hoped that someone would put her in her place.

I got my family's children settled which wasn't an easy task. The house had double quarters for two families with a shared kitchen space. It was located on the white sandy beach. The waves could be heard crashing closer and closer to the house. The air was as if a constant breeze from a fan from heaven. It was as I would picture paradise (without the woman from hell).

Gloria and I straightened up the mess then headed for our sleeping quarters. It was just the opposite of the huge beach front house. It was a detached little outhouse looking building. We walked into a one bedroom with two bunk beds. The stench of the flooded bathroom floor was horrific. We did our best to clean up the filth that another white family had left. We were determined to make it work and so we did. It was about midnight when we finally could feel comfortable to lie on those two beds. Oh yes, we didn't have air conditioning and the big house blocked all of the view and the breeze. We knew that we were assigned for the same hour and off a half a day on Saturday and a full day on Sunday. That sounded reasonable. We were like wild heathens that Saturday night. We got a ride to the colored bars and clubs. The streets were packed with fine men who were all out trying to pick up any honeys that would. We didn't get home until daybreak – we made sure that we watched out for each other. She more so than me. I was bound and determined to have a blast. Money was no object. It was the liveliest block party that two hot kittens in the beach city could ever have. Gloria and I made a pact whatever happens in Tampa stays in Tampa. We barely made it home on Monday morning. Our rides had flaked out on us because we hooked up with two fine gentlemen who later dumped us when they got what they wanted from us. We were dead on our feet. The least bit of noise seemed to have been amplified including those waves, I had the worse headache. Mrs. Shalle had a lame brain idea that I was to prepare gumbo for the entire crew from a recipe that I had prepared before and it had turned out scrumptious then. I was half drunk during the preparation and burned it beyond salvaging the singed seafood from the black burned pot, "Carrie the cost of the meal will be coming out of your salary." She barked. The next weekend got better. The wild, crazy night spots were covered very well by me and Gloria. One night we met our match. Two men got us to go to their place. It was fun at first but became out of hand. They wanted us to strip and dance in the nude for a crowd of men who they had invited to their pad. It appeared that that was their line of business judging from the set up in their living room. There were costumes galore from princess to barbarian queens. I wasn't in the mood for any of it. I could see us being molested and our body parts being found in several places. We talked fast while they were in the kitchen planning their floor show. We had to hitch hike fifty miles that night to get back to the maids' quarters.

The next day we were at it again. it was Sunday our regular day off. We decided to go to the colored beach. Neither of us had bathing suits. We discovered that they had rentals. I was quite skeptical. I didn't want to put on a used suit not knowing what bug ridden pussy that had been stuffed in it. Gloria got a bathing suit that fitted her (it still had a price tag on it). We paired off with two life guards who were mediocre. There were very few beach goers that day. I kept on my shorts and top. My partner convinced me that no one was looking. So I took off my top and got into the beautiful balmy waters. I frolicked and squealed loudly. It felt so good to have the water around me as it carried me and Frank from the shoreline. He undid my top button further then the zipper of my shorts. The ocean claimed my shorts but I kept my panties. I was so busy trying to get my short back that I finally noticed that we had continued to drift out and – I CAN'T SWIM – I was screaming and waiving my hands trying to grope my arms around his neck. I was totally panicked realizing that Frank wanted one thing from me. In my quest to stay alive I pulled him down under the water. I swallowed and breathed in so much salt water. He shook me sharply and screamed at me, "Carrie, calm down! We are going back to shore but you have to stay calm!" I wondered if I would see my mother again. I said as we neared the shore, "I want to go home." He was walking in the deep water but had me and my half naked ass above him. We rested on the shore. He must have thought that I would show my appreciation to him for saving my life. The only thing that kept him from going down on me was my period had came on from all of the excitement and commotion of my near drowning.

Back home Mrs. Shalle was true to her promise that I would have my salary reduced because of my carelessness plus the incident of my breaking a crystal glass the week before we went to Florida. She and the mister argued in their back room. When she came out she had the money in cash as usual so that she wouldn't have to report it to social security. I counted the money in front of her and thanked her because I had never had that much money at one time. I promised her that I would be careful. Mr. Shalle drove me home that Saturday night. They didn't need me to babysit.

Joe Henry wasn't at the apartment. He was expecting me to return on Sunday. He must have drove by and saw the lights on thinking that there were burglars inside because he came inside quietly up the stairs with his pistol drawn, "Who dar?" he said loudly. I was coming out of the bedroom. The living room was dimly lit. I saw the gun as he was turning into the living room. I said, "Joe Henry it's me. We came back a day earlier than was planned." He answered, "Good cuz I needs some money." (there weren't any hello's, kisses or hugs just demands). I said, "I need to buy me a few personal items and we need…" With the gun still drawn in his right hand he used his left back of his fist a blow that landed on the left side of my head. My ears were ringing as I lost my footing. He yelled, "Whar' izit? I needs it rat naw!" I tried to talk him out of his rage, "Joe Henry please let's talk!" I begged as I was getting up off of the floor. It only angered him more. I grabbed my pocket book and ran to the bathroom and locked it quickly just as he lunged toward me. I heard a loud thud on the door, he must have ran into it. There was a moment of silence then he began banging on the thin door insisting that I give him the money. The next unexpected occurrence was his fist rammed through the frail thin door. I got inside the bath tub and stood there pleading to him as he was reaching in and unlocked the door. I put the small pocket book on the floor and backed away then back into the bath tub cringing awaiting to be assaulted by him again. He picked up the pocket book. He counted the money and smiled sadistically and sneered, "I tolt cho' tha' dis is ou' money." He slammed the door after he threw the purse at me. I became so angry and went after him. It only made him laugh out loud. He pushed me as he grabbed the purse again. he emptied it completely spilling all of its contents on the floor. "Naw you see who cho made me do, you pick dat shit up of tha flo'" He left and slammed the door as a car horn was being impatiently blown outside our apartment. I ran to the window thinking, "I wish that he would have an accident and die tonight." He walked toward the car waiting at the curb for him. He jumped in on the passenger side. I got a glimpse of his driver. She was a fair skinned woman. I could hear laughter from both of them as she sped away on the wrong side of the street.

The next week was crucial because my mind was finally made up to not take any more crap from Joe Henry. I found out that he had been missing out on going to work because of his night life. He told me to stay at home with him. He only wanted me to call Mr. Wade and lie for him that he was too sick to work. I went to a phone booth and called my boss also.

I made one more last ditch effort to talk to him but he wouldn't listen. He acted as if he didn't need to discuss anything with me especially what he did with his money (my money was his). I knew that he had the pistol in his jacket. I grabbed it and went to our bed and pointed it at him. He jumped up startled by my desperate action. He said as calmly as possible, "Carrie, naw you gwine hur' somebody." I thought, "you aint nobody." He said insistently, "Gimme da gun." I pointed the gun to his head, "You need to tell me who you've been with and why you treat me the way you do. You've treated me so badly, why Joe Henry, please tell me why?" I cried uncontrollably. He answered, his voice steady, "I'll te' you eva thang jus gimme da gun Baby." I did a double take. I hadn't heard that term of endearment for quite a while. He was walking toward me with his hand out, "You don' wanna hur' me naw do you?" he said with so much self assurance – something that I no longer possessed. I jumped backwards to keep him from grabbing it. I said, "No" as I pulled the trigger and aimed above his head. My warning to him that I had had enough and I meant business. "Carrie, you' gwine ki' me den whar you gwine be, aint no otha man gwine love you lak I do." I pulled the trigger again missing him only by a couple of inches from his fucking cold heart. There were two huge gaping holes in the wall of our bedroom and I for one didn't care. He was in his boxer shorts. He started putting on his pants as he continued to plead with me to give him the gun. I ran out of the apartment with the loaded gun still in my hand but at my side. There were several occupants of the building that had heard the disturbance that I was making. An older lady came to her door who must have been aware of who I was and knew what a terrorist that Joe Henry had been in our community for about one year. We were the talk of the town. She said, "Baby don'do dis, he aint wurt it." We had a stand off for about a half an hour. Nobody called the cops because they all knew what turmoil that Joe Henry had put me through. I really didn't have a plan as I stood there on the corner with my hand gun. I had no more pride left so I wept for everyone to see. I could hear some grumbling about, "She sho' don't need to git huh' se'f in trouba' ova tha' niggah." Laura Lee came up to me, "give me tha gun Carrie." I did and Joe Henry came and took it from her. I walked back to our apartment, walked past him as I glared at the man that I had married 'for better or for worse'. Such a big man who was actually a wimp, to jump on me, a woman. He was twice my size and growing bigger and more muscular than what he was when we married.

I went inside and secretly started packing all of my belongings while he stayed outside talking to Laura Lee's husband who was absolutely afraid of Joe Henry as most people were. It would be best to wait a few days before I made a drastic move to end the charade. I pretended that everything was good with us and thought that I was over the tantrum that he began teasing me about. He went to buy some cigarettes one evening at which time I called a cab to pick me up and all of my glad rags and took me out to my mother's house. He was already on the prowl. The coast was clear.

Mother and daddy both knew that I had been suffering because of the many attacks on me made by Joe Henry. Nobody said, "I told you so." I had suffered enough and I needed a safe haven. I felt it until Joe Henry decided to come out to my parents and gather his property (me). I went back because he promised with his right hand up to God, "I'm gwine do betta by you. I love you Carrie." I was mesmerized by his charms. My knees would buckle when he touched my face. "We gwine mak it huh?" I nodded my head yes as I followed him out of my safety zone.

Mrs. Shalle seemed glad to see me at first when I showed up for work that Monday. Or was it that the bitch was preparing some scheme to pay me back for not showing up for work for a week. A week after I returned she had me walking her two small kids back and forth to school and to day care while she slept the day away. The bags under her eyes seemed to have gotten bigger and redder. Maybe it was all of the liquor that she consumed.

I finally got up enough nerve to ask for a raise. You would have thought that I had stolen a government mule or kidnapped one of her children the way that she came down on me. I told her that I knew that I was doing a good job and that there was another white family that wanted to hire me. She argued with me and tried to even reason that "the kids would surely die if you go." I just stared at her. There wasn't anything about what a fantastic job that I had done over the year that I had worked for her. The youngest boy, John, started pleading , "Cara, please don't' go we want you to stay." It was sincere coming from a little boy whom I dearly loved. She wouldn't budge and neither would I. I valued my work so I left just before Christmas. She came in on the day of my departure. She said musically, "Carrie I have a present for you before you go." She handed me a box that was rather heavy. It didn't have the usual Christmas wrappings. "Open it" she beamed in front of her kids who seemed so excited. I opened it – it was a set of her used Melamac dinner ware consisting of four of each: plates, cups, saucer soup bowl and a platter. When I said used I meant used (with burn marks from the stove and scratched). She said gleefully, "Here are some tree decorations for your apartment and oh yes, a Christmas tree." (it had some of the limbs missing). I said, "Thank you." She hugged me. Before I left I explained the real reason for my leaving. I didn't like the way she treated me and the way that she screamed at me (she needed to know). She said, "I did it because

I felt that you were just like on of my children." I thought long and hard because I remembered that she hated coloreds – me included. She seemed absolutely frightened of colored men. So my question was, "how did I become to be her little picky ninny child?" I didn't buy it. It was time to go. I was a seventeen years old woman and about to make a big step for the best.

My family had always believed in the Baptist ministry. Some of my family members had been introduced to another spiritual concept. At first it was Aunt Carrie Mae and then my brother Tommie (Boy Baby) wanted something different. They were on fire for new information that came from the Seventh Day Adventist Church (SDA). My mother quickly followed suit. She went to bible studies and asked me if I wanted to get my soul saved also. I was so deep in quick sand I couldn't go any place else but up. I began going to bible studies and to the Sabbath meetings (held on Saturday). We studied the same Holy Bible but actually followed the Ten Commandments and the teachings from the apostles. At last, I began to have a purpose in life. God was my salvation. I sang in the choir again. I even joined the church's trio with my sister Lottie and Denise Nelford (who was another church member. She had been sexually abused by her Uncle). We were asked to sing on many occasions at church and sometimes at conventions.

Denise was about twenty eight years old who had not been allowed to mature to her fullest potential. She resided with her bed-bound Aunt (an accident(?) caused by her Uncle). Both she and her Aunt were simply petrified of the beast. He was brutal in all aspects. He demanded that Denise do everything including lifting her Aunt from the wheel chair. I saw her as she maneuvered her with no problem. She was a strong young woman and had an even stronger grip on what thus said the Lord. The man pushed her to her max on one of his rampages. He was about to whip her with a strap – she snatched it from his grip and told him, "I will kill you if you ever put your hands on me or Mama; you get out of her house." He had plans to kill his wife and take over her house. Denise grew up that day. She persevered as I knew that I too would eventually.

I wanted to be a part of the SDA church experience. There would be barriers that I was willing to overcome. I needed to get back with the living. Joe Henry was doing everything that he could to dissuade me. He said, "You ain't gwine use any my har' earn money to give to those preachers; I aint fat'n frogs fa snakes."

Miraculously another day job was found with a much nicer boss. The lady of the house was a RN and so was her mother. She lived with the couple, their two boys and a baby girl. The job lasted about three months earning twenty five dollars a week. I was able to save a lot of money even after I bought a weeks supply of groceries. Mr. Hudnall, the store owner, would have one of his helpers to drive me to the apartment because I had too many bags to walk five blocks homes. I began to feel that things were getting better. However, Mrs. Lockly told me that she was going to let me go because her husband was laid off plus her mother had just been diagnosed with cancer of the cervix. I was referred to another white family who needed my help. She too was a registered nurse. I recognized her immediately when we first interviewed. She was a country nurse who visited public schools to give kids their vaccinations. The man of the house was totally creeping me out, the way that I would catch him gawking at me when his wife wasn't looking. The bastard had the nerve to playfully lay his hands on my knee when he drove me home. He had so much junk piled on the back seat, so he said, "sit up heah" as he patted the seat. He continued, "I don't mind no colored sitting next to me." With that being said I made sure that we cleaned off the back seat for the next trips because I didn't want to come up missing if he decided to advance his hands. There were too many strange things happening in Meridian with the whites and the coloreds. I didn't know who I could trust. I worked for them one more month. I had saved up enough money that I kept stashed away in the closet. Joe Henry had been giving me money to buy groceries also. He wasn't privy to the amount of money I had made on the past two jobs. I wasn't going to allow him to take money from me and spend it on God knows what…or who.

My mother and father were having a holy war with each other. He didn't want her to work and she needed that outlet as her purpose in life. Mother went to California to so called, "help Tommy and his wife

Jewel." They had moved there in search of a better life for them and their two small children. mother had stayed with them as long as she humanly possibly could. She told me that Jewel was so mean to her that it became unbearable for her to continue to stay. Jewel had tried to turn Tommy against her. He was always in the middle because he truly loved his mom. They had become so deep into the SDA experience. Mother found a job near Tommy. Her employer was a member of the church that she attended every Sabbath. She talked about Mr. Mosley all the time. She had a glee in her eyes whenever she talked about him or her position. She never did say but I think that she was secretly in love with him, however, she was a true Christian to her vows (unlike me). She had found her niche in life and so she blossomed. Her face was aglow during that time while she was in California. Deddy talked with her frequently on the phone to put pressure on her. He told her that if she didn't come back soon there wasn't going to be a home for her to come back to. Janie was there with her. Mother stayed as long as she could. She then became ill. She tried to be strong but the situation of my daddy pressuring her was slowly but surely chipping away at her body, soul, and spirit. Her eyes began to look tired, the face that had shined with a glow was etched with sadness. She went home and daddy was moved to the room that had primarily been the kitchen. He, however, found his way to her bedroom when the spirit arose.

I was back and forth to their house so many times. I had either ran away from Joe Henry or he had put me out of the apartment. He always knew exactly where to find me when he got tired of taking care of himself. I would always go without putting up a fight because I wanted to continue to go to church.

One Friday night we had started out like two love birds. I was talking to him about my parents and how my dad was treating my mom. He disagreed and sided with my dad. Thus started world war ?? (I had lost count). One love bird was turning into a raging caged bird that was about to do what he did best. He started in on me about what a slut that I was and that without him I would never amount to nothing, "You needs ta do sump'n wid cho hair, yo got a onion head wid it slicked bak lak dat, wid yo' haf white ass, you needs ta git ou' in da sun." Not only was he tearing down my character. He hurt me so badly when he attached the way I looked (my self image). Both were equally important to me. I started to cry. He said, "you kin save yo' tears; yo is so ugly when you mess up yo' face." With that he was gone. I was left alone for the last time I thought. I found my straightening comb and my cheap hot curling iron. In two hours I was a different person after a refreshing bath, make up and a cute little black dress. My hair was perfect. I took a few sips of beer that was trying to keep cool in the Frigidaire. I left the apartment with a glimmer of confidence.

I walked down to Phillip's juke joint. I knew deep down in my soul that it wasn't a good move. I should have been at home studying my bible and praying but I didn't. Joe Henry's car was no where to be seen. Bill came up behind me and playfully put his hands over my eyes, "Guess who?" and I said, "Santa Claus or could it be Brier Rabbit?" Then I continued, "I must be the big bad wolf?" He picked me up and spun me around as if I were a piece of paper. We were both laughing so hard. He asked, "What cho do'n down heah?" I told him that I was looking for my husband. He said knowingly, "I knows exactly whar he is" with a big grin all his teeth were showing. He didn't have the same charismatic style that Joe Henry and Phillip had. He reminded me of a mountaineer. So rough around the edges yet he had an extremely funny characteristic that I needed to elicit. My eyes widened as if to say, 'tell me more.' I was flirting with him, but I did what I had to do to catch Joe Henry. He said, "Now don' git mad, he at sum women's house." He took a swig of his port wine that he had in his jacket pocket, he then gave me a swallow. He coaxed me to take as much as I wanted. I followed him out of the door. Phillip came out. He said, "Bill, now yo know yo' wrong." He looked at me, "Carrie if'n I wuz yo I would'n go wid Bill." Well he wasn't me. I got into the familiar car that Bill and Joe Henry had just fixed up.

We drove around the corner real slow with the headlights off. He pulled up to an old house, parked the car and told me to wait out here. I didn't see any signs of Joe Henry or his car anywhere on the street. Bill went and knocked on the door as if to ask if Joe Henry was inside. I got a strange feeling that Bill was trying to fool me. The older lady that answered the door seemed to have known him and gave him a hug before he got back inside his car. He said with disappointment, "She sed he wuz heah a few minutes ago." I asked, "who was the woman that he was with?" He drawled, "Naw Carrie, don' cho' go'n git mad, promise you wan' do nut'n crazy." Irritated I said, "I promise." He said, "Joe Henry's wid Thelma Hackman, hez mak'n a foo' ou' cho." We were driving away from the neighborhood. There was anger in his eyes. He said with so much conviction, "I'll take care o' you, Joe Henry's wrong ta trea' cho' lak dis." We were traveling at a higher speed in an unfamiliar area. I asked, "Where are we going, Bill?" I saw several corner stones on a hillside. It was a colored cemetery. Ironically there was a freshly dug gravesite awaiting the next tenant. He began talking again, "He's mak'n a foo' out cho', he 'n dat gir' iz probly laugh'n at cho' rat naw." He stopped the car and began grabbing at me. I hadn't realized just how drunk that he was until I noticed how slurred his speech was and the wine bottle was practically empty. He was out of control, tearing at my clothes. "Bill noooo please don't" I cried. Another car pulled up next to us and was parking. It must have been an area that young lovers went to neck (he wasn't my lover). I screamed as he tore at my panties. Then they were down. The more I screamed the stronger his hold was on me. Like a panther, he was on me. I tried to reason with him that those people in the other car would see us and it will get back to Joe Henry. He said, "Damn Joe Henry" as he had attempted to penetrate (his dick became soft as doctors cotton when I mentioned his brothers' name). I tried to be cool and calm as though I was going to go along with the program. I said, "Bill let's go somewhere else so nobody will see us." Out of the blue, he became angry at me. He said, "I knows 'bout cho you aint no good to Joe Henry." He began to cry loudly as if angry for the whole world. My consoling him didn't help. I tried to think fast, "We'll finish this later I need to go by the apartment to see if Joe Henry's there." That seemed to have appeased and sobered him up a tad. I pulled my panties up and my torn dress down. He kept looking at me as he drove me to my apartment. There were no lights on inside and Joe's car wasn't parked in its designated parking slot. I thought I was home free as I was about to open the door and jump out and run. The door was half way open. Bill grabbed my left arm as my right leg was kicking the door open trying to escape. He growled, "Whar you thank you go'n bitch?" I struggled and his grip tightened. I pleaded, "Bill please let me go. I've got to go home, Joe Henry will kill me when he finds out what you've done to me" I shouldn't have said it that way – or any way for that matter. He had renewed strength, anger and determination. "We gwine finish wah' we started lak you sed!" I reasoned, "I didn't start anything." No amount of pleading with him helped. I reassured him that I would never tell anybody about what had happened. He laughed sadistically, "You aint gwine say noth'n any how ta nobody, I'll see tah tha' " he was driving like a mad man. I sat as close to the passenger door as possible. I was able to open it when he came to a half stop. I almost escaped but his long arm and hand was like a vice. "Git bak in heah bitch o' I'll sho yo wha' fo'!" He reached over across my lap and yanked the door handle off. "Naw sid' dow'!" He yelled with his fist in my face. We were traveling in the direction of his parent's house. He took several gulps from another bottle of liquor. It smelled like whiskey. He held it toward my mouth, "heah, have some." I was totally sober. "No thanks. Please Bill take me home." He said, "You needs ta tak some of dis 'n relax." I pretended to take a sip. He had parked on the side of the road. He began breathing heavily as he was pulling off my clothes. He was having trouble with his belt buckle with his left hand because he kept me pinned to the door with his right hand, "Come heah gir' I knows wha' cho' needs" as he pulled me kicking and screaming. It seemed to excite him the more that I struggled. He flipped me on my back on the front seat. He came down so hard with his mouth. I felt his teeth as he tried to get me to give him some tongue. I moved my head side to side. He bit my bottom lip for I could taste the rusty taste of blood in my mouth. There were no lights in the car. He kept fumbling with his zipper as I fought like a rag doll. He finally got his dick out – he thrust it inside me with such anger. I felt so violated. He was taking something from me even after I had begged him not to. There was no love, joy or positive emotion. He took something that his brother had, and violated it. I literally felt sick, "Bill I'm going to throw up right now." I made a sound as if up-chuck was imminent. A car was coming up from the rear. He jumped up like a scaled cat, and threatened, "You don' mak a soun', you heah?" The car past by at a slow pace. I got a good look at it. It was his father's Cadillac. Bill quickly pulled up his pants and warned me again, "You don' te' nobody" I still felt nauseated and insisted I get out to vomit. He got out and attempted to hug me, "I'm so sorry I wuz so ruff." I saw that the Cad was backing up to where we were parked, they must have seen us. I felt sick but it would have to wait. My hair was tussled, my dress torn. I began running toward the car as it continued to back up toward us. Mammie Dell was driving it. She didn't seem to recognize me at first then she asked, "Is Bill okay? I thought that he was having car trouble" when she passed by. She said, "I wuz gwine go he'p him" I ran to the house where Muhdea was standing at the door looking confused, "Carrie wha' cho do'n dow' heah? And whar's Joe Henry at?" I was in such a daze as I rushed past her I hadn't thought about what I would tell Joe Henry's family. Billy's car pulled up into the driveway and he got out quickly. He kept his eyes focused on me as if to say, "I dare you" but I didn't care. I told them a part of the truth that we had gone in search of Joe Henry and then we thought he was down at The House. None of them seemed to believe nor bought the story that was so full of holes. It was even an insult to their intelligence. They all agreed that it was best that I go back home that night because of Joe Henry's temper. He would surely polish me off from what Bill had started.

When we left Bill was lying across the bed with all of his clothes on and his pants unzipped. Mammie Dell drove me back home – we were both so quiet. I felt so dirty and ashamed. It served me right to get raped. I had it coming to me with the way that I was dressed, all of the make up and that 'come hither' look. I had nobody else to blame but myself.

Surprisingly Joe Henry was already at home when we got there. Mammie Dell came in with me. She told him that she and I had gone down to Phillip's earlier then drove down to the country to get me out of the house – if she said it then it must be true. He had a puzzled look on his face. Before Mammie left she looked at me and shook her head. Then to Joe Henry she said, "You needs ta star' tak'n betta care o' yo' wife, sheza good gir' and you aint right. Why don' cho' take huh' wid cho' when you go ou'? shez gwine mess aroun 'n git huh sef kilt." He hung his head in shame, "Okay Boot" He never did ask what had happened to me with my busted lip, torn clothes and bruised ego.

That Saturday morning Joe and I arose bright and early. I cooked him some breakfast and fixed him a sack lunch to take to work. We were barely speaking to each other. Neither one of us wanted to be there but didn't know how or when to say good bye. He said that he was going to be a little late. I figured he'd be back Sunday morning. I washed out a few of my things by hand – we had been getting our clothes washed by an old colored couple who was trying to open up a wash, fluff, dry and fold business in our neighborhood. I pulled out the little suit case and a few plastic bags. It frightened me to think of me being on my own. I needed the closeness of Joe Henry when he made time for me. I put the bags and suitcase away. I knew that Joe Henry loved a spic and span clean apartment. I spent most of the morning cleaning it. I fixed his favorite meal – fried chicken, rice and gravy. I didn't try making any more biscuits to avoid getting him angry at me. So light bread it would have to do. I sliced tomatoes and waited and waited – until four o'clock that morning. He was lit up like a Christmas tree. There was no appeasing him with the home cooked meal I had prayed "Lord give me courage give me wisdom." I think that satan intercepted my prayers. Joe Henry insisted I tell him who I had been with. It was the most foolish thing that I could have uttered from my split lip (and the dumbest). He was about to become violent and enough was enough – "Joe Henry sit down, I do have a lot to tell you. I'm tired of you asking me and you beating me." I explained my pitiful rationale for the past three years of my being unfaithful to him. I began with, "You accuse me of being with 'some nigger' when we first got married, and I honestly hadn't been with no man except for you. You beat me unmercifully for crimes that I hadn't committed. You've gotten several women pregnant, yet you made me pay for your anger at them and for the crime that was yours." I stared straight ahead afraid to look into his eyes. I continued slowly and deliberately, "I had my first sexual experience while I was working with the Shalle's. It was with four men while I was in Florida. There was another time with a man who used to live up the street from here." He sat there dumbfounded as I got the burden of infidelity off of my shoulders. "There was another man that you thought was yours and Phillip's friend. His name was Cleo the real handsome man that got killed in a car accident," I groped for courage as I whispered, "and your brother Billy." I thought as he was trying to process the devastating information that I layed him with, "Let's see did I leave anyone out?" He began pacing and then literally running from one end of the apartment to the other. He picked up the bric-a-brak ceramic figures that I had been decorating our apartment with. He slammed everything that he got his hands on. He was breathing hard his nose flaring and for a short time, at a loss for words. I said as I sat on the far end of the couch, "I'm so tired of you asking me about who I've been with. I've answered you so you have to tell me about your women." Wow – was I not the brightest star in the sky – he said with conviction and sarcasm, "I ain't go' ta' te' you a fuck'n thang." He started demanding that I tell him details of who the men were, he wanted to know where I met them, "did thay mak you fee' good?" How big wuz thay dicks?" I had made a big mistake – I should have confessed my sins to God but…

Let the beatings continue. He went into second gear, "You gwine die ta'nigh'. Immo' choke da' live'n shit ou' cho'." He drew back and crowned me harder than he had ever done. I saw red and I knew that it would be my last night on this earth. I lost my balance as he slapped my face over and over again. I ran to the bedroom which was surely a rat trap. There was nowhere to run. He grabbed me and threw me on the bed. His hands tightened around my throat. I had given him enough ammunition to polish me off, which it seemed that he was doing as he put more pressure around my scrawny throat. My screaming, begging and pleading was stopped. I went limp under all of the pressure. But something happened that he stopped for a moment, I was able to get just enough air in my lungs to grunt so hard – he jumped off of me because I had done just what he had said he was going to do, and that was to choke the shit out of me. It wasn't a pretty site nor was it a bed of fragrant roses. He got up off of me, it was all over him. He got so busy trying to clean the pasty bomb shell goo off of his clothes. He had forgotten what he had set out to do and that was to control and humiliate me. I got up and drew a tub full of water. All is fair in love and war and I had to use whatever tactics that was at hand. I had taken all the bed linen off of his bed (not our bed) and threw them in the trash.

It seemed that he had gotten his second wind after he had gotten a bath and was putting on his leisure wear. I put on my robe as I heard him gather his key ring. I went to see what he was doing. I needed to know…

"I thought we were trying to work out our problems." He was about to go down the stairs. He turned and said, "fuck you bitch." He was walking down the stairs. I reached for a heavy liquor decanter that I had filled with green color water (my decoration) that was on the banister. I screamed "you are not going to leave me up here alone any more." He looked at me with so much contempt then turned to continue to descend down stairs. Before I knew what happened I had brought the decanter down as hard as I could on the back of his head. It made a strange thud sound. The bottle remained in my hand. He staggered then broke his fall by grasping the side rail. He was still groping as his legs began to give way. Blood was oozing from the site that I had struck him. "God, what have I done?" His eyes rolled back in his head. He sat for a minute then stumbled back upstairs mumbling incoherently. I was so scared that he was going to die. I said, "I'll call the ambulance." He answered quickly, "No, I'll be a'ight." We both apologized because we were both maxed out and at the end of the rope. He made me promise not to discuss the incident with his family.

He found something to do early Sunday morning. I knew that he wouldn't return anytime soon. I finished packing and called a cab to take me to the trailway bus stop in downtown Meridian. I put on an old hat (disguise) and old tattered clothes that nobody would recognize. I had already discussed my plan with Boy Baby. He would pick me up at the Los Angeles Trailway Bus Station Tuesday morning – free at last. I was so scared traveling alone but nothing could ever be as bad as my life living with Jack the Fucking Ripper.

I was out of the frying pan into the fire. I didn't see it at first because I was so excited about seeing so many new things. It was so thrilling to see all of the bright lights at night. They reminded me of sparkling jewels that I had only seen in jewelry store windows. I was amazed at all the mountains as they stood majestically even from a distance. It was incredible to see them up close. The rock formations were a reminder to me that God had created those magnificent mountains and they were still standing. He was my creator and had brought me through such an ordeal yet I was still above ground and able to see how great he was. It took me in a round about way to realize that he must have had better plans for me, away from Meridian. I had never traveled any further than to Jackson, Mississippi or Lisma, Alabama and yes, to Florida. I had been given a second chance. It was going to be so much better as I smiled thinking about Lottie who was already living out in California with her little girl Cheryl. They were staying at Boy Baby's house along with mother and Janie (Mother had decided to go back again).

The bus trip was tiring. I had to be extra careful not to talk to any strangers so I had been forewarned. I was still in one piece when Boy Baby came to pick me up in his V.W. bug. We drove back partially on the freeway. That was an experience in itself. I figured that I would never be able to drive under such fast pace conditions. Boy Baby was briefing me on everything except – when we got to his house – my first educational lesson was it was Jewel's house (I wished that somebody would have told me earlier). She had Boy Baby on a short leash, and when she cracked the whip he jumped. He certainly didn't get that from Deddy.

Lottie and I shared a room in the back of the house. I was made to feel uncomfortable when I ate the food that Jewel had cooked. She complained that PEOPLE were eating her out of house and home. Lottie had a job in a nursing home and she bought food for she and I plus she gave them money for the room. It was never enough. Janie was babysitting for them without receiving payment, although she was much younger than me she knew how to handle Jewel much better than I ever could.

I found a job in a drug store that had a snack bar for its shoppers. My salary was less than minimum wage. It was based on tips mostly. Sometimes it was good but most of the times business was slow. I didn't have the go-getter personality that some of the seasoned waitresses had. They would lure customers to their station after they would have sat at my assigned tables. That lasted about two weeks. I had worked so hard and had nothing to show for it. That was the first salary paid to me by a check. It was basically the same as the salary I had back home with the Shalle's. After Uncle Sam had deducted its two cents worth from it. There was a young man that I had met there just as I was about to resign. He was totally smitten by me. He seemed to have been a real nice person, not pressuring me into anything such as sex. He just wanted to talk a lot. He walked me back to Boy Baby's (excuse me) Jewel's house. He sat and talked with my brother who seemed to trust him enough for him to take me out to eat and to a drive-inn movie. He remained a gentleman and I wasn't interested.

Boy Baby had became a vegetarian. I wasn't. they wouldn't allow me to bring any meats into the house. However I could bring money in for my room and board. Lottie could tell that I wasn't happy and becoming more upset about my arrangement. There was so much pressure to attend church every Sabbath. I was nagged until I gave in to their strenuous rituals that the members were expected to practice if you want to be saved such as: no make up, no sleeveless dresses, no jewelry (except maybe a wedding band – they mostly allowed a wrist watch to be used instead of the band – it was debatable), no short dress attire above the knees, no pork, no shrimp, no catfish, no blues, no – it was a lot to give up and the list got longer and longer including nooooo dancing. Ouch – I gave it all up and joined a SDA church headed by pastor Robertson. He seemed to have had hate in his heart. He had the air of a pompous arrogant man who was above his congregation. He professed to be a prophet. I was urged to be baptized and be saved. I got baptized and tried so hard to fit into an unhappy lifestyle. I believed that God wants things in moderation, not a people who were keeping the Sabbath Day and hating their neighbors during the rest of the week. Another thing, one cannot eat nor pay their way into heaven.

There were so many temptations that seemed to have doubled when I saw so many many couples at church. They seemed so happy as they held hands while they worshipped together. I began to get a burning desire, an itch that could not be scratched except by one man. I did everything that I could to forget about him. Lottie had talked to folks back home. She said that he (Joe Henry) had gone out to my parent's house acting so meek and lowly to get close to our family to get information about my whereabouts. I didn't want to give in to him so I told Jim that I would go to the drive-in movie again. We went to a Mexican café before the show. He brought me tacos and shrimps I hadn't tasted meat for so long. It was glorious to bite into something that wasn't vegetarian and it looked and tasted likemeat. We saw the movie – Lawrence of Arabia. I fell asleep on it and him. I apologized to Jim because I felt so bad since he had made his intentions known to me. He wanted marriage and I wasn't a free woman. It was sad that there still wasn't any sparks. I broke it off with him.

There was a young enterprising doctor from Meridian who was opening up a medical clinic and he was advertising for a receptionist. I interviewed for the position. It paid better than the waitress job and I would be off on Saturdays – Tommy's rule – so that I could go to church. I often wondered why the good doctor needed me since his business was so slow. It was in a rather large building that had been transformed from what had been two separate warehouses. The upper level had been gutted out and in its place was a drafty eerie sounding echoes. I was forever looking over my left shoulder and was sure that my childhood ghosts had found me. My responsibilities were to keep the floors clean. I even swept and mopped them daily. I swept the sidewalks out front of the office. I learned how to clean and autoclave his medical instruments. Most of his clients must have came after hours because I made appointments that were few and far between. The phone seldom rang. He did have a patient who was anxious to talk with me especially when he knew that Dr. Warden took his two hour lunch break everyday at the same time. One afternoon he waited to come by after the doctor was out of the building. He talked a big game on how much stamina he had and how he was gonna make me the happiest woman on earth. He certainly was looking fine with his stylish suit and tie, his hair was neat and trimmed. I was at my wits end with desire so I finally gave in to him. He wanted to have me in the Good Doctor's personal office and I agreed. I didn't have any shame or feelings of remorse only – Poh lil' thang. It engorged as big as a number two pencil and no motion of the ocean was going to help Mr. Pencil Dick. I was so frustrated when he finished, "Wow" he said, "that was good." For him but definitely not for me. I heard Dr. Warden's car in the back as he was parking. I had to rush Mr. Pen – I mean Dr. Warden's patient (who needed a penile transplant not implant). I told him "You have to hurry because he's coming through the back door at any moment. He's back sooner than I had expected him." His patient had seated himself in the waiting room and tried to talk his smooth talk to Dr. Warden who looked at us as if he knew what had happened on his leather sofa in his office. He told me about a week later that his business was so bad that he didn't need me anymore (he did move his business practice back to Meridian). There were rumors that he had been murdered because he was married to a white woman.

I received word that Joe Henry wanted to talk to me. I phoned him from a phone booth. I needed some privacy and didn't want Boy Baby and Jewel into my wax. I saw that I wasn't making any headway with my finances. So I informed Joe Henry that I was coming back but was thinking about getting a divorce. "Carrie, we don' needs ta tak 'bout tha' rat naw, lets wai' til you git back heah." Tommy was beside himself. He argued "When you leave a hog in a sty wallowing in all its filth, when you return he ain't gonna change, he will always be a hog." I knew that Boy Baby was right. I had a lot of respect for my big brother for trying to look after me while I was in his (Jewel's) house. I needed some time to think.

I went on short walks through the neighborhood and to the corner produce market. It was there that another man approached me. He had been watching me each time that I went in to buy some fresh fruit. He said that he lived in an apartment in Hollywood. It certainly would be good to have some company because I was drowning in my dire loneliness. I could tell by the way that his pants fitted him in front that he was happy to see me and that he was eager to please. I got into his car. We stopped and got some take out burger and a fifth of wine. His apartment turned out to be a room and a small bath. We listened to music and danced. I felt so fancy free after taking a shower together. The man was packed in every place that mattered. He saw that I was staring at him with so much longing. I must have been drooling and licking my chops. He kept dancing in front of me, as I sat mesmerized by his exotic movements. He tauntingly asked me, "do you want this?" as he touched his engorged penis. He reiterated, "do you really want it?" I said, "yes" as I continued to stare in amazement at how huge it had became. I laid down and watched him as he continued to arouse me with his joy stick. I held my hands out to him while he was lowering the shades and dimming the lights. I was lying on the edge of the bed. He came over smiling at me knowing that he had me just where he wanted me. He said sweet and low, "close your eyes, I got something for you." I was expecting some strawberries (from the product market). I opened wide. He was standing next to the bed as he began breathing deeper and deeper. I felt something warm and hard on my lips. He played with my mouth with his dick. It was beautiful as a sculpture. I licked the shaft, the head then looked at him as he was getting so much pleasure. I had never had oral sex before then. It was intoxicating as he was allowed to slide it in and out of my mouth. Every fiber in my body was alive with desire. I tasted a little bit of the creamy cum. I grabbed his taunt bottom. He pulled away and said, "not yet baby, I want this to last longer." I was breathing so hard and was about to whimper still reaching for him. He said in a whisper, "you need to help me now easy does it." I had never felt that kind of desire that was so different. We restrained ourselves as he kissed me on my breast then my lips. I opened my mouth then he was inside with his penis. I let him go as deep as I could without gagging. He screamed out, "I'm cumming baby!" He stood there frozen as I let some of it ooze down my throat and the rest squirted on my face and then onto the bed. We embraced each other for about an hour, then he was ready to go at it again. He became so hard as he climbed on top of me. I screamed so loudly and clawed at his body. He gave me just what I needed since I had arrived in California. When we finished both of us were too spent to move. He finally said, "I have someone that I want you to meet." I was still a bit tipsy and didn't know how to respond. He was searching for the right words. He said in other words that he thought that I could bring in a lot of money for both of us. I got up and immediately sobered up as I was putting on my clothes. I said, "You got me so wrong, I don't want to earn money for turning tricks." I began to panic as I looked out the window and saw that the sun was setting. "I've got to go, will you take me home?" He answered in a rather sleepy voice, "I can't, I don't have the car anymore. It was borrowed." I was about to turn on the water works. He saw the look of a frightened young girl and said, "You'll have to take the bus back home." I saw so many buses going in all directions. He got up, put his pants on, "You'll be fine. Here is some money for the bus fare." He counted out forty dollars from the wad that he had stuffed in his bill folder. He explained the bus line that I needed to take and the transfers. He hugged me as I walked out. He said, "You know where I am if you change your mind."

I safely got on the bus. I saw him as he stood in the window of his hotel room. I was going in the right direction back to Tommy's house. I asked a lot of questions to assure that I got on the next transfer. It was good when I got to South Central area that was more familiar to me. I never did contact Mr. Delicious. I did learn something about myself from him – yummy – I must have had a death wish judging from all of the men that I had encountered since arriving in Los Angeles. I was in harms way. I might as well have stayed in Meridian for the choices that I was making wasn't conducive with what a professed Christian would do. It wasn't a moment too soon to get out of Tommy's house. I let Joe Henry know that I would come home but I would not take any more of his crap.

Joe Henry had moved out of the projects one month after I left. He had quit working for Mr. Wade and had opened up Joe Louis Café in downtown Meridian. He was staying out in the country at The House during the week and on the weekends he was sleeping in a rat infested cubby hole over the café. It had been used as an office by the previous owner. There was a toilet with a sink about twenty feet from the makeshift bedroom. The place had been so popular years ago. There was an extra large dance floor. I remembered seeing people dancing as I passed by when I was much younger. They even had had a live band that could be heard up and down the block on 5th Street especially on Friday and Saturday nights.

Business was no where comparable to what it used to be. It was as if trying to revive a dead man. He had opened it up in hopes that he could compete with Phillip who had a mindset of business first, good times later. Joe Henry was so excited for me to see his new business venture (just like the apartment). In his minds eye it must have been the most fabulous place with so many potentials. When we arrived he asked me to close my eyes and don't peek. I waited till he fumbled with the key ring that had multiple keys that he may have had since his childhood. He led me inside as I continued to keep my eyes shut. The blast of stale beer and cigarette was pungent enough to take my breath away. "Tah dah! You can open your eyes." It was the most dreary place that I had ever seen. The four booths were in dire need of upholstering. The long bar had obviously been the brunt of many bar room brawls. There were so many slashes on the padded edges. There seemed to have been bullet holes at the far end where the outdated cash register was stationed. There were supposed to have been ten bar stools – four of the seat had been removed and only the stem was left as a reminder of what used to be. The other six were lopsided and beckoned the patron to sit at their own risk. As I looked around my mouth was open in sheer shock. Each area that I was shown outdid the previous. I didn't want to burst his bubble but someone would eventually have to. The next stop on the tour was to the kitchen. He had bought all of the over used stoves that had blackened grease that had been caked on it probably since the place opened. It was an accident ready to happen with all of the grease. There were no windows only a vent that went nowhere because it too had became clogged with filth. I felt faint from the foul odor where food was to be prepared. The old refrigerator moaned and groaned as it was dying a natural death. He said that it only needed to be defrosted and would be okay. The floors were disastrous with the same gooey film that stuck to the soles of my shoes. I walked back to the front of the café and he followed. It was then that he admitted that it was a little (I muttered a lot) rundown and all that it needed was a little elbow grease. (I thought that it had enough grease in it already). Even the old neon signs were faded and flickering erratically and was trying to stay on when he flicked the switch on. I wanted to run but had came back all of the 2,000 miles from California. It was as good as it was going to get. I promised him that I would help him as much as I could. He knew that I had plans to continue attending church and wouldn't be available from Friday evening until Saturday evening at sunset. That was the time that he needed me the most. I moved all of my clothes upstairs after he had bought another bedroom set so that we could have some privacy. I stayed out at my parent's house on the Sabbath. I had forgotten to bring extra knock about clothes for after church. I made a surprise visit to the café. It wasn't an intentional act of spying. When I walked in dressed in a gorgeous suit, I had on a hat that matched my outfit. I looked smashing as if I was auditioning for a fashion magazine. All eyes turned to me. Suddenly the café was so quiet you could hear a rat pissing on cotton. I kept walking in my self assured stride. There were so many people (mostly men) who were seated in the booths and at the (workable) bar stools. I heard someone do a cat call and then a whistle. I was really working it as I switched over to the far end of the bar. Then I became devastated when I saw Joe Henry as he stood next to the bar and Cassy Gipson was busy bursting black heads and pulling his ingrown hairs from his face. He had his eyes closed and she had her back turned away from the doorway. I said, "Joe Henry!" loudly. Everybody turned towards me and the lying cheaters too who were so shocked to see me there on the weekend. I exploded forgetting about being a Christian. I told her to get her fucking hands off of my husband. Joe Henry meanwhile was making it worse by saying that it was nothing she was only helping him out and he had asked her to groom him before he shaved. I wondered then asked, "Is she here to bathe you too?" Cassy became angry and acted like I was the outsider invading her space and she wanted to jump on me. Joe Henry told her that she had to leave. She screamed at him as she glared at me, "I ain't going nowhere!" I ran back to the kitchen and came back with a butcher knife. I knew that I was in my rights to be with Joe Henry as he was still my husband. She said as she was leaving (I had the knife drawn and would have plunged it into her gut), "You should have stayed where you were in California, when you moved you loose and that's the Mississippi rule" she added tauntingly. The more she talked the angrier that Joe Henry became. He yelled out as he was pulling his pistol out just enough for her to see it. He lunged at her, "You git ou' heah you stank'n bitch!" She was shocked but she did leave screaming profanities at both of us. He needed an Oscar for his award winning performance for my benefit. I decided not to return back to my mother's house that afternoon. I stayed with my husband to try to salvage the marriage that was doomed again.

My family was flourishing with the birth of baby(s). Joyce was the first to give birth to her son named Antoine; Lottie had her first born daughter Cheryl; Connie and Tommie G. had a girl named Patrice; Tommy (Boy Baby) and Jewel had their first child Andre; Bennie had her son, John Jr.; Janie's son was named Dion; James and Jeanette's first born was Brian; and Willie and Vivia had their oldest child, Wendy. All these "first-borns" arrived within a span of 4-5 years. They were all beautiful/handsome. I began to get maternal instinct I could picture me as a mom. I knew that I would be a good parent. I wanted a child so badly. I told Joe Henry who acted like he wanted the same as me. During sexual intercourse he would say, "I'm gwine pregnant cho'" It never did happen but not for a lack of trying. I went to see Dr. Stoddard who examined me. He said there was no reason that I couldn't get pregnant. So he prescribed hormones to regulate me and antibiotic because I had some kind of infections. I took the pills religiously. I became so sick. I thought maybe I had a tumor after about two months of taking the medication. My stomach stayed sour. Lottie had just given birth to her second daughter Tina (Bug). I was happy for her but too sick to get out of bed. I went back to the doctor and explained all of my symptoms including I had not been regulated (I had a strange period). I'm too sick to continue to take these pills." He examined me again. He said, "It worked you are two months pregnant." He asked, Is that what you and your husband wanted?" I was ecstatic as I smiled uncontrollably. I said, "yes of course sir he wants to have children." I shook his hand and we wound up hugging. I literally floated out of the office. I couldn't think of anything else except that I was going to have a baby!

Joe Henry picked me up at the doctor's clinic. He asked, "Are you a'right, whaz wrong wid yo' stomach?" If I kept it in any longer I would burst so I blurted it out, "Joe Henry I'm pregnant, we are going to have a baby." He looked at me as if I had just landed on the earth from mars. His words would always be etched and would echo in my brain. He stopped the car and looked at me with so much disgust as he screamed, "What tha God damn hell do I needs wid a baby?" The words hurt so bad, I could never describe how badly I felt. It cut deeper than a knife. No matter how he felt I wasn't going to give my baby up. It was his child too so he would have to accept it.

At six months along I was still trying to help out at the café as I had promised. My belly was beginning to show. I was so proud to be carrying Joe Henry's child. He began to come around that he was going to be a father. He took an interest when the fetus was kicking or tumbling. He felt my tummy and would say, "He gwine be a football player." I began to tire easily so the doctor warned me to stay off of my feet.

Joe Henry usually wouldn't leave me alone in the café. One evening during the weekday he left and was gone about an hour. He said he had to run some errands and get some supplies. He left the pistol in the cash register. He came back as I as selling a pack of cigarettes to one of our customers. He was carrying a little boy who was about six months old. I was in a state of shock so I just stared at them in dismay. Joe Henry had a diaper bag in one hand and the child who was asleep with his head nestled on Joe's shoulder. I asked him in hopes that wouldn't tell me the truth that time, "Joe Henry, whose baby is that?" My heart began to pound and the child that I was carrying in my belly moved suddenly and with such force I had to stop and rub my belly to calm my unborn child who must have been reacting to the tension that I was feeling. Joe Henry was groping for words and once they were uttered they didn't make any sense to me. He said, as he was patting the child's back and swaying (in a swinging motion) in an attempt to keep the child asleep. "His momma don' wan' him no mo'. She tol' me ta take'em." I had so many questions all crowding my mind. I wished that it had been a nightmare. The sleeping child began to squirm about in Joe's arms. His eyes were focusing on its new surroundings and the only familiar object was the person who was holding him. He clung to Joe Henry for dear life. He must have also felt the tension that was surrounding him. I tried to ease the scowl that was apparently on my face. He allowed me to touch his plump hands and arms when he felt that I wasn't a threat to him. I held out both my hands to him and he allowed me to cuddle him. We all sat down in a makeshift office space (that was actually a large walk-in closet). Joe took the little boy who was fretting as he looked for the familiar face. I waited for a response. "Carrie dis is Tweedy Boy Brandon." I continued to wait, "Why do you have this baby and why are you bringing him to me?" He was looking down not daring to give me eye contact to assure me that maybe it was his nephew. We were facing each other, "Carrie, he's my baby, Cassy is his Mama." Oh God – I had been warned to stay as calm as I could during my pregnancy so that I would have a healthy baby. Maybe he was trying to make me miscarry by getting me so upset. That wasn't going to happen. The baby that I held in my arms was Joe Henry's. He had finally fessed up but why now? How could he do this to me? I caught myself and answered, "evil for evil, tit for tat, goose and gander." This was his ultimate thus far. I was carrying our child which I wasn't about to do any harm, nor would I hurt the innocent baby boy that favored both his parents – I wanted to scream – the voice inside of me warned me, "You'll hurt your baby that you're carrying." I kept quiet.

Tweedy Boy began to fret again, Joe Henry found his bottle and took him from me (forgive me Lord – love thy neighbor – I'm wrestling to overcome). Tears had welled up in my eyes once again – and as I write this – I was glad when a customer broke the tension. He sat down and requested a pack of Camel cigarettes. He lit one then requested, "Give me a quart of Falstaff beer please." I had stopped smoking and drinking. I thought about it that I shouldn't be selling liquor or cigarettes. I must have been getting a test from God.

Joe Henry was taking care of his son – Phillip came by and talked with Joe Henry who had just gotten his son quiet and had made him a pallet on the floor to take a nap. They argued back and forth. The last word from Joe Henry was, "He ain't go'n no whar wid dat bitch, she used him ta try ta trap me." The word about Joe Henry's baby must have snowballed out to my mom. Lottie came by and told me, "Carrie, you are a fool if you let him do you like this, he don't want you and he definitely don't love you." She added, "Mother said you can come home, you don't deserve this kind of abuse." I stayed for two more weeks. Cassy's grandmother had come by while I was away and took the baby. She was not one – that I had been told – that Joe Henry wanted to cross. He finally gave up after keeping the baby for three days, and I was still pregnant.

Meridian was having its fair share of growing pains. There were so many changes that were being made. Shopping malls were sprouting up in every direction of the city and on the outskirts of town. All of the new businesses meant new job opportunities for so many families – that is if you were white.

Coloreds were still looked upon as second class citizens and less than that because we didn't know how to exercise our rights to vote that could change the course of our lives. Most of us were too afraid to take the first step in the voting process. We needed to be registered to vote and to some whites that meant that we were dissatisfied with the way things were with being the so called inferior to whites who continued to act superior to us. We were supposed to know our place and stay there. One of the main suppression that we experienced were our extremely inferior segregated schools. Education was and will always be the cornerstone for the foundation of successful lives. It would open up so many doors that we didn't know were even available to us because we had been brainwashed all of our lives. We were told that we were less than whites and even their dogs. We had been accepting that they would always have better jobs than us. I was yearning to be empowered through higher education. I wanted for me and my family to have the same opportunities as those who had been born so called, 'fortunate' to have the right skin color. I'd always felt that there was more to it than what I had been taught by my parents – we were all created equal. God wasn't a respecter of people's race but by our deeds. The child that I carried would have more to be proud of than I. I would see to it. I wanted the same God given rights as those who didn't know of any other life style. To keep us down by keeping us in the dark was so cruel. The saddest thing about our state of being were the shackles that kept us from moving forward had been unlocked for a long time yet we continued to self imprison ourselves behind many open doors. I'm sure that those who were evil enough to benefit from our ignorance of the bondage must have found it amazing that we refused to let go of our way of life because change is unknown and that was frightening. We were ripe but not quite ready to stand up for our rights to higher education, the key to our self worth, self esteem and self actualization. It was time for growth. All things happen for a reason, "when the student is ready then the teacher will suddenly appear" (The Twelve Steps). We were all excited that there was a movement that was to help us coloreds to register to vote and to boycott the white owned businesses that continued its' unfair practices against my race. Some offenders who were in official capacities were the major culprits. Some of them were the leaders in the Klu Klux Klan – an organization of white supremacy.

It was about the middle of the year of 1964 when Joe Henry and I had heard about the group of people called The Freedom Riders. They were seen up and down the streets of Meridian. Joe Henry mentioned that he knew one of the young men in question. His name was James Chaney. Joe had started serving breakfast at Joe Louis Café. He and his lazy bone waitress prepared the meal early every morning for a construction crew that was stationed in Meridian for three months. Joe said that on the last day that the Freedom Riders were in town they had came by and ate breakfast. Their last meal must have been at Joe

Louis Café. The devastating news came back to the townspeople that the officials had reported, 'that the bodies of all three men had been found, shot and buried near Philadelphia, Mississippi.'

Lottie's mother in law lived in Philadelphia. She became worried that the elderly woman may be in harms way. We both drove down there to assure her safety. While we were there we went in gathering (asking perfect strangers for monetary donations for our church in turn we handed out pamphlets). We went to a nearby neighborhood and went door to door. Most of the people were edgy and afraid to answer the door for us since the murder of those Freedom Riders. I noticed that during all the time that we were there, out in the field, there was a German Sheppard that followed us. Usually I'm afraid of all dogs no matter what size they were. I felt safe in its presence. This animal stayed with us until we were safe inside the old lady's house later on that afternoon. We didn't get any contributions but we did get something much greater and that was protection from above. Angels do come in so many forms.

I was staying out at my parent's house because of all the commotion and dangerous conditions there in town. Joe Henry didn't want me and his unborn child in harms way. There were several colored churches that had been set afire because of meetings that were being held to inform the coloreds how to register to vote. My father came home one evening and said that the church that he attended frequently had been burned down to the ground. It was located on highway 45 the route that we took to go to The House. Mount Pleasant – the building – was destroyed but not the dreams that so many parishioners had. They kept the faith that there was going to be a brighter day. It wasn't too long before they had erected another building on the same site but was built from a more solid foundation. They used bricks in building it. Some times when we go through the fiery furnace we become stronger as the precious metal of gold.

My pregnancy was coming along very well except for those pesky infections that I was experiencing. The last time that I had seen the doctor about the problem he told me that he was bound by law to report it to the health department. I had STD (sexually transmitted disease). He asked me about my sexual contacts. It was my husband only – I added that I had sexual intercourse three months before I got pregnant with a man in California. He said that I would need to have surgery under general anesthesia to remove the Bartholomen's gland that is located in the vaginal area. He did an incision and drainage of the excruciatingly painful abscess. He told me that he needed to treat my husband with antibiotics also. Joe Henry agreed to the treatments. I didn't get any more abscesses again. I did share more information with the Good Doctor about some of the women that I knew had sex with Joe. He reported it because there was an epidemic in Meridian at that time.

It had been decided that it would be best for me to continue to stay out at my parent's home to complete my pregnancy. Through it all I was reasonably happy as if though I had invented being in the family way. I resembled a may pop (I may pop at any moment). I was near my due date and I was hoping that the baby could just wait to be delivered at least until after the family's Christmas dinner. Mother did what she did best on Christmas. It was a feast to remember. After over indulging I began having more gas than usual. On December the 26th, 1965 I felt a gush of warm fluid stream down my legs and onto the floor. I looked down, I stood in a puddle of blood, I yelled out, "Mother, come here, something is wrong!" She came quickly. I saw horror on her face. "Where is Joe Henry?" I said, "He's over at the café." She made several attempts to call him. "WE can't wait for him." We both knew that an ambulance was out of the question because they were busy already with the multiple Christmas holiday car accidents and calls for house fires from faulty lights on decorated trees.

Deddy wasn't at home. Tommie Gathright drove me and my mother to Mattie Hersy County Hospital (I didn't have insurance). By the time that I got into the emergency room, the new red over coat that mother bought me was soaked with blood. My baby wasn't moving as well as it should have. I had to have an emergency c-section. I must not have been under the anesthesia too well because I heard them say, 'we may loose both of them.' I was feeling so much pain in my pelvic bone as if they were using a saw. I literally tried to jump off the operating table. More anesthesia was administered. The next thing that I recall was in the morning. I was told that my baby was going to be okay. The nurse said that he was born a little bit blue (cyanotic) his color was better. She wanted to know what race was his father. His skin was so fair. He didn't have colored features, neither was his hair that was somewhat sandy. I thought he was going to have grayish eyes like my mother. They were warming him so I had to wait to hold him I looked around and saw that I was getting blood transfusion. It was my fourth unit. I was attended by Meridian's finest obstetricians. She had ordered that I be placed in a Trendelenburg position (my head lower than my heart and feet) to raise my extremely low blood pressure. I had gone into shock after loosing all of that blood.

I got to see my beautiful baby boy. He was absolutely gorgeous. He looked so much like his father. I was in and out of consciousness. Joe Henry was finally located and he came to visit. I must have cursed him out. I told him, "You get the hell out of here." He relayed that to me after I was on the mend. He said he was trying to get people to donate blood – we named our baby boy Joe Henry Mathis, Jr.

Joe Sr. and Bigman had made a last ditch effort to open up another café (hole in the wall) after Joe Louis folded. It was on the outskirts of town in an area that even the poorest colored folks didn't want to go. Even if they did it would mean going through a muddy red clay maze to get there. Oh there were some attempts by a few of his cronies to stop by and give the Bopsy twins some business. They would get their vehicles stuck on the unpaved road to the joint. There was limited inventory such as sodas, nabs, beer, tin cans of sardines and crackers, bologna sandwiches (and White Lightening sold under the table). He and his dad were their own best customers. They ate and drank most of their profits. The building had been an old house that had been purposely gutted out for the purpose of a juke joint. Several enterprising people who saw potential in it had opened it with high hopes, but closed it down faster than grease lightening.

Before Joe Henry closed it down completely he told me that he wanted me and Jo Jo to come over and spend the night with him because I was getting antsy and acting cranky. Jo Jo was six weeks old. It was time to "let's get it on." I packed up a few things for my baby boy including his formula since I wasn't producing enough breast milk for my hungry little man.

Generally speaking Jo Jo had been a good baby but while there in the see mo' holes than walls (it was drafty) he began to get sick. It started with mild wheezing then coughing. He was crying inconsolably. We both thought it was colic. Joe Henry said he had experienced this with Tweedy Boy. He tried blowing cigarette smoke on the soft spots of Jo Jo's head. He continued to cry even more. There was no calming him. I tried walking with him then burping him. Joe Henry took him from me and began blowing the smoke directly in Jo Jo's face. He coughed several times then turned a grayish color. He started crying again but that time it was much weaker. I noticed his little chest was drawing inward when he breathed (retraction). Joe Henry was still trying to blow more smoke in our baby's face who was lying limp. I grabbed him because he was gagging and gasping for air. I yelled angrily, "Joe Henry, take us to the hospital now or he's going to die." On the way there I held him up against my chest and patted his tiny back. He started crying a little bit lustfully. His color was somewhat better when we got to the ER he was whisked away from us. They drew blood works and placed him on a ventilator for a while. They put in an IV. The emergency room doctor scolded both of us for the ignorant act of blowing smoke in our child's face, "You could have killed him". They kept him overnight in an oxygen tent. I took him to my moms house. My needs would have to wait, my son came first.

JoJo grew up wanting to be just like his daddy. He was The Man at head start. He had been given the titles: The Teacher, The Judge, Jury, and The Peace Keeper. All of his playmates were afraid of him. He had no fear of anyone.

Joe Henry and I continued to try to stay together. Our marriage was in shams. JoJo needed a male figure so that he could learn how to become a man. I was so busy studying to get my GED so that I could apply for an upcoming LPN – Licensed Practical Nurse – course. Joe Henry offered to watch JoJo because quite frankly no one else wanted to do it. His father had spoiled him so badly till I really didn't trust anyone else but his dad and Muhdea to keep him.

I was still staying out at my parent's house. Joe Henry brought JoJo back home to me. I noticed that there were a lot of scratch marks on Joe Henry's arms and face. He said he had fallen, I thought, "That must have been some fall." He remained distracted, angry and acted distant. My bubbly little two and a half year old boy was so happy to see me. He climbed up onto my lap and playfully started punching me. He was laughing. He said, "Cassy did that." (he showed me). I got a demonstration of what his daddy had done to Cassy. He was stuttering, but was able to get the gist of the fight over to me. Of course Joe Henry denied the whole thing. He said that JoJo had seen too many movies. I studied harder than I had ever done while I was in regular school. I couldn't depend on Joe Henry.

I was getting beatings, slapped around and humiliated by Joe Henry for no apparent reason. I went to see a lawyer to file for a divorce. I informed Joe Henry of my plans. He grabbed me so hard on both of my arms and shook me my teeth rattled. He said in a threatening tone of voice, "Bitch, I promise you if'n you go through wid dis you aint gwine see JoJo eva agin, and anotha thang if'n you eva repor' me to da cops, I promise I wi' ki' ya."

My husband was a man of his word. I had seen him in action as he would pick a fight then beat the tar out of the unsuspecting victim. He started a fight with me while we were in town shopping. Joey was staying down in the country with Muhdea. Joe Henry slapped me so hard I had ringing in my ears. There were several witnesses but they didn't do anything. I was able to get away from him. I ducked around the corner and stayed hidden from him until it was dark. I hailed a cab and went out to my parent's house, who had turned in early. I told Lottie what had happened and asked her not to let him in if he come looking for me.

About ten o'clock I heard a loud commotion. He had came out quietly and parked his car and sat outside stalking me like an animal. He pushed past Lottie. I heard her say, "She's not here" I dashed into my parent's room and hid in their small closet. The rifle that my daddy used for hunting was propped against the wall. I hid under a pile of fresh laundered clothes. He was calling my name, "Carrie, Carrie!" he was getting closer and closer. He banged on the door then pushed it open. They were sounds asleep. He had a shot gun pointed at them. Loudly he said, "Whar iz she?" My father bolted up in a sitting position in bed with a surprised look on his face. My mom just lay there with the covers pulled up to her nose. She was looking up with her hand clasped in prayer. My dad said calmly, "Joe Henry you needs ta git a grip on yo' sef', dis heah ain't no way ta handa yo' bizness." He kept talking, his voice was with authority and no nonsense. "I ain't se'ed Carrie Ann and if'n I did she wouldn't go wid cho lak dis, naw, yo put dat gun down fo' you hur' somebody." Joe Henry put the gun down to his side and started crying like the boy that he was. My mother had turned as white as a sheet. I came out of hiding and went over to console my weeping husband then apologize to my parents for putting their lives in jeopardy. I felt like the lowest animal as I slithered out of their house to go down in the country to stay with my husband. He wanted to hurt me because of my filing for a divorce to be free from him. I had to walk an even tighter rope without a safety net. I wasn't proud of myself. I vowed that I would one day make my parents proud of me. I was so proud of my brave father and of my mother who continued to love me in spite of it all.

JoJo started pre-school and all he wanted to do was play. For a three and a half year old boy what else should a kid his age be expected to do? He always had such a pleasant expression on his little mischievous face. Looks can be deceptive because he wanted to dominate whom ever he was playing with. He didn't care how big they were. I got a call one morning because he had jumped on a little white boy in his class. The child got a bloody nose from the blow that had landed on his face. His parents were a prominent white couple in Meridian. They were demanding that me and Joe Henry pull Joey out of the school or they were going to take legal actions against us. The school had just became integrated. Joe Henry thought that it was amusing how his boy had handled himself. I, on the other hand, was faced with the prospect of retaliation from the white parents. Connie worked there part time as a school secretary. She had witnessed what had happened and urged us to pull JoJo out of that school until things could quiet down. Her afternoon job was at Mr. Barton (where I had attended as a little girl). She held the position of Executive Secretary. She agreed that she would, "watch JoJo to make sure that no body would hang him because he was so bad, just kidding" she said, although I new that it was true.

I received a call while I was attending class at Meridian Jr. College. It was Connie who sounded frantic. She said almost out of breath, "You need to get over here now!" She wouldn't give me any details. I got a hold of Joe Henry who picked me up at school. He broke all the rules of the road with his break neck speeding. When we arrived, the school grounds were swarming with policemen. Connie met us out front. She was in tears, "JoJo is missing." The ground began to spin. I went and sat down inside, "What happened to him?" I asked frantically. She answered, "He was playing with some kids who were a bit older than him. I think he must have tried to follow them home." The police officers were seen going door to door in the immediate neighborhood to search for him. There was an older couple who were sitting on their front porch. They recalled seeing a little boy who fit the description of JoJo. They saw him playing with a group of children as they were walking home. The old man pointed in the direction of 31st Avenue which – "Oh no! that's the Sawashee Creek bridge!" I screamed. I tried to keep my composure. I thought if he turned to the left he would have to cross the – I20 (interstate). I said firmly, "I want him found." My mind raced with all of the what if's, I coulda, woulda, shoulda. Suddenly someone called out, "We found him." I ran outside the school. Joe Henry was already in the front awaiting the news. One of the police officers was lifting him out of their cruiser. He had a lollipop stuck in his mouth as he was laughing and talking with the policeman. There wasn't a scratch on his body and his clothes were dry. He saw us, "Hi Mommy, hi Daddy. I was playing with my new friends." I swooped him up and hugged and kissed him as I twirled him around. Joe Henry had tears of joy as he held on to both of us. Reality hit me in a matter of seconds. I scolded him, "Don't you ever do that again, you've got to learn to obey those who are taking care of you and learn how to follow their rules, do you understand me?" He answered very sadly, "yes Mommy, I understand." He saw how his daddy was beside himself. He truly did love his son.

The police officers were wrapping up and had wrote their reports for the record. They came over and told us what had happened. He was found sitting on the bridge railing throwing rocks in the raging water below. He was seen spitting in it also to see it splash in the water that had claimed so many other colored children in that neighborhood.

I was so proud of my accomplishments of getting my GED and completing the trade school course to obtain my LPN license (Licensed Practical Nurse). I had my training at St. Joseph's Hospital and was hired immediately after graduation. I loved the work that I was doing, it was something that I could do to give back for humanity. I had a sense of pride that I had never experienced. There were a few draw backs. I found that there was a disparity in my salary in comparison to my fellow white hirees. I had heard a long time ago that coloreds have to work harder and longer to be hired and to keep a job. There was something in my subconscious mind that always kept me motivated to reach higher and higher. Maybe one day I could just work smarter, because of my race, it would take time and patience.

We were struggling to keep our little family together so we were staying at both of our parent's homes. There wasn't any accountability to either family. We both felt that they were our parents and that was what we expected parents should do – take care of their children – I was twenty three and Joe Henry was twenty five years old.

My daddy was an excellent mathematician. He began to put 2+1 = 3 more mouths to feed. He called me to the dining room table one afternoon when the house was so quiet (you could hear a rat pissing on cotton). You could hear a pin drop. He said after he cleared his throat – by that act I knew that it was serious – "Carrie, I knows you and Joe Henry been really try'n to git ahead, I se'ed you through yo' nu'sin scho' and naw yo's wok'n so you and yo' famly needs ta star' pay'n fo' yo' keep heah." I looked at him in disbelief. My daddy couldn't no, no he wouldn't tell me to pay him for staying in the house that I grew up in. It was home – crying – how could he? My poor little aching heart was crushed. I told him that I would talk it over with Joe Henry the next time that I saw him. When it rains it pours. I got a telephone call from Joe Henry who had been dodging me after his last pay day (he wanted to play the daddy and my husband game but didn't want to help with expenses. He had often told me, "I ain't fatten'n frogs fa snakes." It was early Monday morning about five o'clock. He was whispering, "Carrie, I'm locked up in jai' and dis is da only call I kin make." From what he told me, he was in deep shit. He and his drinking buddy Sam Sterling who worked with his dad across from Joe Louis Café had gotten in trouble with the law. I really had to strain to hear him as he continued, "I'm in a lota trouba' you gotta git me outa heah, call Phillip and ask him to call Mista Lucus' tell'm whar I'm at." All of the information I got wasn't registering. I felt the silence as he was trying to prepare me for the worst. He continued, "They locked me and Sam Sterling on suspicion fa murda'!" My jaws dropped. It was like pulling a tooth to get all the information that I would need to help him – he said, "Sam was ou' wid his gir'friend (S. Sterling was married with two children). "He bean date'n huh fo' a whi' you probly kno's huh. She goes to Pleasant Hi' chućh." He described her and said her name sounded like petticoat. I asked her, "Is it Pettymire?" and he assured me, "Yeah! Thas' huh." I was flabbergasted and angry. I asked, "What were you doing with her and who killed her?" He answered with his voice trembling, "Carrie you gotto believe me I didn't do it, S. Sterling did it." It wasn't making any sense, "What do you want me to do? What do you want from me? You should have been home last night like you said you would." I wept as I felt me and my family was going backwards. He interrupted my thought. He said, "I'm gwine loose my job if'n I do't git outa heah, I needs you to trust me Carrie, I did'n do nut'n wrong. Call Phillip" he begged, "and te' him to git me outa heah." Phillip bailed him out. Joe Henry said, "We gotta git outa town and quick." He later relayed the story that S. Sterling had been arguing – a lover's spat, they all had been drinking – I believe that there was a fourth person that witnessed the fatal accident. Joe said that Sterling's girlfriend was acting disrespectful to him. Joe Henry gave him his hand gun that he kept under the car seat at all time. He told Sterling to "shoot the bitch." He yelled it several times until she had her brains splattered all over the bed. Another nigger bit the dust and it was okay with the law enforcers. Joe Henry bought another hand gun since his was confiscated.

He had ran out of fresh ideas for making a living in Meridian including a small sandwich shop in the west end. He worked at a paper mill that paid minimum wages. There were several women who were after him to pay child support. My salary would be factored in as family income. We talked about getting out of town and start fresh. There were two options, either Tennessee. He argued that was too, "close to heah." We settled for California. I resigned my position at St. Joseph's – not a moment too soon. I was about to be framed for stealing drugs by the night supervisor. I had been working in their four bed ICU – Intensive Care Unit. I worked alone and gave injections for pain, nausea, etc. when I counted the narcotics on one morning the count was off. You see the night supervisor had came and helped me when it got overwhelmingly busy. She offered to at least give the narcotics, we both had to sign out for them. She helped herself to some of the narcotics. She didn't know that the hospital was investigating her already because she had offered herself to other unsuspecting LPN's over a period of time. I had worked so hard to get my licenses to do something so stupid to jeopardize it. I had no regrets when I left. Joe Henry simply didn't show up on his job.

We both spoke with my brother Tommy Jr. in Los Angeles and he gave the okay for us to stay at his house. Wrong move. We should have asked the boss of his house because she rode us like we were criminals when we arrived. She didn't seem to like JoJo. She said that he had poisoned their children's minds and made them act bad. Joe Henry went to work with Tommy the next day of our arrival. He was started at a descent salary at Special Made Accordion Doors. He learned the business routines quickly.

Jewel loved to gossip which she did constantly. She would backtrack and tell so many lies. She was literally running me crazy. I began to have severe headaches. She saw me taking aspirin then told my family that I was on drugs and that they needed to do something about it before I became addicted. What I really needed to do was to get me and my family out of that crazy house. We stayed there two weeks – we found an apartment about six blocks from them in a business section of South Central LA. It had wall to wall carpet (excuse me that would be roaches). You could hear them crunching under foot especially at night. They covered the entire kitchen and would scurry for cover when the light was flicked on. We were better off with the roaches than at the house that we weren't' welcomed.

We had settled into the roach motel just in time for the big earth quake of 1969. I found my first job at Good Sam Hospital. I commuted by bus in the afternoon and Joe Henry and JoJo picked me up at night. we weren't able to put Joey in school yet. We found a neighbor who ran a child care in her home. We hired her to care for our son. It sounded like a good place.

We went to pick him one evening that my scheduled had changed. He sat in the back seat very quiet. I thought he must be sick. It was extremely dark. I reached back to check if he had a fever. As I touched his face I felt a welt on his cheek. I screamed, "Joe Henry stop the car!" which he did. JoJo climbed over the seat. He said, "it hurts Mommy, it hurts bad." We pulled over for a closer look under the street light. His entire body was covered with welts. His fair skin had bruise marks also. Joe Henry and I were to the point of hysteria. I said, "You tell mommy who did this." I began to cry. He was stuttering as he told us that his babysitter had beat him. She had threatened to kill him if he told anybody and that was why he was so quiet. Joe Henry was furious as he was headed back to the sitters house. I said, "We need to report this to the police" which we did. The police officer talked with JoJo who was crying uncontrollably. "I'm scared Mommy." Upon examination it was found that the weapon that had been used was a large leather belt using the metal tip of it to beat him so badly. He kept saying "I was thirsty Mommy Franny didn't want me to have any water." I cried like a baby shaking my head side to side. How could she do that to my child! They took pictures of his injuries. They also took X-Rays. Afterwards they went to the sitters house and arrested the fifteen year old daughter whom her mother had left the little children in her care. We found out that JoJo had asked her for water one time too many and she snapped. She had warned him to stop begging for water because he would have to pee a lot. He liked flushing the toilet. The police officers told us not to try to contact them, they would handle it. Well they did. She was arrested and released the same night. the day care was put out of business.

I wanted and needed to work but I didn't trust anybody to watch over my very active son. It was about the same time that my Aunt Carrie Mae heard about what had happened. She was more than happy to take care of JoJo. They were excellent company for each other. We rented the big house in front of Aunt Carrie Mae's very small rental home.

I continued to work across the city, basically downtown LA. We were living in the El Sereno area which was predominantly Mexican. As in all neighborhoods, there were some very nice and others who were questionable. Our house was directly across the street from Evergreen Cemetery. It was an old house that had been owned and occupied by a ninety year old colored (black) lady. She had been ill for a short while. She was stubborn (claimed her daughter) and had refused to go to the doctor and to the hospital when she was found down. She hadn't been eating for days and had fallen. She was found by her daughter lying in her own urine and feces. She was pronounced dead by the coroner. She was in a semi sitting position obviously trying to get in her old rocking chair that she had bough fifty years ago.

We went to look at the house. It was as good as it was going to get. There was a hint of old urine smell in the house especially in the room across from the kitchen. We were told that she used to urinate in a container and throw it out of the screened window. Her daughter (the new owner) had painted but there is so much that paint can cover including certain odors.

Joe Henry's commute to his job was much closer and so was mine. We bought the old furniture that the old lady had left including her old rocker, dining room table and six chairs, an antique ugly bedroom set (we bought our own mattress). A chrome dinette set with four chairs upholstered in bright yellow plastic. I did my best to fix up the house with curtains, a hand-me-down modern sofa and chair from Joe Henry's boss in Burbank. It was a battle that I eventually gave up with trying to redecorate. It was the old lady's house, she was the winner.

We went to church regularly at El Segundo. Our family was going to make it. I began to breathe easier and felt secure about our marriage. Joe Henry and JoJo came to pick me up after my swing shift at Good Samaritan Hospital. I couldn't stop smiling I was so happy until one evening I was taking a bath (located out on the back screen porch). I didn't hear the phone ring but I heard him talking. I went inside quietly as he asked playfully, "When wi' you le' me come ova an' see you?" I stood there with chill bumps all over my body not saying a thing. He still didn't realize that I was listening to everything that he was saying. He said in a lowered sadistic laugh, "That ain't noth'n she kin do 'bout it, wha' she don' know wan' hu't huh and besides I'm biggah dan she is." Without thinking I ran over to him – my robe opened – and snatched the phone out of his hand. He was just as surprised as I was by his reaction. I quickly walked away from Joe Henry and I said into the receiver in a voice so icy cold, "This is Carrie, I'm Joe Henry's wife. You need to get your own man and don't you ever call here ever again." With that being said I slammed the phone down and looked at Joe Henry who was so busted. There wasn't anything that he could say to make it better. I had heard enough. I asked, "Who is she?" He answered with his head turned away from me, "She's from back home." I learned later that she indeed was from back home and had followed him out here (I wondered how she had gotten our phone number).

I began having bouts of crying spells and I had the stomach flu that my family had also. Theirs eventually cleared up and mine continued. It must have been cancer? I fretted, it couldn't be anything else. I went to a walk-in county clinic. They ran tests and they came back. I was afraid to tell Joe Henry the news. He acted like he was happy when I told him because I had reminded him that I wouldn't stay through another pregnancy if he ever reacted the way he did with my first pregnancy. My flu symptoms lasted for seven more months.

JoJo was six years old and the apple of his Mommy and Daddy's eyes. They were inseparable. JoJo wanted a baby brother. I reassured him that I would do my best but couldn't make any promises, "We will love it even it it's a girl." He answered questionably, "Okay Mommy." His feelings meant a lot to me because I knew that he had been in the lime light for so many years. He may have a problem adjusting to either gender. He had to know that he would always be my little man (Dough Dough Bird).

I was on cloud nine again. However I was so scared that I would have more of the same complications I'd had with JoJo. I had the worst back ache and vaginal itch. I warned Joe Henry that I would not stand for anymore of his infidelity. He was so assuring. I had to believe him. Although I loved my job I had to resign and became a full time mother to my boy. Thank God, Aunt Carrie Mae was there. A God send for him.

Joe Henry's job assignments took him out of town a lot. One night I heard someone at the front door. I knew that Joe Henry would always knock then call my name before coming inside. The only thing I heard was the door squeaking as it was flung open. I did what any mom would have done to protect her sleeping child. I ran through the living room with a hand gun – shoot first and ask questions later – the bullet went through the screen door. JoJo called out, "mommy it's me, don't shoot me." He was standing behind the opened front door out of my sight. The room had only a dim night light. He was crying as his little body was shaking. I stood there frozen almost in a state of shock when I realized that it wasn't an intruder and I wasn't having a nightmare. I tried to reassure him that mommy meant him no harm. He said through his sobbing, "I thought I heard my daddy at the door." He had slept walked as he had done so often in the past. He promised me that he wouldn't answer the door again. I became frightened to have a loaded gun in the house for so called protection.

I didn't sleep for the rest of the night. I felt so guilty I had almost shot my Dough Dough Bird. I took a nap after I had walked him to the 1st Street School. You would think that I would have been able to rest. The old lady of the house came and sat next to me. I couldn't move. She wouldn't say a word to me. She just stared at me as if I was an intruder. I struggled to wake up. Nightmare was my best friend. I couldn't talk or move but I knew that I would eventually awaken and be happy that it was over. I thought, "if only I could move my finger I would awaken." I tried and couldn't and didn't until the phone rang, "Thank you Lord." It was a wrong number I think, they didn't respond to me.

It was close to my due date so Joe Henry wouldn't take any assignments out of town. I confided in him that I had always wanted a boy first (JoJo) and then a little girl. He tried to keep me from getting my hopes up too high. I was getting more nervous by the minute. I was to have a planned c-section because of my past episode. They didn't want to take any chances.

On November 7, 1972 early in the evening Joe Henry and I had tried to make love, I think he was trying to induce labor because he was just tired of taking care of me and he just wanted it to be over. We would have to wait another six weeks after the baby was born. Shortly after the failed attempt I felt a gush of fluid in the bed as we slept. I awakened Joe Henry, so I thought. "Joe Henry its time my water broke. The baby is coming." I didn't see any blood. I became so happy and excited that it was going to be over soon.

Joe Henry got up and was trying to help me stay focused. He put on his shoes and was putting on my maternity dress (we laughed about it many times later on). His voice was trembling. He got Joey up and took him over to Aunt Carrie Mae. We drove quickly over to the County General Hospital (we didn't have medical insurance). It was decided that they would proceed with the c-section because there had not been any labor pain after the show.

My mother was en route by plane. She had been called by my husband as we had planned. I signed all of the necessary pre-operative papers for the c-section and to have a tubal ligation (my tubes tied). I started screaming after I had signed it, "No, I don't want it if it's another boy, I want a little girl." The nurse tried to reason with me that they couldn't leave the consent blank. I either signed it or not. I couldn't see why they couldn't bend the rules this time. It was important to me.

On November 8, 1972 my baby was born. I was awakened by the anesthesiologist, my mother stood at my side on the right side and Joe Henry on the other, "Carrie she is beautiful." I had my little girl, I cried tears of joy and so did Joe Henry and mother. I said, "JoJo will love her," I added, "he said he would." God had answered my prayers for both of my children.

She had the prettiest head full of black hair. Her mouth and eyes were just like her daddy's. her nose was more like mine. She was absolutely adorable. I couldn't take my eye off of her. All she wanted to do was sleep. I tried to awaken her to feed her. She was too tired. I was in excruciating pain and developed complications of a collapsed left lung. They placed a chest tube for two days until it re-expanded. Later it was found that I had pleurisy. The doctor ordered a full course of IV antibiotics. I knew that I was in good hands there. The nurses and doctor were very friendly and professional even though I was black. I watched them as they performed multiple technical tasks throughout my hospital stay.

It was finally time for them to discharge me and my baby girl. They seemed so in love with my Vanessa Yvette Mathis. I was already in love with her also. She was such a quiet baby – mother and JoJo met us in the car. JoJo asked, "is it a baby brother?" I answered him, "No, JoJo she's your own baby sister. Hold out your arms and hold her." He did it so clumsily yet determined he wasn't going to drop her. She began squirming then crying loudly. He said, "I don't think she likes me." I tried to reassure him that she was just hungry. I got him to smile and he helped me feed her. I prayed that he would want to help take care of her – his little sister – he was almost seven years older than her. Time would tell.

Vanessa was turning out to be a daddy's little girl. There wasn't nothing that he wouldn't do for her. And whatever he did for her he had to do for JoJo who was finding it hard (he had been the only child for a long time) to share the spot light. I knew my mother came out to California to tend to the baby. I wanted to do it myself. My mother was sleeping a lot. I was afraid that my baby would slip off of her lap. I never did tell her that. I told her that it would help me more if she would help me prepare meals since she was a fantastic cook. Everybody was happy with the arrangements.

Mother continued to be jokingly aka Grandma Globe Trotter. There were so many grandchildren being born. She would pack up and fly to wherever that she was needed. That was the most important thing for her. I had often wished that she could have gotten that sense of belonging with Deddy.

Motherhood was a wonderful experience for me. Both of my children were thriving. Vanessa looked like a rolly polly rendition of Muhdea and of her daddy. She was growing out of everything that she had as a newborn. My princess didn't have a baby shower as most babies would have had. She needed so many things like clothes that we couldn't afford to buy for her. I tried my hands at hand stitching little Mammy made dresses for her. She was beautiful in anything I put on her. The older she got the more that she favored her Muhdea. Joey teased her that she must have been adopted because she was darker than all of us. He went even as far as to tell her, "I'm better looking than you and my hair is better than yours." He still begged me for a baby brother. I told him that he had to be a good brother and to love the only sister that I would ever be able to give him.

Life seemed to be getting on track and much better than we had had since we'd been married, until Joe Henry started going out of town on his business trips. He packed his own suitcase. I saw that he had his dress clothes and a new pair of Stacy Adams shoes packed. There was a new pair of short silk boxer shorts and a bottle of expensive smelling cologne. I was assured that it was just in case that he ate out in a nice restaurant, he would have everything.

I was so busy being the doting mom and the wonderful wife. Before he left, I kissed him one of my sexy lingering kisses at the front door, "that should hold him over." I thought.

He was away from home over a week. I was so lonely. Upon his return I was so excited and wanted to be with him in the naughtiest way. He dragged himself inside and he seemed so tired. He barely paid me attention. The kids felt left out also. He sat in the living room and played a record that he had just bought. He played it so loud over and over again. It was a new release from Latimore – Let's Straighten it Out - He seemed angry and distant. He wouldn't talk to me. I figured that my bubble had finally burst. He refused to come to bed that night. he drank a fifth of liquor until that morning. I was so tired from the lack of sleep and so were the kids. I kept JoJo home from school. Joe Henry was finally asleep on the sofa so I checked his pockets. There were two unused rubbers and a receipt for a motel in San Diego. His job was supposed to have been in Arizona. My blood was about to boil over. I went into a mad rage screaming as I shook him, "Who were you with?" I had the two rubbers and the motel receipts. I threw it into his face, he looked confused. I could smell the heavy odor of liquor on his breath. He jumped up off the couch (he still had on his dress clothes and had taken his shoes off). He screamed as he lunged toward me, "You God damn bitch, don' ch' eva go search'n in my pocke'" I ran and escaped his advances into the children's room thinking he wouldn't hurt me in front of them. He ran after me as he lost his balance because of his socks. I had just waxed the kitchen floor the day before. It had a beautiful shine that made it slippery. He broke his fall on the door to the children's room. He came after me again, that time he caught me and slapped me harder that he had ever had. I thought that we were beyond that. It landed on the left side of my face. He had used the back of his hand and the ring that he wore cut into my face. I felt blinded for a moment. JoJo had been watching cartoons, and didn't like what was happening. He yelled, "daddy noooo!" as his daddy had picked me up and held me (my body was horizontal to the floor) over his head and literally threw me across the room – I was lucky to land on JoJo's roll-away bed. JoJo went after his daddy, "Are you trying to kill my mommy?" I cried as he began to wrap his little eight year old body around his daddy's leg. I jumped up and was able to run out of the room. I was limping. I thought my leg and back had injuries.

I looked back and JoJo was trying his best to save his mommy and he must have because Joe Henry caught himself as he was about to attack our son. He put him down gently and started crying (so was JoJo). I heard him say, "God, what am I doing?" Vanessa had awakened and

I joined in on the chorus. She looked so frightened. I walked out of the house to the front porch. My body was shaking as if I was having a seizure. I was in so much pain and despair. I looked at the calm neighborhood. My parents were two thousand miles away. I had no where to run. I didn't have any money. "Lord, what am I supposed to do, where am I supposed to go?"

Joe Henry had gotten Vanessa changed and had calmed JoJo down. He brought both of them out on the porch to where I was. They came over to me. I must have looked so disheveled no matter what they loved me and gave me a hug. "Come inside," Joey said, "Daddy's not going to hurt you no more." Joe Henry came over and hugged me also and looked at my face. Tearfully he said, "Carrie I'm so sorry please forgive me. I promise I wi' neva eva hu' cho agin" I felt nothing but hate for him at that moment. I was so belittled and humiliated in front of my children. my face was swollen and I had a black eye. There were bruises over my entire body (I was too afraid to report it to the authorities and they wouldn't care if I did). He must have felt guilty, he said, "I'll take the children to get something to eat." He turned to me as he shook his head. "Do you want anything?" I requested some aspirins. He brought back a bucket of KFC with all the trimmings. I couldn't stop crying which made my headache worse.

I began to finally drift off to sleep after about three hours lying in bed planning and came to the conclusion, "I can't take this anymore."

I put in an application at El Sereno Community Medical Center after the swelling and black eye went down. I didn't have any trouble getting hired as a LVN as their treatment nurse. My starting salary was $12.25 per hour. It was just a few blocks from home. Aunt Carrie Mae had moved back home to Meridian. Another lady and her husband moved into the back house. Mrs. And Mrs. Jackson. He was white with an attitude and she was – I'm not sure what race she was. I do know that she took care of JoJo and Vanessa until I found out that she drank excessively. I saw that she had passed out on their stoop. She was totally nude in a puddle of her own vomit. The sun had baked her to a crispy lobster color. We saw her husband when he found her (as he had many times). He stepped over her seemingly lifeless naked frame.

She was taken to the hospital after one episode by an ambulance where she later died. She had a stroke. JoJo loved her so much.

Me and my children had attempted to attend a Seventh Day Adventist church in the community. Most of the parishioners were predominantly white, with only a few blacks and fewer Mexicans. I didn't get that warm and fuzzy feeling when we attended. I felt that we were being snubbed. The welcoming committee would look the other way when we arrived each time. There were smiles, hugs and kisses but not for me and my kids. Vanessa wasn't used to being so confined to one area. She became so unruly that I was told to either leave her in the nursery or it was nicely put in an insulting manner to bring her back if she was able to behave herself. Children have a sixth sense to detect if they are loved or hated. I refused to put either of them in a position where they weren't welcome. JoJo had already told me that he didn't like going to that church, "It's no fun there mommy; they don't like me." Who was I trying to fool? I was responsible to introduce spiritual food for my children and I failed to do it because there were so many so called barriers. So I gave up and started back sliding. When Joe Henry had a beer, Carrie Ann had a beer. If he lit a cigarette, so would I only I had to sneak and smoke because, "It ain't lady like fo you ta smoke, I always pu cho ona pedestal." It was one of his ways of controlling me. I got tired of sneaking around so I told him, "I'm smoking." He knew that I was making more money than he did. He didn't want to break my face. So smoking was allowed.

We both wanted to have nice things for our children. I made sure that their needs were met before mine. Joe Henry's needs came before the children. I stayed in a state of frustration (forsaking all others). I felt left out I knew that I would never be number one with him. I continued to want and wait.

We had discussed buying a house because the house that we were renting was slowly but surely falling apart at the seams. The landlady didn't really care about the house only collecting the $75.00 a month for rent. It took us about one month to find the right house for us at the right price. Although we thought it was a stretch and above our heads. We became so excited when we looked at the big picture and was told that we were new home owners of the house that was fifteen years old. We put down $500.00. the previous owner paid the points. The house sold for $35,500.00 we had to put in new carpets and draperies in the living room before it was inspected. We had a thirty year conventional loan at $145.00 per month. It was nineteen hundred square feet. There were four bedrooms, two and three fourth baths, a large living room, and a kitchen/family room combo. Joe Henry claimed the two car garage one side was used for his tools and storage. We were so happy.

Vanessa seemed to have been having multiple problems of adjusting to our new home. She had nightmares every night. it was like clockwork. We would all be asleep. She would awaken and screamed in a blood curdling voice, "MOMMY, DADDY!" she literally flew down the hallway to our bedroom. We found out later that it had been JoJo who had been frightening her with stories about dead people who were in her closet and under her bed. She wouldn't eat because he taunted her unmercifully. She thought the food was poisoned. She would either hide food in the trash can when I gave up coaxing her or JoJo would eat whatever food that she had left on her plate especially fried chicken.

Both our moms decided to visit our new home at the same time. Imagine two more women in our house for two weeks (if it don't kill you it will make you stronger). They were as different as night and day. I had to cook two versions of everything. My mother was on a special diet of low fat, low sodium and low calorie (she was SDA), no pork. Muhdea liked everything that she could have cooked in her food especially her, "vegetable" (vegebas) she thrived on anything that the pig had to offer. I was truly thinking about running away from home, enough was enough. One more week and they would have been left there alone. Joe Henry would come home from work and refuse to come out of our bedroom during the last week of their stay. The weight of the world was lifted when we saw both moms take off on their flights back home. They would always be welcome – one at a time – to 5244 Coney Road, our home.

There seemed to be a freeze on my salary. We needed more money to take care of our two growing children and the household. We had developed a good system for paying bills. I would balance the bank book after depositing both our checks in the same checking account. Joe Henry would get spending money and I would get half the amount (maybe because I was half his size). He would spend his quicker than John stayed in the army – then he demanded that I share with him. He kept tabs on what I spent. However, I wasn't privy to his spending habits. I informed him that I was going to get my own bank account and a credit card. He hit the ceiling, "You mus' have anotha' niggah on the side" No, I didn't but I should've when he received a summons from back home to pay child support. The lady's name wasn't familiar to me. Of course he denied the whole thing. Our bank statement indicated that it was overdrawn. I had been so meticulous with balancing it. There were several hundred dollars unaccounted for. He said he needed more money and that I had better not start trying to keep up with him because he was the man in this house. I applied at ELAC for prerequisites for their RN course. I was so driven. I knew that deep down within myself that it would only be a matter of time. Joe Henry had put me out of the house that weekend. I took Vanessa with me to a community hotel. He kept JoJo with him. He had started beating me again. I never did know what his intentions were when he would reach for me in bed. He would start out lovingly then for no reason he would snap. He jumped on top of me. He was choking me. He refused to seek help for his psychological problems. He often said, "if'n you don't like it, you can leave, dis is muh house."

I must have been going through some kind of metamorphosis stage. There were so many good looking guys who were approaching me. I did the most natural thing, I responded. I, the butterfly, was coming out of my stagnated form. I continued to study and was placed on the Deans Honor list with a 4.0 GPA.

Being accepted to ELAC RN course was one of my major accomplishments (for the exception of my two children) and then finally passing my state boards with an extremely high score. Joe Henry must have known (he confided in Tommy Jr.) that I was motivated to excel for many reasons. He was on the top of my list. I was hired by the same hospital as a new grad awaiting my license. My interim salary was $17.32 per hour and would be evaluated after a three month probation. Me and my classmates from ELAC got together for a house party. It was totally wild. There was an abundance of booze, snacks and marijuana being passed around. Several people coupled off and was so wound up they stripped and the orgy was on. That time I was the looky-loo. I was appointed the designated driver.

Joe and I were well over due for new furniture because we had brought all of our old stuff including the old overstuffed rocker. Out with the old and in with the new. I felt like a queen with all of the beautiful modern furniture for the living room, dinette set, a king-sized bedroom set for us and a white canopy bedroom set for the princess. JoJo had pissed his dad off (it didn't take much). I wasn't allowed to decorate his room. We discovered that he had taken a knife and had cut his bed. He seemed to be so angry about everything. My thoughts drifted back to before I graduated. My mother wasn't doing too well back home. She was taking care of Bennie's children and was having an extremely difficult time acclimating to the dreary weather that Mississippi had to offer in the winter. The roof had started to leak and the bathroom stayed backed up into the bath tub. The odor was deplorable. I had spoken with her several times long distance. She seemed to have the need to tell me more than she ever had about daddy's affair with Wilona Milson. He didn't seem to care who knew about it. She said, "Carrie you are doing something for your life by getting more education and I'm so proud of you. That is something that Joe Henry will never be able to take from you." She had always known how he had manipulated and bullied me into giving him all the money that I had then he'd spend it on other women. I think she was talking about something even deeper than my education would open up doors which was the key to my eventual success. She had seen that no matter what beatings and blows that I had endured I kept getting up and with added strength.

She went into the hospital that night for congestive heart failure (CHF). She stayed a while then was released home with Willie and his wife Vivia. The doctors felt that she didn't need to be in the depressing surroundings at her house. That was basically what her problem was. Her blood pressure and diabetes was reacting to her state of mind. Before hanging up I said as I always had, "I love you mother, I'll see you soon." There was another call form Lottie about one week after mother had been discharged. Lottie said, I think you had better come home, mother is seriously ill." I arrived at her bedside the next day. There she was, my beautiful mother. Her mouth was twisted and she was paralyzed on one side. She'd had a stroke. She recognized me as I took her hand and leaned over and kissed the face that had been with me throughout my childhood. The hand that had prepares so many meals and yes had spanked me when I needed it. Tears were in her lovely grey eyes. She cleared her throat, "I want a drink of water." There was a syringe that was at the bedside. I slowly allowed a few drops into her mouth, "to wet your whistle" I said. She attempted to smile but couldn't because of the facial paralysis. She closed her eyes and drifted off to sleep.

My whole family was there in her private room. We all joined hands and had prayed at her bedside. Afterwards we were requested to limit two visitors at a time. Her condition was listed as grave. They turned their heads if there were more visitors than what was allowed.

Her primary doctor asked to see all of us. He was straight forward. She had suffered a massive stroke. She was in congestive heart failure. Her blood pressure and diabetes were out of control. She had gone into renal failure. He wasn't sure if she would make it throughout the night or through the next week. It was decided by our family that if her heart were to stop, we didn't want any heroic measures. She wasn't to be placed on a ventilator. I went to her bedside and said, "good bye," and that I would see her later, "I'm going home tomorrow." She shook her head, "okay." I arrived home that night. The phone rang - - - - - "Carrie, she's gone, our mother is gone." It was Lottie who had always stood in for mother.

Dazed I went through the motion. Me, Joe Henry and the kids drove back for the closed casket funeral – what a lady – a lady knows when it's time to leave.

Afterwards I threw myself into my RN training as I had promised my mother I would do. I kept looking around for her to walk in for my graduation. My family was there – Joe Henry, JoJo and my little Van. The gaping hole was left in my life with my moms passing but I knew that she wanted me to be happy.

Joe and I threw a house party for my graduation. We invited twenty five people, only three people showed up then left early because there was another party that the strippers were going to. I had already enlightened the invited guest of my husbands bad temper and of his jealousy. Well duh! I should have kept my big mouth shut.

I had been driving an old old Chevy station wagon. It was beat up it looked like a clunker. It didn't want to go too fast. I didn't want to push it. I wanted a new Corvette, one evening we all piled into Ms. Clunk - the wagon – we went shopping for my dream car. It would have cost too much just for insurance and for upkeep alone. We drove out of the car lot that evening in my first new car (I made sure that my name was the primary owner on the deed). It was a 1984 Trans Am, red, hardtop convertible. It was hot – I got personalized license plates – PRN4CAM.

Bigman became ill (prostrate cancer) and was hospitalized for weeks after he had it removed surgically. Joe Henry flew down (alone) to go see him. I called to speak to him and found that he had been out partying practically most of the time. Joe returned back home and received a call that Bigman died shortly after he got home. He was 93 years old.

Just before we left home to drive back home to the funeral, Joe Henry went outside to our back yard with his daddy's old shot gun. He screamed in a pitch that was blood curdling as he looked up to the heavens. His fist was clenched as he made a gesture of defiance, "You God damn bastard, you took my daddy! (Bang, bang, bang) now you take me you son of a bitch." He flung himself on the patch of grass next to the patio. I refused to go anywhere near him for fear of a lightening bolt that would surely strike him. I prayed that our two children would be safe. Our trip through Texas was the worst ever in all the years that we had traveled through there. The lightening bolts came so close to our car till it shook. Our visibility was zero. Joe had a death wish but it wasn't God's time for him to go. Joe Henry's family had moved from the infamous house to another old house. It did, however, have running (cold) water in the kitchen only. There had been a bathroom out on the porch but it was no longer in service. Its flooring had rotted and wasn't safe to use. The outhouse was out in the back with plenty of newspaper.

Muhdea was so stoic. She had finally gotten her wish Bigman was dead. She would no longer have to worry about him throwing a drunken fit of rage. She actually took his passing very well. She stayed busy taking care of Bobby. We stayed down at the newer house with her. They had a phone that rang constantly. It was in the same room that Joe Henry and I were assigned. It rang one evening when Joe was feeling somewhat frisky. Muhdea ran in without knocking (no locks on the door). Not a pretty site. I'm sure of staring at ones sons' ass as he was about to do the down stroke – she came on in anyway, shook her head at the both of us – I couldn't look her in the face for a while but soon got over it. The next time the phone rang I answered it. It was a woman (I think). She sounded like a man. She drawled in her baritone voice, "you te' yo' man he needs ta' buy his babe sum mi'k." I answered, "you tell him yourself" as I slammed the receiver down. Some things will never change. I had to be strong for Muhdea.

We made it back home safely and settled into our routines. It was nice being able to afford some of the finer things in life that we wanted. Joe Henry had always wanted a motor cycle since he was a teenager. His parents had bought him a used one which he wrecked after about a month.

We went shopping in a Honda motorcycle shop in Alhambra. We saw the honey that we both fell in love with. I don't know who was the happiest or the most excited. It was a huge black trimmed with gold Honda 1000 Goldwing Windjammer. It came equipped with a removable radio tape player. We had to have it. It was our toy. He bought extras for it for my comfort and safety. A sissy bar and back rest with saddle bags. I made sure that when he took it out I was perched on the back.

There was a younger Mexican couple who lived a half a block down from our house. They drove by our house one afternoon on their Harley Davidson because they had been admiring our bike parked in the driveway getting spruced up.

Joe Henry got on theirs and the rest was history. He loved the power and the rough sputtering sounds that it made. Ours had a whining sound that I had come to love. We were all so excited. We promised that we would all get together soon.

They came back sooner than we had expected. The next weekend they stopped by for drinks and suggested that we ride out to Santa Monica beach. It was rather hot and we all needed to cool off. Jose said his wife was game but was afraid to ride that distance on the back of their bike that didn't have a back rest. She did however feel more comfortable on a bigger bike that had more protection – like ours.

She climbed up on the back of Joe Henry and clung to him like Velcro or a wart on your ass. He was in sheer heaven for all of the attention that the beautiful young lady was giving him as we rode down the freeway. Jose saw the same thing that I was staring at and he slowed down behind Joe and out of site. He started coming on to me. I had had enough to drink and was uninhibited and I began flirting back at him. My arms were wrapped tightly around his slender waist. He looked so good in his leather jacket and I in mine. I started playing with his navel and pulled the hairy areas round it and on his chest. We kept an eye on Joe Henry and his young rider. He continued to lead. They had their game going on. Two could play at the game. I reached again under his jackets and cupped his firm chest then pinched his hardened nipple. He laughed, winked at me in the rear view mirror and gunned the motor. It sounded so good. He almost lost his passenger because of the thrust forward. I was laughing so hard he unzipped my jeans and found that I was so lubricated. He licked his finger then touched me again until I wanted to scream. He said that I smelled and tasted good. It was wonderful just throwing all of my cares to the wind.

We were close to the beach. The salty air was moist and the fishy smell was pungent. The gorgeous orange sun was setting. Joe led the way to a liquor store. We got a pint of Cutty Sark and some Michelob beer. We got settled on the beach just as the sun was setting. We had taken a few sips of the liquor. We had two blankets. Joe Henry and Lupe on one and Jose and I on the other. I didn't trust the situation. I needed to keep an eye on someone who had became lost in another woman right in front of me. I could tell that she had climaxed as she let out a long sigh of relief. We all became sober afterwards.

Neither of us mentioned it when we returned home. Jose made several attempts to see me when he knew that Joe Henry wasn't home. One evening I was sitting at a desk downstairs in the guest bedroom. I had the door opened. He tapped on it and entered quickly. He came in expecting to get some desert that he didn't get on the beach. He began kissing me gently then with urgency. It wasn't safe so I told him he had to leave. He and I heard my daughter (Vanessa) calling for me. He left and I never saw him again. I'm not sure if Lupe contacted Joe Henry again. I didn't want to know. That was weird even for me.

It was Memorial Day and our family was going to meet Janie and her family for a picnic in an Alhambra park. Joe Henry wanted to ride the motorcycle but since we had to take so much picnic supplies, it would take two trips. I went on the first round to stake our claim on a table and set things up. Joey was to bring Vanessa in his little old fixed up car. They came and we all waited for Joe Henry to return back to the park. He never did. It was getting late and we were getting impatient. He must have stopped to get him a drink. I let my imagination run wild since I had so much practice. The Alhambra police officers came to where we were and reported to me that there had been a serious motorcycle accident and that Joe Henry had been hurt. They said that he had refused to go to the hospital because he didn't want to leave his bike for he feared that someone would steal it. I rode back to the scene of the accident on Valley and Amar Avenue. His bike was being towed away upon my arrival. Joe Henry was still able to stand but the bike was totaled. He had been thrown off of it. By his account, was thrown several feet by a car that hit him from the rear he landed in the path of an incoming car. He rolled over by some cat instinct to avoid getting hit again, what a lucky man. They looked at me and said, "if you had been a passenger, you would certainly be dead." Joe Henry had many cuts and bruises. There were no obvious broken bones, not even his spirit. He continued to refuse to go to emergency because we had no insurance on the bike" he argued. That afternoon he wasn't able to walk and was having delayed pain. Although he had had a helmet on during the accident he was acting as if he had neurological problems. I called an ambulance which took him to Alhambra Hospital. They poked at him, did a battery of tests and X-Rays. They medicated him for pain by IV. They were about to take him for a CT scan of the brain at which time he got up, put his clothes on and demanded that JoJo and I take him home right away!

Our motorcycle was left in impound because they had jacked the charges up so badly. It would have cost us the amount that we paid for it to get it out of impound.

We loved to entertain. Joe Henry would barbeque he was the best and I was his helper. I prepared the baked beans, potato salad and kept the beers and drinks flowing. Janie and George and their children had came over as we often visited each other. George was so rude to JoJo's company – a young white neighborhood boy (young man) who was about nineteen years old, a year older than Joey. The food was great but Janie and George left earlier than usual because he hated Sol because he was white. Sol seemed naturally disturbed by George's behavior so I tried to console him by telling him that some people would always hate each other. Joe Henry had gotten so drunk I helped him get into bed. Joey and Van were wiped out so they both went to bed. I was tired and my last guest was not budging to go home. He was still acting so hurt. I said, "Sol, your daddy is going to wonder what happened to you." He answered, "He won't care, he knows I'm safe over here" (their house was adjacent to ours). He was still tearful. I said as I held out my hand, "come here" I didn't see it coming – he took my hands and I held him like I would any person that was in an emotional distress. I told him, "You're going to be alright. I knew that he had recently lost his older brother whom he loved so dearly. He had shot himself in the head. His brains were splattered all over the room. There wasn't a note, no good bye's just emptiness that I too felt behind his untimely death. He and his wife and their child had spent so much time over at our house. Sol was hurting and I was doing my best to sooth his pain. The music was still playing in the living room. I had purposely kept it on so that my family wouldn't be disturbed.

I opened up a fresh bottle of beer for myself and he asked for one for himself. He came so close to me and just hugged me so tightly, I figured he was missing his mom whom he seldom ever saw. I hugged him back. We both began swaying to the music and being the dancer that I was I added a sense of delight to a person who was in need of comforting. He stopped and was still holding me. I had my head on his shoulder. The music had stopped a while ago. I looked up at the handsome face that I had never noticed in that light. His hair was reddish blond and so was his moustache. His piercing eyes were slate grayish blue. He was looking down at me and was smiling. He said in his southern drawl (he was from the south) "I've thought about you a lot." I pulled away from him and was walking away. I answered him sternly, "Sol, this is wrong" before I could finish my response he kissed me ever so gently on my mouth. I pulled away from him again and said not quite so convincingly, "this isn't right." He held me closer, as our bodies touched, at which time he kissed me on the side of my mouth then inside of my mouth. Something inside of me said, "stop!" the weaker side of me said, "more, more!" I could hear Joe Henry snoring so loudly in our bedroom. I went down the hallway to Vanessa's room and she was down for the count and so was Joey in his room. I knew that we were doing something that was so wrong, but it felt so right and down right wild to feel his young hard body. His kisses were magnificent. We both were at a point of no return. He said as he took my hand in his, "come with me, I want to show you something." I asked as I was beginning to hold back, "where are we going?" He grinned and said, "over to my house, you'll be back before your family awakens." I asked " where is your dad?" he answered, "He's gone out for the night on a date." I left with him, my family was asleep. I locked the front door as we left. He kissed me again in the driveway not really concerned about our neighbors. He said with conviction, "I know what you've been going through with Joe Henry." Well, that sealed the deal, say no more. I followed him to his house and into his bedroom. He had a red velvet spread on a round bed and there we made love for the first of many times. He was young yet masterful and knew how to please me.

We heard a noise coming from the hallway. I was so nervous thinking that Joe Henry would find out. I bolted up. It was his father returning back home earlier than Sol had expected. I think that he saw me. I rushed out of their house. Sol wanted me to stay but the moment and the thrill of it all was lost. His dad didn't say anything to me thereafter except for his usual pleasantries.

Sol and I had many other encounters such as going to a motel on the beach. It had a Jacuzzi in the room and x-rated adult films. He drove us in my car. I would meet him about two blocks from my house. We especially loved going up to the foothills in Pasadena. We would pack a picnic lunch, some wine and a big blanket near a stream of gurgling water. We enjoyed each other so much until one fateful day I received a message from his dad. Sol had been in a serious accident. The car that he and some of his friends were riding in had went off the narrow winding road up in the mountains. One of his friends had been killed, the other two were serious and had been air lifted and taken to different hospitals. Sol had a broken neck and multiple significant trauma of major organs. He was in the hospital for months in a halo to immobilize his head and neck. I was finally able to go and visit him at the rehab hospital. He barely recognized me on my initial visit. His recovery was slow but sure. We drifted apart, however, I must say that the last time that I saw him he was basically the same young man that I had known and loved. He was at a night club with a date. We hugged knowing that it was the end of a chapter of our lives.

Joe Henry and I were just going through the motion of being married. He had severe mood swings and I was the brunt of all of his anger. He would spend most of his free time downstairs in his garage fixing cars or outside washing them. He repaired anything that was broken in the house. One thing that he couldn't repair was all of the damage that he did (I allowed) to me or the self inflicting damage that we had done to ourselves.

We tried so many things that should have brought back some of the sparks that had been siphoned out of our marriage, including going to x-rated movies. Joe Henry took me to the Pussycat Theatre in Hollywood. He wanted me to see the long playing film - Deep Throat - Most of the movie-goers were older men who were scattered throughout the audience. We got a seat near the rear and close to the isle. After my eyes became adjusted to the darkness I noticed that someone (a man) who was seated four seats from us was watching us more so than watching the movie. About halfway through the multiple scenes that didn't have a real story line only scenes of an actor with the biggest dick that I had ever seen. (his name was John). I don't know who the leading lady (I think it was Linda) was but she (or the trick camera) sure could swallow all of that dick. The man that was seated near us came closer and began masturbating and watching us for our reaction. I kept nudging Joe Henry to look at the offensive man. He only shrugged his shoulder, laughed and kept watching the movie. For me, there were no sparks that night. I got so bored until I drifted off to sleep. Who wanted to be a looky-loo? Certainly not me.

We received a phone call from Mammie Dell that Bobby had been sick but she thought that he would eventually be okay. He had been taken to the hospital twice suffering from severe intractable abdominal pain. He wasn't able to eat although he tried. What small amounts that he consumed, he vomited it right back up. Muhdea thought that it may have been an ulcer. She figured that if she could get him to hold down a bland diet (corn bread, mashed potatoes with butter and lima beans) he would be better. They took him back up to the doctors clinic. He was so weak and had lost so much weight. X-rays were done and lab works completed. After about one month they had a definitive diagnosis that he had end stage stomach cancer. There was a growth about the size of a grapefruit in his stomach. It was inoperable. The cancer had metastasized throughout his body. The only thing that could be done was to allow him to go home on pain management. He became skin and bones, a living corpse before the Grim Reaper came to claim him. Joe Henry took his death quite hard.

We went back home to Mississippi for Bobby's funeral, of course we traveled by car as we had done so many other times, we could have been blind folded and found our way.

Muhdea didn't handle Bobby's death too well. His passing had taken so much of her energy. She was going through the motions of her daily routines but it was as if she was a zombie who had a blank stare, and for the first time in all the years that I had known her, I saw anger on her face when she would drift further into herself. She allowed herself to cry for the child whom she had raised but he had never matured into manhood. Apparently it ran in the family because I was married to someone who didn't know how to be a man either. I must say one thing that Joe Henry did help his mom in her grieving process. He held her when she looked so lost. He was able to get her to laugh with the help of our two children.

Muhdea eventually moved in with Mammie Dell and her husband who Muhdea couldn't stand. It may have been a good thing because the energy that she had been using to grieve was then spent on, "I hate dat niggah, I hope he do try ta hur' somebody. I wi' shoo' da shi' ou' him if'n he eva try ta come afa' me!" She was still feisty and I believed that she could probably "bust a cap in his butt" because she probably still packed a pistol in her apron. If not, she bluffed enough where we all believed it. She was still the Matriarch of the Mathis family. Everybody and their grandma adored her. She had tried so hard to fit into her new environment in Mammie Dell's new brick house. She was so unhappy because most of all of the familiar things that she had in the second house had either been thrown away because of the unrepairable state that it was in when she moved. She held on to a few of her possessions of keepsakes although it was meager it held sentimental value to her. She gave Joe Henry and I some of her old skillets and dishes. Some of them were chipped but we kept them. It was a piece of our history (something from Muhdea). She began to talk to herself and have conversations as if though Bobby was still there with her.

Back home Joe Henry was having trouble keeping up with the work assigned to him at the shop. He had been placed as a foreman on his job and my brother (he said) was working under him. Joe was having problems with reading some of the plans for complex door installations. He would come home so angry and had so much animosity. He complained constantly about Boy Baby who was actually a gentle person who wouldn't intentionally harm anybody. I figured that the hatred stemmed from the love/hate that he had for me. He confided in me that he hated everybody, that included all races, creeds and religions. He knew that his admitting something so profound would hurt me because I had always tried to be a positive person. His negativity was wearing me down until I got fed up! It was getting worse each day with so many complaints of what someone else had done and how much he wanted to kill them, "I just wan' ta take my gun up tha' a shoot tha' shit ou' all of them in clud'n dat brotha o' yos." He complained about the way that he drove too fast, too close, music too loud, talk too much, he hated Christian music, garlic breath. The list went on and on. I didn't have the nerve to tell my brother for fear that it would get back to Joe Henry and his short lease, and a gun that was cocked at all times. It was about that time that I had decided I needed to get out of the so called marriage.

I posed the subject for the sake of discussion of divorce to Joe Henry. He didn't want to hear of it. He did however say, "If'n you eva decides ta go, you wi' go wid' ou' nothin' diz iz my house and eva' thang in hit dat includes des cahs (cars)" We had a big fight (or I had a bad beating). He went out of the house in his usually huff, slamming the door behind him. I didn't want to be there when he returned therefore I left shortly after him, and took Vanessa with me to the same hotel. She went willingly but in the morning she awakened and begged me, "let's go home, Mommy please. I miss my daddy, I want to be with both my parents."

Seek and ye shall find. I found myself in yet another triangle. I did most of my meat marketing one block from our house. I liked their cuts of meat especially the way that they sliced my order of very thick bologna, just the way that I liked it. I had grown up on a good old bologna sandwich and my family also. Joe had asked me several times to keep a good supply for his lunch. He didn't, however, ask me to get involved with one of the butchers who was responsible for making deliveries. He was fifteen years my junior and was married with two children. his wife spoke Spanish only. They had recently moved from Mexico and she was pregnant with their third child.

Rigo Gomez and I flirted unmercifully whenever I went in for my weekly order. The other butchers were aware that we had a thing for each other so they would call him from the back so that he could come to the front and wait on me. Sometimes I would see him in the company truck making deliveries. He would motion to me to call him. We were the most unlikely pair of hot blooded people. We met in motels and would spend the afternoon making wild passionate love. I knew that there was nothing else to it and so did he. I paid for the hotel room and whatever drinks that we wanted. He rocked my world for three years. He almost got fired because he wasn't to be found for about four hours on one of the days that we were together. We had worn ourselves out and went to sleep thereafter. I was basically black-balled from phoning him there again and he was no longer allowed to wait on me. Wow! What a man! I missed him so much. It was an outlet for coping with my husband.

Joe Henry had refused my request for him to get counseling for anger management and severe mood swings. One evening he came home so irritated and wanted to take his aggressions out on me. I actually knew what was bothering him. He had received a phone call from Mammie Dell the night before. Muhdea had fallen, however, she didn't have any apparent fractures. She did, however, have some mild weakness of the left upper and lower extremities and bouts of confusion. It lasted for a while, "She okay naw and has anotha appointmen' at da doctah's office ta follow up da blood test" she drawled.

Joe Henry went directly to his hidden liquor bottle that he kept in our bedroom. I followed him there for fear of what he might do. He turned up the bottle and downed about one fourth of a fifth of Chivas Regal. Afterwards I wished that I hadn't asked him to express his feeling. He started about his hate for his job. Then he lit in on Tommy's case again and all of the mistakes that he (had so called) done that day. Everybody was out to get him. I actually tried to change the subject, but he was bound and determined to pour out all of his negativity and laden me with all of that hatred that he kept bottled up inside (except for beating me as his outlet). Again I tried to change the subject several times but he was a man on a mission. I would be just as miserable as he was. There was so much torture in his face and his voice seemed tormented by some evilness that had apparently consumed his whole being. He was pacing as if though he was trying to escape form some satanic being. He blurted out as he raised both of his arms to demonstrate the gravity of how deeply he felt, "I hate eva body" he stopped pacing and glared at me and said, "and you'se included."

I had prepared his favorite meal of collard greens, fried chicken, twice baked potatoes and corn bread. I fixed his plate as I had always done and it was expected. I sliced some ripe tomatoes and onions that had been soaked in vinegar. He sat at the kitchen table and began to eat. I sat down to eat with him. He got up abruptly and pushed the plate away from him. He began pacing again with a look of doom plastered on his face. I trailed behind him not knowing if he would turn the looming gloom on me. I took my chance. I asked, "Joe Henry, what's wrong" He answered, "not a fuck'n thang bitch." I felt that I had had enough and responded, "I'm not a bitch, you aught to be ashamed of yourself the way you talk to me." I was about to let the water works flow. Surprisingly he said, "Carrie, I'm so sorry, I'm so scared 'bout Muhdea." He started to cry then in the same second he began clutching his chest. Sweat was pouring down his face. He seemed to be trying to control his breathing. I said in a matter of fact tone of voice, "You need to calm down Joe Henry. Go sit down while I call an ambulance." That was like me striking a match and throwing it on some gasoline. He growled, "he'll nah, you ain't gwine call nobody. I ain't go'n ta no hospita' fa' dem ta ki' me, you want me dead anyways" I talked in a lowered voice, "at least sit down and be quiet." It was like talking to a charging bull in a China shop. He wouldn't allow me to do anything for him – he was the man – Joe Henry got up and went over to the kitchen sink and took two aspirins then went back to our bathroom. The smell of liquor was on his breath when he returned back into the kitchen. He said, "hit wuz gas" when he went past me. He sat down to finish his meal. Just as he had taken another bite, he jumped up again with the most horrific look on his face. He clutched his heart again with both hands, "Carrie it's something wrong." It looked as if thought he was having a heart attack. I picked up the phone and was about to dial 911 – he yelled, "naw" I said as calmly as I could, "If you don't get help right now you could die. I think you are having a heart attack." He looked so frightened as he listened to me. Then said, You wi' drive me to da hospital." He gave me two choices, to watch him die at home or to drive him to the hospital as he had insisted. I drove like a semi maniac while I did observe all of the stop signs (well, maybe not coming to a complete stop) I was going over the speed limit but not dangerously. No matter what had happened in the past, Joe Henry was a human being and he was still my husband. I got him to the hospital where I worked. As we pulled up to the ER I noticed that he had slumped over still clutching his chest. His color was ashy. I honked the horn just as I parked in front of the ER doorway that was actually slated for ambulance only. Time was of the utmost. The ER crew of nurses, a doctor and a respiratory therapist came running out when I yelled out, "Help! Help! I think my husband is having a heart attack!" I was scolded, "You should have called an ambulance." I responded defensively, "He refused to come by ambulance." They all were instrumental to getting him out of the car and on to the gurney and oxygen was placed on him immediately. That frightened look was still on his face as tears rolled down his cheek. I squeezed his hands to assure him that they were going to take good care of him. He thanked me as they were performing so many blood draws. Blood pressure and continuous EKG monitor of his vital signs. I was asked to leave but be available in the waiting room. I knew the routine so I didn't argue or ask for special privileges. He was put on a morphine drip and they ran multiple CT scans. It was found that he did indeed have a coronary. There was blockage in his heart arteries. An emergency PTCA (Percutaneous Transluminal Coronary Angioplasty) was performed. He did well thereafter. He promised his doctor that he would follow the diet, take the prescribed medications and above all stop smoking. He was given a list of do's and don'ts. I knew that life that we had once would get worse. Joe Henry had a way of vowing/promising things that he knew he wasn't going to keep. The low salt and low fat diet was the worse culprit that they could have ever given to him. He had so many medications and took whatever he wanted. "I'm not take'n tha' shit." He absolutely refused to cooperate. He threw tantrums with his food, "I ain't eat'n shit." He would fling it up against the wall or on the floor. Either me or the kids would have to clean up the mess.

Our children were beside themselves to try to get their daddy to follow the restricted regime. I found that he was smoking and drinking. Joe Henry had never been placed in a position where he had to follow rules. He had been allowed to go through his childhood being non compliant to the laws of the land and the laws of God. He continued to have the same attitude as an adult (over grown boy). He made his own destiny which was self destructive.

Joe Henry began having more mild chest pain. He was popping so many nitroglycerin tabs like they were candy. It was decided that he would need extensive surgery because another P.T.C.A. wasn't indicated. He had a triple bypass Graft (CABG) surgery, thereafter he was on a ventilator. I prayed that he would be okay. I didn't want to see him die. They had a problem getting him weaned off of the ventilator because of his history of being a heavy smoker. Me and the children were glad when he was finally discharged home. I insisted that he follow the restrictions that were ordered. He started progressive exercises and seemed to have been following orders a lot better after the surgery. He wasn't getting disability. So I worked extras and harder than I had ever done before. I went walking with Joe to keep him focused and motivated. I worked the night shift so one night I was assigned to CCU with a Filipino RN who was pregnant. We were so called, 'working together' positioning a 300 pound patient who was comatose. The nurse didn't use any of her strength and I used too much of mine "on the count of three." My poor body mechanics was partially at fault for my back injury that I sustained on my job. I felt something go crack when I straightened up. The next day thereafter I was flat on my back (for eight months).

Neither Joe nor I were collecting any disability because I was told that I should have reported it when it happened. Well I was walking fine that night at work and it progressively worsened. We stretched what little savings we had. I cashed out all of my retirement that I had saved from my employment. We were spiraling downward so fast. We both wondered what else could happen. We were hitting rock bottom. We were going to loose our house if we didn't rebound. Joe Henry wasn't ready to return back to work yet.

We received the dreaded call from Mammie Dell that Muhdea had worried so much about Bobby's death and now she was beside herself with her beloved baby boy so sick and so far away. She had a massive stroke and never did recover. Our Muhdea died at the age of 86 years old. Joe Henry wasn't able to travel and attend her funeral. We tried to console each other. We were both practically on our backs like two turtles. I was finally authorized to get physical therapy and rebounded. I was instructed not to lift anything greater than thirty pounds I wouldn't be able to work as a regular staff RN.

It was 1989 when I applied for another position at the hospital (that I claimed to own a piece of the rock). I was hired for the position that I had requested. It was totally out of my league and out of my field of expertise. Above all it went against my grain for what I had gone into the nursing field for. But what else could I do? My job description was discharge planning, utilization reviewer. The position that I held overlapped so many other specialties such as social services, financial counselor, quality management and coders. I filled so many hats. With the added accountabilities my salary was increasing. I began to feel good about myself. Although I wasn't a bedside nurse I was able to offer information and support during and after a patient's hospital stay. My evaluations were very good. I was the only black in the department that had twelve positions. The majority of my coworkers were white, there were two Filipinos. They were paid more than a dollar an hour more than me. We weren't supposed to discuss our salaries with each other so that the disparity wouldn't be discovered. I still held on to the notion that as a black woman I had to work harder especially since I was in a new position that was predominantly white women. Staying focused was a challenge when every day brought on more rude awakenings that I wasn't indispensable. There were so many staff RN who wanted my position because they had burned out in their role as bedside nurse. My coworkers were the ones that tried to do the most damage when they discovered that I was doing so well in school at the University of Phoenix to obtain my BSN degree. It was so petty and should have been obvious to my superiors, however that's not how it was taken. They reported me to our supervisor that I was leaving work undone, leaving the premises too early, and found fault with my documentation in the chart especially about an AIDS patient. No matter what the charges, I stayed above ground.

Joey and Vanessa were growing up so fast. I got so much pleasure just observing them as they developed into teenagers and young adults. It brought so much pride to me to be their mom. They on the other hand had other desires rather than being a child. JoJo was dating one of his classmates that he had known since Jr. High school. They seemed to have been smitten with each other and were inseparable. Vanessa on the other hand had so many road blocks since she was proclaimed as Daddy's Little Girl. He didn't want to allow her to have any boys to visit her at home. Nobody was good enough for her. Joe Henry was afraid that she would become pregnant and he was adamant he wasn't going to take care of another man's child. He developed two sets of rules (I fought against it to no avail) one for his son "You go git'em son, jis be careful and don' git no babies" he said that kiddingly but I knew different. He had often told me as he chuckled that rape was an assault with a friendly weapon. His rule for Vanessa was, "you kin star' dat'n when you iz 21 years ol'" She didn't think that it was funny. She began staying out of sight. On the phone constantly. She was rebellious with me and refused to do any chores around the house. I felt that it was because she didn't have as many privileges as JoJo. I had to punish her by taking away her phone in her room. She didn't seem to mind and she still stayed in her room with the door closed. I found out that she had borrowed her friends phone. It fit right into her phone jack next to her bed. When she wasn't using it she would unplug it and put it under her mattress. Once she forgot to unplug it. It rang as I was in her room. She got up quickly because she knew that I was going to do a Rambo on her. I wondered how she had learned to be so sneaky.

One afternoon I was getting ready to go to work when I got a call from Van's school. She had been absent for three days. The school had a note that had been signed by me. They compared it to my signature card and it was slightly off. She had signed my name on a note to excuse her from classes. JoJo had written the note for her. The truant officer had picked her up at a local park with a group of her school mates of several older boys and girls her age. They all looked like floozies. I had to punish her by taking away her TV and the attached Atari game. That next morning she was about to leave home with a pair of jeans that had so many holes cut out. I could see her butt cheeks and "Oh my God!" There was a hole that was cut so close to the cu---. "No, hell naw! You're not leaving this house with that on, you go change." Her girl friend was waiting down the stairs – so she had an audience as she was resistant and argumentative. "Mom, all the girls at school wear jeans like these." I guess she thought I would back down since she had her entourage. She knew that I wasn't hearing it. I couldn't allow her to leave until she had changed. I showed her who's boss.

It appeared that every time that Mammie Dell called was to inform us that someone was dying or dead. She said, "I'm jus callin to say hey and give ya'll a report on Alain." Joe Henry was glad to hear that she was doing fine. He was on the mend, he chest sutures were itchy and irritating him. He was becoming his old (hateful) self.

Phillip phone Joe Henry a couple of evenings after Mammie's call. Joe Henry was ecstatic about his brother's phone call. They cracked a few jokes. I hadn't seen Joe Henry laugh so much. Then Phillip slowly lowered the bomb, "Billy…" I saw Joe Henry turn so pale. He sat down in his easy chair that he kept next to the kitchen phone mounted on the wall. Phillip continued, "Bill's oldest boy is dead." I knew that although he was aware of my past indiscretions, he still loved his brother. He got as much details that people knew back home. The boy had gotten in with the wrong crowd at the age of fifteen. It was reported that his buddies saw him as he laid down in the middle of the highway (I-45) in front of Mount Pleasant church on a dare. His buddies had tried to coax him to get up – the traffic was generally quite fast on that stretch of roadway as it had passing allowed. He wouldn't get up. The eighteen wheeler never saw him as he was ran over. He was reported to be unrecognizable. They had a closed casket funeral. It hurt Bill so badly that soon after he and his wife separated. Billy moved into an old house near Tommy G's moms house. In about three weeks we got another call from Mammie Dell that Billy's body was found charred beyond recognition from a house fire that everybody thought was suspicious. It appeared as though it had been purposely set afire but by whom? Some speculated that he had gotten drunk and was smoking in bed. There wasn't a thorough investigation as far as the law was concerned it was an open and shut case. One niggah bit the dust…next!

Over the years I found that I could temporarily loose myself in the arms of another man easily. It was a second nature that I had developed to so call protect myself from Joe Henry. But who was going to protect me from Carrie? I wondered how many times could a person hurt another knowing that what goes around will certainly come around. I felt that I was so entangled with so many evil things in my life. I knew all that being said, but I continued to suffer the Spirit of God. I begged for forgiveness but I felt how could He hear me? I had defiled myself so badly. I wasn't worthy of saving.

So little time I thought. What should I do? I did what had came so natural to me for so long. I met and became involved in men that I met on my job. There were two security guards. The black one was everything that I would have wanted in a man except he had no ambitions in life. He was built like a hard brick. His skin was smooth mocha, mm, mmm good! He towered over me as if he was a chocolate sculpture ready to be devoured. It lasted for about one year until his mom became ill. She went into renal failure and required hemodialysis. He moved her into his apartment so that he could take care of her. We drifted apart then he must have taken another position in another organization. I was involved with another lucky person that lasted about three years. We excited each other with acts that were…

Joey was dating and eventually married his childhood sweetheart. She became pregnant with my first grandchild, Nairobi. The sun and the moon rose in her. How delightful she was. Her mom was going to beauty school to become a model. She was an extremely pretty Mexican girl. It became so cumbersome for their family for her juggling trying to be a mom, model and a wife. Their marriage was against our better judgment but it wasn't anything that we could do about the multiple problems that they faced as a mixed couple. One evening we got a call from the police department that Joey had been arrested and was in jail for assault and battery. It was reported to us that he and Ana had had a tiff and he called the police. Upon arrival to their apartment, they saw what a big strapping muscle bound man that he was so they took him to jail. Me and Joe Henry put our house up to bail him out. When he got out he went back to his wife and baby. Vanessa in the meanwhile wasn't in the limelight that I was aware of and was... "Mom, I'm not feeling too good. I can't keep food down" she cried. She didn't have her usual makeup on, she had a pitiful ponytail. Her skin was ashy with pale lips. It reminded me of the time when she was ten years old and had fainted when she came out of the orthodontist office. "Well, lets just get you an appointment to see a doctor, mean while you need spinach and lots of liver." I said with concern. I was thinking out loud that she should see a pediatrician since she was sixteen years old. "I'll make an appointment today." She interrupted me and wouldn't give me eye contact. "Mom, I think I need to see a doctor who delivers babies." I shouted, "Wha, what are you saying Vanessa?" She continued to look down at paper that she was doodling on. She answered, "I think that I'm pregnant. I haven't had a period for two months and I'm sick at the stomach." I argued that I too had been irregular when I was her age (16 years old). We kept the appointment. Her pregnancy was confirmed which wasn't the worse thing that could ever happen to her. It was telling her father that his princess had allowed some boy to touch her and defile her as he had done to so many women, and who had became pregnant by him. His rule was don't do what you see me do, do what I say. I tried my best to come up with a master plan on how to inform him. There wasn't an easy way to tell him – just do it.

Vanessa went to her daddy and was about to blurt everything out as he was walking down the stairway toward the front door. I stood in front of her and said the words that would change all of our lives, "Joe

Henry, Vanessa is pregnant." It seemed as if though there was an echo with an amplifier. His reaction was what I had expected. It reminded me of when I had given him the news about my first pregnancy. His facial muscles were tense. His eyes could have bore a hold in me if he had continued to glare at me. His chin was a dead giveaway that he was about to strike or cut me down verbally. He chose the latter as he said angrily, "I blame you dat she's pregnant. I tol't cho time and time agin tha' she wuz'n s'pose ta be date'n" He wouldn't even look at Vanessa who was still standing behind me on the stairs. The look of terror seemed to have intensified on her face as he hissed at me, "You git yo' God damned ass ou' my house and take tha' black bitch wid cho." He hurried back up the stairs to our bedroom to where he kept an arsenal of guns that were kept loaded and ready to bust a cap in anybody that got in his way or who didn't agree with his philosophy of life.

Not wanting to take any chances I grabbed Vanessa's hand and ran out of the house. She was shaking like a leaf. She was my daughter and my responsibility I felt an overpowering new found strength at that moment. I vowed that I would protect her. My vows that I had made to him – to forsake all others – were long gone. I wasn't about to allow that mother fucking – I caught myself before I allowed myself to continue to be manipulated. I tried to calm myself as I told Vanessa to get in the car and lock it. She did so quickly. I jumped inside my car and was scrambling to start it just as he appeared. He had followed us outside with the gun. How predictable he was. He began hitting the window with his fist on Van's side as I was backing out, my heart was pounding so hard. He fired a couple of shots as I sped away from the house that had never been my home. Vanessa seemed to be in a state of shock. We stayed at the safe haven hotel for the last time that night. We called the house the next morning, the coast was clear. We returned back to Joe Henry's house my thoughts were, 'for the last time'.

I parked my Trans Am in front of the house. As Vanessa was packing her things I was on the phone to secure an apartment. I took it sight unseen. I called the bank and found out how much money that could be withdrawn from the joint accounts. I called in to my job that there was a family emergency and that I wasn't going to be there that day. I later went over to my job and picked up my check. We packed the car with all of our clothes. Her small TV, a small lamp, a few pots and pans, an old place setting for four. She packed her memorabilia's of cards that had been written to me when she was a child. All of her report cards. I left all the family photos, letters from my mom. So many keepsakes were left behind because the car was packed to its capacity. I purposely left Joey's things because I knew that Joe Henry would hunt me down like an animal for taking his son's things. I was so torn just having to leave all of my books. So much of my past wouldn't fit in the small car. I knew that Joey's things would be safe. We had worked diligently for about five hours. I was afraid that Joe Henry would return back from work at any given moment. At last, we were packed and out of his house. He wouldn't have me to abuse anymore or to stand in his way. I was brain washed by him. It was crystal clear it was his house.

Chapter V

Freedom

VANESSA AND I became occupants of a two bedroom apartment that was about five miles from Joe Henry's house. I took the crawl space because Vanessa would be needing a place for the baby's crib and a rocking chair that I bought early on. Although I had the prospect of being Van's sole support, I felt as if the weight of my shoulders had been lifted. I could go to sleep at night and know that I wouldn't be awakened with a gun pointed at my head just because it was allowed or to have someone slapping me around just because they could. I felt that I would no longer have to worry about getting my feelings hurt. Verbal abuse is just as devastating as physical. I DID NOT CRY ONE TEAR!

I felt so damn good about my new freedom. I was so scared but oh, so happy. I couldn't say that I could be Carrie again because I really didn't know who the real Carrie Ann was. I had tried to define myself at a tender age of fifteen, had stayed in a marriage that should not have taken place. I did it so that questions still remained, who am I?

Within the first week of our move I had used my financial planning skills to budget and was able to buy a floor model refrigerator (the price had already been slashed) upon delivery I found a nick that happened at my apartment. I paid only twenty five dollars for it. I furnished the apartment with cute, cheap (real cheap) furniture. It was mine.

We stayed there six and a half months. I didn't mind being right next to the freeway (I-5) with all of the constant traffic and freeway noise. Neither did I mind the railroad track (with the trains whistle blowing throughout the night) that ran parallel to the freeway on the opposite side of the apartment. It was a dust trap, and I did mind that my Vanessa and my unborn grandchild had to breath in all of the fumes and dust.

I looked for and found another apartment in Alhambra. It was perfect, so I thought. I purchased a floor model RCA TV and an exotic white laminate queen sized bedroom set, a dinette set of beautiful state of the art black leather chairs, its seats that was mounted on crystal clear arms and legs. (I had it custom made). The table base was made of the same crystal clear material. That material had been used by astronauts during their outer space exploration (so the salesman had said). I got rid of the two day beds that I had initially purchased for us.

The day that was slated for our move was the day that my third grandchild decided that it wanted to be born. My second little grand bugger (Leilani Paige Mathis) who was Joey's second child with Ana. She looked more like Joey than he did himself. She was such a beautiful honey bunny. I didn't get to be there for her birth because I was afraid to be in the same company with Joe Henry who was using every tactic to make me look like a villain that had left him destitute. I had left everything in tact upon my departure except for me, my life, Vanessa and the child that she carried. I wanted to begin anew. Something that I had never dreamed that I could do on my own. My ultimate goals was safety for Vanessa because I didn't know what might happen to her if her father would find us. We needed to be further away from his house. I know that it was a false sense of security but I held on to what would be best for us on a daily basis. Lani had been born eight days ago on September the eighth. I knew that Joey was at odds with me but I needed his help. He was the son that most mothers would give their eye tooth for. I only had love for him and his sister.

I started the movers and JoJo came to my rescue. I took Vanessa to the hospital. I was back and forth from East LA to Alhambra. (freedom comes with a price). I was there at Vanessa's side as my mom had been with my two deliveries. On September 16th I saw Jasmine Elyse as she was being born, my beautiful Jasminelly (nick name) who without her I would never have had the courage to leave my existence in my self imprisonment. I only had to say enough and mean it. I had allowed so many things to happen in my marriage/my life. I closed that door – another door opened.

As I was leaving the hospital so exhausted I was approached by someone who looked so familiar. We stopped in the hallways said our hellos. I gave him my new phone number and the new city that I had just moved to. He was one lucky man I thought as I walked away. Sleep came easy for me that night. It was a new beginning for me and the newborn that Van would be bringing home tomorrow. Ring, ring, ring! I was awakened to a bright, beautiful sunlit day. I answered, "Hello." I knew immediately it was him. ■

Chapter VI

Family Photos

Mother was pregnant with me during this family portrait. She is the beautiful lady on the back row.

Photo taken after the movie. Left to right: Gladys, Melvin Jr. and me, Carrie Ann at the age of five.

Pictured from Left to Right: Joe Henry, approx. 4 years old; Phillip, 6 years old; the twins at 9 years old, Bobby & Billy.

Mother, Deddy at home with Willie and Janie.

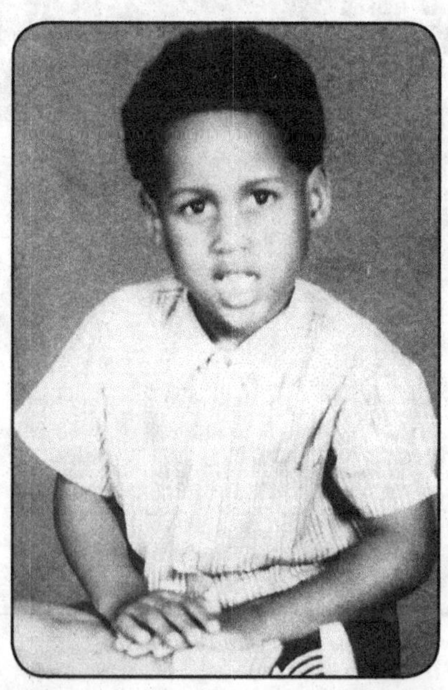

Joe Henry Mathis, Jr. (Joe Joe), my son, age 3 at Head Start (year 1968).

Vanessa Mathis at age 3.

Joe Henry and I at home.

Family Photo at my fathers' house. Back row, left to right: Willie, Janie, James, Bennie and Tommie Front row, left to right: Carrie (me), Lottie, Deddy (Tommy Lee) and Joyce

East Los Angeles College

Dean's Honor List

In Recognition of Outstanding Scholastic Achievement

This certifies that CARRIE A. MATHIS

has scholastically qualified for the Dean's Honor List

College President

June 21, 1980

Date

Dean of Student Personnel Services

Celebrate

My graduation photo taken at East Los Angeles College, June 1983.

Chapter VII

Glossary

Frequently spoken words, phrases and language fillers used predominantly in the southern region of the USA.

A

Af'a – after.

A'ight – alright

Aw' – all

As nutty as a fruit cake – psychologically unstable.

As happy as a dead pig in the sunshine – elated.

A piece of a man is better than no man – settle for a half stepping man.

As funny as a barrel of monkeys – hilarious.

As soft as a doctor's cotton – softer than regular cotton.

As full as a tick – stuffed, over ate.

As crazy as a betsy bug – a term of endearment of "you are so crazy."

As easy as climbing a tree not near as dangerous – it's simple to do without any harm to you.

As easy as shitting in a well not as dangerous – it's simple to do without any harm to you.

As useful as a tit on a bull – not usable; it will never work.

As sho' as yo' born – for sure.

B

Bet'n – better than.

Baghettiz – spaghetti (plural).

Bone tired – too tired to continue.

Barely mit'lin – barely able to make it, but still trying.

C

Ca'h – car.

Chunk – pitch/throw the ball.

Cho – you.

Comp'ny – company.

'Cuz – because.

Crazier than a road lizard – term of endearment; crazy or psychologically unstable.

Colder than a well diggers ass – extremely frigid.

Cheap stream strutter – trout; headless trout.

Cow chips – chunks of dried cow manure.

Cool your lilly – calm down; relax.

Chip up onjuns – diced onions.

Comb 'da kitchen – comb the kinky hair on the back of the neck.

D

Dis'heah – this here; this.

Dis – this.

Do'n – doing.

Dagh'dah – daughter.

Dat – that.

Darkees – negros.

Dog gone! – darn it!

Dang! – darn!

Drap – drop (the ball).

Don't throw the baby out with the bathwater – getting rid of the good with the bad.

Do dad – memory lapse.

Do hicky – memory lapse.

Drunker than a skunk – intoxicated.

Don't let your mouth overload your ass – you'll get your butt spanked for back talking; defiant.

E

Eyes too big fo' yo' stomach – putting too much food on a plate and not able to eat it all.

F

Fit' n' ta – fixing to; about to.

For goodness sake – wow, exasperation.

Flappin yo' lips – argumentative.

Fart busta (burst) – passing gas; flatulent.

Fat n' fine – velouptous woman; healthy man.

Fattening frogs for snakes – refusing to pay monetary responsibility to wife/child while they are living somewhere else.

G

Goosy – tickle.

Gallix – suspenders.

Garray – porch.

Gwon' – go on, get out of here!

Gwine – going to.

Good golly Miss Molly – Wow!

Glory be! – Wow!

Goodness gracious alive! – Wow wee!

Great gooby do moo! – unbelievable!

Great day in da mon'n! – unbelievable!

Goody goody gum drop – a childs, "gotcha!"

H

Hard headed – unruly, misbehave non conforming brat.

Hip slappers – gospel singers, usually a trio or quartet singing acopella style.

Hush yo' mouth! – that's incredible! Wow!

He was tow down from the flow down (floor) – drunk, intoxicated, not able to stand.

Hot headed – agitated behavior.

How'z yo' hamma' hang'n – how are you doing?

Hotter than a pussy with the pox – extremely hot.

He/she didn't stay no longer than John stayed in the Army – visit was cut short.

Head fuller of kuck-a-bug (nappy hair) aka buck shots – unruly, kinky, short hair.

Hard headed and a soft bottom – a brat that's about to get their butt spanked.

Heer'd – heard.

Heah – here.

Huh – her.

H'it – it.

He' – hell.

Hizun – his.

I

I'll be dog gone – unbelievable.

If you like it I love it – I'll stand by your decision.

If you can't stand the heat get out of the kitchen! – walk away from the problem or deal with it!

It'll all come out in the wash – the truth will eventually be known.

I'll be a monkey's uncle! – that's incredible!

I HEARD that! (said with an attitude and melodiously, emphasis on <u>heard</u>) – I agree with you!

I'z yo' huz'ban married? – are you married and does your husband play around.

I ain't stud'n you – I'm not thinking about you.

If'n God had meant fo' me ta fly, he'da gave me wangs – afraid to fly in an airplane.

I ain't git'n no mo' wawda than I kin swalla' – afraid to swim or to sail.

Im'mo snatch a knot ou' cho! – "you are about this close to getting your butt whipped!

J

K

Ki' – kill.

Knock kneed'ed – deformity of the lower extremities where knees knock together while walking (it's hard to run).

L

'lectwicity – electricity.

Licky de split! – quickly! Hurry up!

Lordy mercy! – I feel for you.

Low down dirty blues – songs that depicts an emotion of sadness and despair.

M

Mon'n – morning.

Mammy made – home made clothes that looks and fit like it's home made.

Make do or do bid'dout (without) – make the best of what you have; don't complain.

Mmm, MMM, mmm (shrug shoulders) – blank look on face; I don't know.

N

Niz – nice.

Naw – no.

Naw'suh – no sir.

Naw – now.

Nabs – small snacks of peanut butter crackers or small bags or salted peanuts, nuts.

No'me – no ma'am.

Nelly 'bout – almost.

Negro round steak – bologna that's sliced thick, ¼ inch, fried and blackened on both sides; sandwich with all of the trimmings, a staple.

Naw ain't tha' cute? – per Deddy, "I think that's sweet, do you?"

Non o' yo' pea pickin' business! – stay out of it! It's not for you to know.

O

Ou' – out.

O'mines – of mine.

Oh! For crying out loud – feeling of exasperation.

Out of the frying pan, into the fire – a problem that's gotten worse burn baby burn.

P

Pu' – pit.

Pooless – police.

Poh thang – poor thing, an emotion of empathy.

Piss haunt – a child's name caller (it doesn't make sense).

Pidgeon toed – a deformity where the (toes) feet are turned inward.

Pot liquor – liquid from boiled vegetables (green beans, peas) boiled with either cured smoked hamhocks, bacon, hog maul, etc. corn bread is placed in the liquid and the rest is history – yummy!

Pissin' lak' a cow – the sound of a person urinating that's a loud and steady stream, usually heard while using a slop jar.

Poot sniffer – a child's name caller.

Poh as Joe's turkey – living in poverty.

Q

R

Roe'ad – road.

Rat naw – right now.

S

Sti' – still.

See'd – seen.

Stank'n – stink; putrid.

Sto' – store.

Sump'teat – something to eat.

Shoty – shorty; Deddy's nickname for Mother.

Spraw'd – sprawled.

Shut yo' mouth! – unbelievable!

Stank lak kiyarn – per Muhdea – putrid.

Straighten up and fly right – do as I say now! Get your act together, now!

Shame faced'ed – bashful.

Shit or get off the pot – handle your business or let someone else.

Siditty – snooty.

Smelly, lak a pole cat – putrid odor.

So quiet, you could hear a rat piss'n on cotton – no sounds heard.

Stink lak tha' air breaks from a ho'bos ass – putrid.

Strike a match – bathroom deodorant.

Show nuff! – surely.

Sick n' tired! – enough.

Scarce ass – skinny, boney.

Shucks! – shoot/shit.

Snaggle tooth – missing front teeth.

Slew footed – a deformity where the feet are turned outward.

T

Ta'k – talk.

Tha' – that

Tha'y – their (e.i. they gwine git thay butts kicked).

Tinanchy – tiny.

Tongue lashing – scolding.

Tough tiddy – too bad.

That's a crying shame – empathy.

That's a low down dirty shame – empathy.

Tarbly well – I'm okay.

Tired to da bone – can't go on.

U

Uncle Tom – a Negro man seen as a sell out to his race.

Ump ump ump! – I feel for you, too bad.

Ugly as sin – homely.

V

W

Whaz – what's.

Wawda – water.

Wha' – what.

Wid – with.

Whi' – while.

Wha sen' eva – whatever.

Well shut my mouth! – umbelieavle.

Whatchamacallit – memory lapse.

Whatchamadoodle – memory lapse or brain freeze.

Whatnot – memory lapse or a brick-a-brack.

Walkin' and eat'n lak a cow – toddler eating on the run (no high chair).

X

Y

Ya'll – you all.

Yo' – your.

Yas'sam – yes ma'me.

Yaaaah hoooo – expression of glee.

Yoooo hoooo – hello, I'm here.

You aught to be shame of yo' se'f! – shame on you.

You getting' too big fo' yo' britches – a child increasingly stepping out of bounds.

You bastard cho! – term of endearment.

Z